Henry Reed

Hilda Tablet and Others

four pieces for radio

British Broadcasting Corporation

Published by the
British Broadcasting Corporation
35 Marylebone High Street
London W1M 4AA
First published 1971
First paperback edition 1976
© Henry Reed 1971
ISBN 0 563 17200 2
Printed in England by
Hollen Street Press Ltd
Slough, Berkshire

Contents

DEDICATORY LETTER

TO

GEORGE D. PAINTER

My dear George,

For a long time I used to go to bed late. As often as not, the reason for this was that I was busy sorting my data. These were usually small details of fact, gathered from the Record Office, the London Library, the British Museum, or from ancient provincial newspapers: details that seemed relevant, if only I could understand why, to the life of a certain great novelist. A *Life* of him was what I was supposed, and still sometimes rashly suppose myself, to be working on. How many volumes it was to consist of I cannot now always remember, but I doubt if it was ever less than one.

My mind would often wander from my subject. Minds do this. And none more eagerly and rapidly, I came to notice, than those of the people I interviewed who had personally known my Author. They were invariably glad to help. From my encounters with them I would retire grateful and moved, full of tea and sherry, and, on one occasion, memories of what must have been almost the complete piano works of Brahms. They were fine men and women. But always, a few nights afterwards, once more sorting my data, I would realise that the main content of their disclosures had concerned, exclusively, themselves.

This struck me as a profoundly interesting fact in itself. After a time I began to diversify my nocturnal labours by a small dramatic study of it. It was called *A Very Great Man Indeed*. (The title comes from Joseph Conrad, though this, at the time, I did not know.) It was meant to be an austere little work, above all complete in itself. No sequel was intended. But, as it happened, there were a great number of sequels: and for this I think I can honourably shift the blame on to the actors and the composer of the music. In the first script, there was one particular scene whose enactment awoke in me a restless curiosity. At the end of it, my *alter ego* Reeve attempts to turn over the manuscript pages of a sonata, which Hilda Tablet is playing on the piano. I used to *watch* this scene, rather than listen to it. It was played with such intense and anxious realism that, to this day, in recalling it, I find it difficult to believe that there was no piano in sight. The piano was far away, being soundly disciplined at that moment by the composer Swann. (This reminds me that you have, of course, a Swann of your own, a most sympathetic fellow, though desperately hooked, as I remember, on a 'little phrase' of music. I hope I am not being unduly smug in remarking that the phrases of *my* Swann have always tended to come in the larger sizes.)

Anyway, the scene fades bashfully out, as radio-scenes do; so does the music. But a short time afterwards, I found myself wondering what would have happened *next* between Reeve and Hilda. And how would Swann's sonata have gone on? And what about Stephen Shewin? I was greatly tempted to ask that the whole cast should come back and do some more. Hence, after a time, and one thing leading to another, the later scripts. Altogether, they totalled seven. The number is sometimes given as nine; but people exaggerate. I have selected the four given here, mainly because there is a faint, barely detectable story-line running through them. They have a happy ending, and I am glad to have managed this, for once.

I am afraid the book is a very poor return for the first volume of your immaculate *Proust*. A bread-and-butter letter perhaps: perhaps we might best think of it as that. Even so, the butter has been mainly provided by Donald Swann's music, Douglas Cleverdon's production, and the willingness of a brilliant cast to re-assemble itself year after year. This, I am sure, you know.

There are a few minor historical points about the scripts that may be worth mentioning. In the second of them, originally broadcast on the night of 24 May 1954, full frontal nudity was heard on radio for the first time, the author being quite unaware of what a trail he was blazing, and the scene itself having been passed on the grounds of unquestionable aesthetic and artistic necessity, fortified by the reverence and tact which the actors brought to it. Mind you, there were some whacking great cuts elsewhere. In these printed versions I haven't, I think, put back anything that was cut in the interest of time or proportion. On the other hand, a fair number of passages, accepted by the producer, and already recorded by the cast, were sometimes, at a late moment, ordered out by higher assessors, on the grounds of indelicacy. To the reclamation of these passages I have given, dear George, a most zealous attention.

Yours, ever affectionately,
Henry

A Very Great Man Indeed

To Hugh Burden

A Very Great Man Indeed was first broadcast on 7 September 1953. The production was by Douglas Cleverdon, with music by Donald Swann. The cast was as follows:

HERBERT REEVE	*Hugh Burden*
STEPHEN SHEWIN	*Carleton Hobbs*
CONNIE SHEWIN	*Gwen Cherrell*
HILDA TABLET	*Mary O'Farrell*
ELSA STRAUSS	*Marjorie Westbury*
NANCY SHEWIN	*Dorothy Primrose*
OWEN SHEWIN	*Denis Quilley*
JANET SHEWIN	*Gwen Cherrell*
BRIAN SHEWIN	*Wilfred Downing*
GEORGE SHEWIN	*Marjorie Westbury*
ADELA	*Diana Maddox*
BETTY	*Marjorie Westbury*
VALET	*Frank Duncan*
T. H. POWERS	*Norman Shelley*
LADY BLACKIE	*Susan Richmond*
MISS RICH	*Cecile Chevreau*
MILLY, MUFFY, ETC.	*Vivienne Chatterton*
RICHARD SHEWIN'S PROSE	*Derek Hart*

Characters in Richard Shewin's novels:

MRS HEPPLE	*Mary O'Farrell*
SCUTCHEON	*Denis Quilley*
MONA STANMORE	*Diana Maddox*
ROSA STANMORE	*Marjorie Westbury*
GRACE	*Diana Maddox*
FATHER TIPPETT	*Norman Shelley*

Reeve The late Richard Shewin has been justly called the 'poet's novelist'. Other and abler pens than ours have done justice to the work that earned for him the title of the Balzac of the twentieth century. It is now ten years and more since he died, but his great series of novels are still strikingly relevant to our predicament today; indeed, Shewin may certainly be regarded as the noblest precursor of the Second Elizabethan Age.

But his literary glory is not our theme. Nor is it any part of our aim to trace the magical spell that Shewin has cast over his younger fellow-craftsmen – though it may be fairly said that scarcely a novelist since him has been untouched by his influence. We have only to think of the late Sir Hugh Walpole, cut off in the plenitude of his powers, or of Mr Graham Greene and Mr Angus Wilson, happily still with us.

The glory of all this, we have said, is not our theme; which is no less than the man himself. Even so, it is in Shewin's actual fiction that we find our first hint for an attempted discovery of the man behind the words – the first clue, we might almost say. At the close of one of his earliest novels, *The Hot and the Cold*, Mrs Hepple and Peter Scutcheon are discussing the death of the man they have both, in their different ways, loved. It may be remarked in passing that Shewin's narrative style has not, in *The Hot and the Cold*, perhaps shaken itself quite free of certain early influences. No matter: it is a young man's book ... Mrs Hepple is talking with Scutcheon:

Mrs Hepple But no, dear friend!

ewin's Prose She all but breathlessly flung the small word at him; so that he, poor Scutcheon, could not fail, almost pointedly, to stare at her 'tone'.

Mrs Hepple You could always find him if you wanted to, even though the dear fellow isn't here any more.

Prose Scutcheon was ruefully to admit to himself for many years after that it was her fine eyes rather than her fine words that 'did it' for him: which didn't however at that moment keep him from all doubtfully putting to her:

Scutcheon You could, you mean, find him in –

Mrs Hepple Yes?

Prose She smilingly invited.

Scutcheon *In the horrid mother, you mean – ?*

Prose *He had all but pronounced, when Mrs Hepple swept the horrid mother so magnificently out of the way, and with her, as Scutcheon forcibly sensed, the horrid brothers and sisters as well, that it was some small minute before he, still hazily, disengaged that she had done this only to sweep them with one of her funny high gestures ever so gloriously back again.*

Scutcheon *Then who, my dear . . . ?*

Prose *He was just about to face her with, when she, instead, faced him, and quite fairly and squarely let him 'have it':*

Mrs Hepple *All of them. The whole jolly lot.*

Prose *She radiantly brought out.*

Mrs Hepple *They all had a bit of him. He was never, poor fellow, his own. They divided him – oh, but with an unscrupulousness! – among themselves. You'd only ever understand him, if, quite triumphantly, you understood the whole family as well.*

Scutcheon *Which –*

Prose *He pertinently blurted.*

Scutcheon *– I almost, you know, don't.*

Prose THE END.

(*brief pause*)

Reeve Let us confess it frankly that that early passage seemed to offer us the very key with which in the end we might unlock Shewin's own heart. 'You'd only ever understand *him*, if, quite triumphantly, you understood the whole family as well.' Yes. Upon that hint we sought. We knew of course that the unpleasant family in *The Hot and the Cold* was in no sense a picture of Shewin's own family. Nevertheless his family was our starting-point. And looking back now, it is a not unmoving experience to recall our first venture into the Shewin penumbra: the day of our first encounter with Mr Stephen Shewin, the novelist's one surviving brother (happily still with us), an interview so graciously accorded, so immediately illuminating, and so reassuring about the soundness of our method. It was a day in April. We were received by Mrs Stephen Shewin, at all times so unsparing in her efforts to help us.

(*most of the following scene is accompanied by the plaintive mewings of cats, varyingly intense. Mrs Stephen Shewin ('Connie') is gentle and charming in voice.*

door-knocker; brief pause; then mewing of cats, behind; door-knocker again:)

Connie (distantly behind door) Is that Mr Reeve?

Reeve Yes. I am Herbert Reeve. Good afternoon. I think you are expecting me?

Connie (a little pause) The door isn't locked. Would you mind just pushing it, please, and *sliding* through? Please? . . . So as not to let Muffy out?

Reeve Yes, I – yes, certainly, I can try.
     (mewings a little louder)

Connie Thank you so much, Mr Reeve. Good afternoon.

Reeve Good afternoon.

Connie You'll think me so very rude, but I can't move for pussies, and I daren't let them out, or leave them in the kitchen while I'm cooking their tea, and I don't like them to get upstairs to my husband while he's in bed; he speaks a little sharply to them at times, and they *mind*, you know.

Reeve Oh, I do hope Mr Shewin isn't ill?

Connie Oh no, Mr Reeve . . . Now, pussy, if I put you down, you'll promise not to go and climb in the sink? What? The sink, yes. Very well, then; and try and be a best girl. Oh no, Mr Reeve, my husband's not ill, he just prefers to stay in bed all the time. Could you just *hand* Muffy to me, please, Mr Reeve, and I can just *slide* her into the kitchen.

Reeve There.

Connie Nice Muffy. Thank you very much. It's so very difficult keeping an eye on all six of them. I expect you'd rather go up to my husband's bedroom; it's the second on the right on the first landing. Don't be nervous, will you?

Reeve N-nervous, Mrs Shewin?

Connie It's . . . I'm afraid it is true he did throw some small object or other at poor Miss Edwards when she was writing *her* book about Richard. But it really wasn't what people said, Mr Reeve, they do exaggerate: it was more of a large teacup actually. No, not just now, pussy. And Mr Reeve; *please* don't broach the subject too soon, if you don't mind . . .

Reeve Oh, of course not . . .

Connie And would you mind stepping over Milly? She's on the third step from the top: she always likes to sit there when she's making her kitties . . . And if you wouldn't mind just *sliding* into the bedroom, so she can't follow you.

Reeve Of course. The second on the right, I think you said?

Connie On the first landing, yes . . . (*receding*) Snow-dove, Snow-dove, where are you, darling?

    (*Reeve mounts the stairs*)

Reeve (*solemnly*) No one could approach a first meeting with the novelist's brother, without memories crowding into the mind, of . . . Hello, Milly. Nice pussy?

Milly Aa.

Reeve May I step over you?

Milly Aa.

Reeve A *big*-big pussy, aren't you?

Milly Aa.

Reeve . . . without memories crowding into the mind, of the touching pictures of brotherhood that occur in the later novels. It is a not unmoving experience to recall our first knock at the door.

    (*knock at door. Stephen Shewin's voice is a quiet, self-pitying and self-satisfied drip, achieved by years of practice; he never whines.*)

Stephen Come in.

    (*door opens*)

Reeve Good afternoon, Mr Shewin.

    (*pause*)

Stephen I am not ill, Mr Reeves, if that is what you are thinking, not at all.

Reeve Oh, I thought, perhaps, seeing you in –

Stephen You may disregard that, Mr Reeves. I spend most of my time here. I've never seen any point in getting up, if there's nothing to get up for.

Reeve Er . . . no.

Stephen And there's been nothing to get up for in my life for a very long time.

Reeve (*regretfully*) Oh, I'm very –

Stephen Mr Reeves: I am less than the dust, in this house, Mr Reeves.

Reeve Oh, I . . .

Stephen You came to ask about my late brother.

Reeve Well, sir, if . . .

Stephen Yes. Others have come here for the same purpose.

    (*pause*)

I am less than the dust in this house, Mr Reeves. I have always been less than the dust. Do sit down, if you would find it more

Stephen   comfortable. Just remove my *Inhibitions, Symptoms and Anxiety* off the chair, if you please.

Reeve   Oh, thank you. Yes.

Stephen   Yes. And speaking of chariot wheels, Mr Reeves, I may say my late brother rode roughshod over my feelings on many an occasion. You know only the outer rind of my brother, Mr Reeves, the gaudy self-display of his so-called literary writings, but inside of that outer rind, Mr Reeves, many strange things beat, ticked and pulsed. Was there any particular question you wanted to ask me?

Reeve   Well sir, if you wouldn't mind –

Stephen   And, Mr Reeves; would you be so kind as to pass me that jug of water from the chest of drawers, please? I like to have it by me.

Reeve   Y–yes, certainly. There.

    (*the jug is put down quietly*)

Stephen   Thank you.

    (*pause*)

Reeve   Well . . . of course, Mr Shewin, there are many things I would like to ask about.

Stephen   I drink a great deal of water, Mr Reeves. Lying here, quietly thinking, staring into the past, weighing, very carefully and thoughtfully, the rights of one thing and the wrongs of another, I drink a great deal of water.

    (*a brief pause*)

Reeve   Yes, I . . .

Stephen   A very great deal. (*after a very brief pause*) It wasn't a nice thing to say, was it? I much regretted it . . .

Reeve   Oh no, Mr Shewin, please say anything you wish, I . . .

Stephen   And to say it to a brother, a *younger* brother. He said to me: 'If *I* hadn't, Steve, somebody else would have.' He knew I hated being called Steve.

Reeve   You mean . . . that Richard . . . Mr Shewin . . . said . . .?

Stephen   Do not think for a single instant, Mr Reeves, that it was the low, common debauchery of it I minded. No. It was his making up nasty little poems about it I objected to.

Reeve   (*rather eagerly*) Poems? I had no idea Richard Shewin wrote poetry. One might have guessed it, of course. He has been justly called the poet's novelist.

Stephen   A private book of them in his own handwriting.

Reeve   Good heavens. And are they extant?

Stephen I wouldn't like to say what they are. I was looking at them only yesterday morning, and they made me feel bitter, aggrieved and depressed: for me, and for him, that he should have sunk so low as to write such things: a brother.

Reeve Do . . . do you think I might be allowed to see them?

Stephen I would have to know you a great deal better than I do as yet, Mr Reeves.

Reeve Reeve is the name.

Stephen Whose?

Reeve M-mine.

Stephen (*absently*) Yes, I suppose it is. Perhaps I shall show them to you, Mr Reeve, perhaps I shan't, time alone will tell. Mr Reeve . . .

Reeve Yes sir?

Stephen If you cared to turn your head, Mr Reeve, you would see a picture hanging on the wall behind it.

Reeve I . . . oh, yes.

Stephen *The Woman Taken in Adultery by Titian*, Mr Reeve. That is the title of the picture . . . And still it did no good.

Reeve I don't quite . . .

Stephen With a brother's wife too, Mr Reeve.

Reeve (*aghast*) I . . . I'm deeply sorry, sir.

Stephen I could have borne it. I have borne much in my life, I have had to, of course. But writing unsavoury ditties on the subject. Shouting them about the place.

Reeve Indeed?

Stephen Yes, in a cheerful and hilarious fashion. And pretending they were my wife's own words:

> *I like to sleep with Richard,*
> > *Better than with poor old Steve . . .*

The coarseness of it all.

Reeve Do you mean that Richard Shewin wrote those words?

Stephen Yes.

> *I like to sleep with Richard,*
> > *Better than with poor old Steve.*
> *Richard doesn't keep telling me*
> > *Just how I make him grieve.*
> *And I know when Richard tickles me,*
> > *Or bites me on the rump,*
> *It isn't for any subconscious reason:*
> > *He does it to make me jump.*

Now, Mr Reeve, that's a cruelly unkind remark to make about my subconscious, isn't it? Yes. I never jibed or mocked at his, whatever it led him to do.

Reeve (*shocked*) But ... forgive me ... I hope I'm not being impertinent, but I had never imagined that Richard and ...

Stephen (*smugly*) And my wife, yes. I would find them in this very chamber, Mr Reeve, I was gravely displeased. But it was the nasty remarks in the poems that wounded, grieved and hurt me. And they were not all. I won't offend your ears by reciting the whole poem –

Reeve Oh, please don't mind ...

Stephen If poem it can be called. I will content myself with mentioning its concluding lines:

> So that's why I leave poor old Stephen
> And hop over to Richard instead:
> Psychology's all right in the proper place,
> But I know what I like in bed.

To think of it, Mr Grieve! Why, if we don't take our psychology seriously, where are we? *Where are we?* Nowhere, nowhere. I've always taken my psychology very seriously, that's why I'm able to do without doctors. I have an anxiety-neurosis, Mr Grieve: an anxiety to *please*, an anxiety to do the very best I can for other people, whoever they may be, but Richard used to take advantage of it, he would take advantage of anybody's. 'You take advantage of my anxiety-neurosis, Richard,' I used to say to him, and one day he said, 'Well thank God it isn't a you-know-what', he said, and that was a very unkind thing to say also, Mr Reeves, because he knew as well as I did that I *had* a you-know-what. Why, Mr Reeves, in those days I just couldn't step off a moving-staircase, I dreaded it, Mr Reeves, dreaded it, and a lot of sensitive people are just the same. It's not a laughing matter, is it? No, no ... No. (*after a pause, very thoughtfully*) No.

Reeve I am very sorry at what you have told me, Mr Shewin. I can understand your distress.

Stephen Yes.

Reeve All we can tell ourselves, I suppose, is that genius is a law unto itself, and that –

Stephen (*sharply*) Mr Reeve.

Reeve Yes, Mr Shewin?

Stephen (*quickly*) Mr Reeve, when you go away, would you be so very kind as to just *slide* round the door, so that Milly doesn't get into the room?

Reeve (*hastily*) Oh, of course, sir, I do hope I haven't . . .

Stephen Oh, don't regard that as an intimation to depart, Mr Reeve. Please resume your seat.

Reeve Thank you . . .

Stephen I suppose you have interviewed other people on the subject of my late brother?

Reeve Well, I intend to, of course; I have plans to call on a great number of people.

Stephen (*subtly*) I wonder if you will be visiting the . . . (*pause*) but no, of course, you wouldn't have heard of them.

Reeve Whom are you referring to, sir?

Stephen I never met them myself, of course. I just knew the address. That was all.

Reeve Well, sir, perhaps you would . . .

Stephen I've no doubt they knew more about him than his unfortunate family ever did. He probably wasn't as mean with them as he was with us. Or as ruthless.

Reeve With whom, Mr Shewin?

Stephen The two Miss Burkleys. You haven't met them, I suppose? Miss Adela Burkley and Miss Elizabeth Burkley.

Reeve (*eagerly*) No . . . But if . . .

Stephen (*earnestly*) The address, Mr Reeve, is in Shepherd Market, and runs as follows: 17 Beech Street, W.1.

Reeve Just let me write that down, will you . . . It's so kind of you.

Stephen I suppose you will never visit me again, Mr Reeve?

Reeve If I may, sir, I should be honoured to call at any time you will allow me.

Stephen Then pray do, Mr Reeve. I am anxious to do my best for you. Or for anyone in the whole wide world, if it comes to that. It is what I live for, after all. I have no doubt that other qualities of my late brother will recur to my mind at intervals.

Reeve (*a little sadly*) What you have already told me does, of course, to some extent upset certain preconceived ideas I had.

Stephen Yes.

Reeve But no doubt things will fall into their place. Your brother, after all, Mr Shewin, was probably the greatest literary figure of our . . .

Stephen Mr Reeve.

Reeve Yes, sir?

Stephen Mr Reeve, when you go away, would you be so very kind as to just *slide* round the door, so that Milly doesn't get into the room?

Reeve Oh yes, of course, sir, certainly. I must be off. And thank you so much, Mr Shewin, for all your very great kindness to me.

Stephen Yes.

    (*door closes gently*)

Reeve (*descending the stair*) It was, as we have said, a not unmoving experience, to see for the first time in the flesh, the Shewin family face; for clearly in the features of the great novelist's brother, Mr Stephen Shewin . . .

Milly (*loud protest*) Aaaaaaah!

Reeve Oh, so sorry, pussy.

Milly Psst!

Reeve Oh dear.

Connie (*at a little distance*) How was he, Mr Reeve? Forgive me for not asking you into the kitchen, but pussies are having their tea. How was he?

Reeve He was most kind and helpful.

Connie Did he mention his brother at all, I wonder? He's always so very reticent . . . (*cat noises*) And I'm afraid there was sometimes bad blood between them, Mr Reeve.

Reeve Yes, he was very frank, I'm afraid, Mrs Shewin.

Connie He is nowadays sometimes, yes. No, pussy. Of course it was a long time ago. I've quite forgiven him.

Reeve F-forgiven?

Connie Oh, one does, you know, Mr Reeve, one has to. And really, he's a very simple man, my husband. I hope you didn't get the idea that he . . . took Richard's wife *away* from Richard.

Reeve No . . . I . . . Mr Shewin said nothing that even made me suspect such a thing.

Connie Oh no, it was *she* who led my husband astray. Poor Richard was very upset. He would never enter this house, you know.

Reeve Wh . . . Wh . . . *Really?*

    (*cats*)

Connie No, not today, pussies. Of course, it's far in the past. Better to forget it. You will come and see us again, Mr Reeve, when the maid is in, and I can give you tea?

Reeve Thank you very much.
(*cat*)

Connie And Mr Reeve, perhaps you'd just *slide* out of the front door? Muffy has got her eye on it.
(*cats*)
Now, (*begin to fade*) I thought a Muffy promised to be a best girl this afternoon . . .?
(*cats fade*)

Reeve (*thoughtfully*) A full consideration of the great richness of Richard Shewin's domestic relationships will perhaps have to wait until later. It is even possible that complete and accurate details are not yet available. What Professor Grilling has called the brother-motive in Shewin's later work offers the student particularly fascinating, if somewhat baffling, material. It is, of course, only the other side of the sister-motive in the novels of his early-middle period: in *The Up and the Down*, for example, or *The Light and the Home*, to name but two. But, as many a critic has asked, where did this intimate knowledge come from? For Shewin had no sisters . . . (*modestly*) We . . . we think we are at last able to cast light upon that question. It was, indeed, with something akin to certainty, that at Mr Stephen Shewin's suggestion, we approached the presence of the Misses Adela and Elizabeth Burkley. Here, surely, if anywhere . . .
(*fade*)

(*the voices of Adela and Betty are only a little 'off', as far as accent goes. They are very agreeable and pleasant; Adela is considerably less bright than her sister, and is obviously unused to the kind of conversation with which the scene begins*)
(*fade in*)

Adela You'd think it would never stop, really. My sister says she's never known rain like it.

Reeve No, indeed.

Adela Beg pardon?

Reeve I said: no, indeed.

Adela Yes.

Reeve You knew Mr Shewin very well, I believe, Miss Burkley?

Adela Beg pardon?

Reeve I imagine you knew Mr Shewin very well?

Adela Well, just ... you know. Of course, he was always very nice.

Reeve Oh, yes, everyone says so.

Adela Very nice indeed. And considerate, too.

Reeve Did he discuss his work very much, I wonder?

Adela Beg pardon?

Reeve Did he ever vouchsafe any information about what he was working on?

Adela Well, he was always very nice, of course.

Reeve I meant, did he ... I hope all this doesn't seem impertinent, Miss Burkley?

Adela Beg pardon?

Reeve I ... hope I'm not taking up too much of your time?

Adela Oh, no, certainly not.

Reeve I ... (*he pauses*)

Adela Did *you* know Dicky Shewin, at all?

Reeve Oh, was he ever called Dicky? I didn't know that.

Adela (*hastily*) Well, no, not really of course. I usually called him Mr Shewin. So did my sister. He really liked her the best, I think. She should be here by now.

Reeve Yes, I look forward to meeting her.

Adela She's blonde, of course.

Reeve (*disconcerted*) B ... blonde?

Adela Almost platinum, really. But it *is* the natural colour, really it is. (*sincerely*) People don't always believe it, but it is. You look at the roots, close to.

Reeve Ah, yes? ... No, I never knew Shewin myself. I was rather of a younger generation, I'm afraid.

Adela Oh yes, I could tell you were young.

Reeve In fact, I never actually saw him; but I sometimes think that people of my generation appreciate him more than his own contemporaries did.

Adela Beg pardon?

Reeve I mean that today one is perhaps beginning to appreciate his real size.

Adela (*baffled*) But ... Mr Shewin was never a *large* gentleman.

Reeve No; his genius, I mean.

Adela Beg pardon?

Reeve His genius.

Adela Was Mr Shewin a genius?

Reeve Well, I suppose it depends on one's standards.

Adela Beg pardon?

Reeve *I've* always thought him a genius, certainly.

Adela Fancy. *(after a reflective pause)* Well. *(after another)* He never said so.

Reeve Oh, no, of course not. He was well known for his modesty.

Adela His what?

Reeve His modesty.

Adela *(with sudden certainty)* Oh *no*. Not Mr Shewin.

Reeve Yes, surely, everyone . . .

Adela Oh no. Mind you, he was very nice. But he was never modest. *(rapidly and definitely)* He was very nice, but he was never modest.
   (door bangs, off)

Betty *(distant)* You in, Addy? It's raining like a bloody –

Adela *(hastily and loudly)* Hello, dear, the gentleman's called. That's my sister. I'll tell her. And I'll put the kettle on. You'd like a cup of tea, I expect?

Reeve Thank you, very much.

Adela Tweeeeet?

Reeve *(startled)* I . . .

Adela I was just speaking to Joey: he's just behind you. Our canary. Tweet?

Joey *(single note, long)* Tweeeeet?

Adela 'Scuse me. I'll send Betty in.

Joey Tweeeet? . . . *(emphatically)* Tweeeeeeet?

Reeve *(politely)* Tweet . . . Tweet . . . It is an interesting fact that, though Shewin always preserved a scrupulous modesty in estimating his own work among his fellow-craftsmen and in intellectual society generally, he was less reticent among humbler people.

Joey Tweet?

Reeve Tweet. Nothing is perhaps more revealing of the true nature of the man than this.

Joey Tweeeet? Tweeeet?

Reeve Tweet. We need not despise him for it. In simple and unaffected company he could appear in what someone, speaking of Beethoven's rondos, has called an 'unbuttoned' mood. That is all it means.

Joey *(enthusiastically)* Tweeeeeeet? . . . Tweeeeeeet?

Betty *(sweetly and cheerfully)* Hellooo . . . I'm Betty.

Reeve Twee . . . good afternoon.

Betty Pleased to meet you. Bobby's putting the kettle on.

Reeve Bobby?

Betty Oh, of course, I expect you're still calling her Adela. Pretty name, isn't it?

Adela (*approaching*) I've put the kettle on, dear. Betty, the gentleman was saying Mr Shewin was a *modest* gentleman. (*gently*) He wasn't, was he, dear?

Betty Modest? My word, no. Nobody could say that. He was an all-the-lights-on man, Dicky Shewin was, every time.

Adela And a looking-glass too.

Betty My word, yes. He was very vexed if there wasn't a looking-glass.

Reeve That *is* interesting.

Adela Why, he *bought* Betty her looking-glass, didn't he, dear?

Betty Yes, dear. Would you like to see it, Mr Shewin?

Reeve Oh, very much, if I may.

Betty It's just in my bedroom. This way, please, just across the passage . . .
      (*slight fade on last words*)

Reeve Richard Shewin's generosity to his younger contemporaries does much to discountenance the charges of meanness sometimes levelled against him. We have ourselves inspected the very large cheval-mirror which he gave, doubtless as a Christmas or a birthday gift, to Miss Elizabeth Burkley of Shepherd Market, London. It is a not unmoving experience to stand before this mirror today, to realise how often it must have reflected the features of Shewin himself, and to imagine him swivelling it (as he is said to have enjoyed doing) now this way, now that.

Betty I suppose you must have been a great friend of Mr Shewin?

Adela No, dear. The gentleman's writing a book about him.

Betty Writing a book about Dicky Shewin? Fancy. A *reading*-book?

Reeve (*modestly*) Well, I . . . hope somebody will read it.

Adela (*kindly*) Oh I'm sure somebody will.

Reeve I hope you will allow me to send you a copy when it's finished.

Adela Oh, thank you, that would be kind. We could do with a book about the place.

Betty (*interested*) It's a thing I've never read, is a book.

Adela Oh, I've read one.

Betty Have you, dear? When?

Adela Oh, when I was in the hospital.

Betty Was it nice?

Adela Not really, no.

Betty No, I've heard other people say that. Well, if you do mention Dicky Shewin in this book, you *will* say how *very* nice he *always* was, won't you?

Adela And considerate.

Betty (*eagerly*) Yes. Put that in: he was very considerate.

Adela Not like the one who came with him the first few times, the one who never even gave his name.

Reeve How extremely uncivil.

Adela Beg pardon?

Reeve I said how uncivil.

Adela Well, some of them don't, of course. But this was a really nasty man.

Reeve I wonder who it can have been?

Betty Dicky always *called* him T.H.P.

Adela So he did.

Reeve Oh, I see! Yes, that must have been T. H. Powers, the novelist.

Adela Was *he* a genius as well?

Reeve (*laughs*) I'm afraid not. Of course, when he was younger, there were people who thought he might go quite a long way.

Betty (*politely*) Well, it wasn't for the want of trying, if he didn't.

Adela (*quietly*) Hush, dear.

Joey Tweeeeet?

Reeve No indeed. Actually I'm calling on him in a few days' time. I'll tell him I've had the pleasure of meeting you.

Adela (*nervously*) Oh no, I shouldn't do that, if I were you.

Joey Tweeet?

Betty He mightn't like it, you know. A lot of them don't.

Joey Tweeeet? Tweeet? Tweeeeeeeeet?

(*brief pause*)

Reeve One is always venturing upon dangerous ground in drawing parallels between an author's fiction and what we know of his life; but it seems to us reasonably clear that the two Miss Burkleys, so courageously living out their spinsterhood in their little flat in Shepherd Market, London, must have provided at least the *donnée*, or hint, for the two lonely sisters, Mona and Rosa Stanmore, in the novel called *The Quick and the Slow*. We are thinking especially of the wonderful 'dying fall' of the closing pages of that moving story.

(in the following passage Mona is played by Adela, and Rosa is played by Betty. Their voices are now normal and well-bred)

Shewin's Prose   *This silence between them: surely it could not be allowed to go on for ever, thought Mona. But how to break it? At last, not quite looking in Rosa's direction, she said.*

Mona   *Did you have a pleasant walk, darling?*

Prose   *Rosa seemed to smoulder for a moment. Then even that sullen fire seemed to die out, and she replied firmly.*

Rosa   *At least I did no harm. The Earls Court Road was not disturbed in any way by my passage along it. I went into the park, sat, watched the birds making their nests, read ten pages of* Les Liaisons Dangereuses, *and returned as I went. I was at no point approached by any undesirable stranger.*

(brief pause)

Prose   *Mona threw her arms round her sister.*

Mona   *(whispers) Darling, don't, don't, don't . . .*

Prose   *She whispered.*

Mona   *. . . don't give way to bitterness. I know you think that life has passed us by. But don't, don't be bitter, darling.*

Prose   *Rosa gently but firmly disengaged herself, and stood up. She looked coldly down into Mona's face as into that of a stranger. Then she said, quietly and slowly.*

Rosa   *Bitterness, Miss Mona Stanmore? . . . What have we to be bitter about?*

Prose   THE END.

(briefest pause)

Reeve   *(rather more energetically than hitherto)* These analogies, of course, must not be pressed too far, if only in deference to the living, many of whom are happily still with us. Above all, we must not forget that the aim of all biographical study is, now as ever, *the exact and objective ascertainment of establishable facts.* And none can be too humble.

(The valet is efficient, agreeable, civil, and answers every question without hesitation. He has some sort of accent, but in view of the restrained nature of his discourse it will not be easy to tell what it is)

Valet   *(fades in)* I did, yes. Yes, I did.

Reeve   And I understand that you acted as Mr Shewin's valet for a considerable number of years?

Valet I did, yes.

Reeve You stayed with him for about twelve years, all told?

Valet I did, yes.

Reeve You joined him, I think, in 1920?

Valet Yes, I did.

Reeve I believe you looked after him during his illness in 1924?

Valet Yes . . . I did.

Reeve And then you went with him to Austria when he recovered?

Valet Yes, I did.

Reeve I gather from his letters that you sometimes accompanied him on his evening walks in Salzburg and Vienna?

Valet Yes . . . I *did*.

Reeve And that you both greatly enjoyed this jaunt abroad.

Valet *I* did, yes.

Reeve You also became Mr Shewin's chauffeur when he bought a motor-car in 1927?

Valet I did, yes.

Reeve And drove him on many occasions down to his country home?

Valet I did, yes.

Reeve You preferred the car to the train?

Valet I did, yes.

Reeve And you always found Mr Shewin a kind and considerate employer?

Valet Yes, I did.

(*Last eight speeches have a steady accelerando; fade on last two*)

Reeve Information of this kind is, needless to say, the very stuff of biography. It is the more subjective impressions that we must beware of, especially when a man has, like Shewin, been greatly loved by the world. It may be added that Shewin returned that love, ay, and more than returned it. One of our modern neo-pessimists has remarked with characteristic acidity: *L'enfer, c'est les autres*: Hell consists of other people . . . We know what Shewin's comment on that would have been. 'Yes,' he would have said, with his familiar wry smile: 'Yes, but so does Heaven.' We have often imagined him saying that. Such a man, and this is our point, awakens an affection among his fellows that may blind them a little to his faults.

It was with eager interest that we looked forward to talking with the novelist, T. H. Powers. Shewin was, of course, considerably older than Powers, and Mr Powers's novels had never reached anything like the large public enjoyed by those of Shewin himself. So that Shewin had become, quite naturally, a hero to the younger aspirant in his own lovely art. We were not unprepared for a little hero-worship on the part of Mr Powers. And why should we despise unaffected hero-worship, God help us?

(*Powers is nearly sixty. His voice, exquisitely modulated and varied, glows like a beautiful trombone*)

Powers So you're writing a book on old Dick Shewin, Mr Reeves? Ye-es . . . Not *much* of a subject, is it?

Reeve Well . . .

Powers Have you ever thought of writing a book on . . . Robert Louis Stevenson?

Reeve No.

Powers That might be a good subject for you, you know. (*musingly*) Or Meredith even – not much been done on him. Gissing might be interesting too . . . or Henry James, of course, always there . . . and Hardy . . . no, perhaps not Hardy . . . too many books on him as it is.

Reeve Well, I feel Richard Shewin will last me a very long time, you know, sir. It's a fascinating theme, his life, isn't it?

Powers Is it? Yes, perhaps it is . . . H'm . . . The 'poet's novelist', what? (*shrewdly*) *You* a poet?

Reeve N-no.

Powers Novelist?

Reeve No, I once . . . No, I'm not.

Powers (*enigmatically*) Ah, then you start with certain obvious advantages.

Reeve Well, I try to think so.

Powers Oh yes, I should. Well, Mr Reefer, I will of course be glad to give you any help I can, about h'm . . . ah . . . Dick Shewin.

Reeve Thank you. I felt sure you would, sir.

Powers Oh, yes. Yes. Where to begin? Shewin, m'mmm, Richard Shewin . . . *knew me rather well*. Ra-ther well. He liked me partly, I think, because I was younger than he was. He liked people to confide in him, you know.

Reeve Yes, he must have exercised a most compelling influence over people younger than himself.

Powers M'm? Well, it would never have occurred to me to put it quite like that, you know. He *absorbed* a good deal from other people, you might say. Yes: shall we put it like that? Yes. A great absorber. A magpie, a dear old magpie sort of chap ... Of course, you couldn't help liking him for it, in a way. One'd find him ... oh, *imitating* one. One's gestures, you know, one's turns of phrases, what? Yes. Imitating.

Reeve *(innocently)* You mean for fun?

Powers Fun? *(lightly)* Good God, no. No, I mean that he would absorb from his friends whatever he could. *Je prends mon bien où je le trouve* sort of business. Yes. You've probably noticed how very derivative his novels are: *(modestly)* I wonder if you've read a little thing of mine called *The Dark Backward and Abysm*?

Reeve Oh yes, of course, sir: I enjoyed it very much.

Powers Still readable is it? Good. Well, you'll probably have noticed that a good deal of Shewin's novel, *The Floor and the Ceiling*, came from it.

Reeve But ... if I may say so, sir, *The Floor and the Ceiling* was published several years earlier than your own splendid novel, Mr Powers ...

Powers *(unperturbed)* Oh yes, yes, yes, yes, yes, we all know that. But you didn't imagine it was *written* earlier, did you? Oh no. I ... I *withheld* my own novel for several years, Mr Reaper, I usually do. It is my wont.

Reeve Of course, I didn't know that.

Powers It is my way. I have never believed in rushing into print. Rather a perfectionist, you know, what? Ra-ther a perfectionist. Shewin ... wasn't. Of course I was very ... very-very fond of the old thing.

Reeve Yes, I believe everyone was.

Powers Oh I wouldn't say that. Of course one can see the significance of it all now, what with the advance of psychiatry and all that.

Reeve The significance of ...?

Powers The old boy's imitativeness, you know. Yes. Hahaha! You know all about that, of course, you moderns, what?

Reeve Well, I ... I *don't*, I'm afraid.

Powers *(coyly)* Surely ... come, come.

Reeve No, really, sir, I don't.

Powers Oh, dear. Well, how shall I put it? Dear me. *(whimsically amused)* *l'impuissance* ... shall we call it?

Reeve Good gracious.

Powers A great worry to the old boy, of course. But very imitative people often are ... *un peu incapable* in that way, shall we say? And of course we all knew about poor old Shewin.

Reeve (*unhappily*) Well, really, Mr Powers, that isn't at all the impression I've gathered from *some* people I've talked to lately about Shewin.

Powers (*chillily*) Well, of course, Mr Heap, you doubtless have superior sources of information to mine; I was merely ...

Reeve Oh, please, sir, don't misunderstand me, I do beg you; it was only that ...

Powers But tell me, Mr Heave ...

Reeve Yes?

Powers Tell me: have you ever, I wonder, thought of writing the biography of ... a *living* author? *M'mmm?*

Reeve Well, no, never ... you see, I have been interested in Shewin almost since I was a boy.

Powers (*benignly*) He's a boy's writer, of course ... So you've never thought of a living author as a subject?

Reeve No, I'm afraid not.

Powers (*thoughtfully*) Interesting, that. Very.

Reeve I do agree, of course, that ... (*tails off*)

Powers (*encouragingly*) Ye-es?

Reeve A living subject could be very engrossing.

Powers (*in dulcet tones*) Very ... very. There have been very good books about living authors. Some of the best, in fact. After all, think of the advantages: you can ... ah ... consult with the ... ah ... subject. The ... ah ... oh, it could be very interesting.

Reeve (*faintly*) Yes.

Powers Especially if he was in the habit of keeping diaries, and was willing to supervise the work ... and that sort of thing. Do you ... enjoy reading personal memoirs, Mr Green?

Reeve Yes, very much. It's been a great setback to me that there are no real Shewin diaries.

Powers Oh, there'd have been nothing in 'em, my dear boy. Just one luncheon engagement after another with this or that rather dubious member of the aristocracy. (He couldn't resist a title, you know.)

Reeve Well, he is said to have refused a knighthood.

Powers Said, yes. But ... does one really know if he was ever offered one?

Reeve Oh, yes.

Powers When?

Reeve The year after he was awarded the Nobel Prize.

Powers (*demurely*) Some writers have refused even *that* award, you know, Mr Weave.

Reeve Refused the Nobel Pr- - -!

Powers Oh, yes. However . . . You were saying that you liked memoirs. I have, myself, written about twenty-two folio notebooks-full of memoirs. (I've knocked about quite a bit, you know.) I think you *might* find them *ra*-ther fascinating. Many interesting people have been numbered among my friends.

Reeve Yes. (*suddenly*) Oh, of course.

Powers Ye-es?

Reeve I'd quite forgotten: how rude of me.

Powers Nooooo . . .

Reeve Two friends of yours asked to be remembered to you.

Powers How kind, my dear fellow, both of them and of you. Who were the dear creatures?

Reeve The Miss Burkleys.

Powers Who?

Reeve Miss Adela and Miss Elizabeth Burkley. They live in Beech Street, just off –

Powers (*sharply*) Mr Treves!

Reeve (*amazed*) I . . . really, sir . . . they . . .

Powers Mr Treves! (*icily*) Is this blackmail? (*loudly*) You, you, despicable . . . *thing!* Is this blackmail, sir?

    (*pause*)

Reeve It is, unfortunately, quite true that Shewin's surviving diaries are little more than engagement-books. But they reveal a good deal of the rich social texture of Shewin's life. For over twenty years he lunched or dined out almost every day during the London season. Many of the people whose names he noted in these little pocket volumes are, alas, no more; but his surviving friends have told us much about the part he played in the dazzling political social life he so well portrays in such novels as *The Bang and the Whimper*. We are especially indebted to Lady Blackie, who can look back on more than seventy years of life in London, and into whose clutches – into whose clu-clusters of celebrated guests Shewin inevitably . . . drift- - - was drawn.

    (*he has become a little confused, and ends rather lamely*)

(Lady Blackie is about eighty-nine; her zest for life has increased with the years)

Lady Blackie *(coughing slightly)* No, don't put out your cigar, Mr Reeve, I like the smell. A little more brandy? I don't drink myself any more, of course; but they tell me it's quite nice. Sir Redvers Buller used to tell me it was the best brandy he'd ever tasted. And to this day, Graham drinks quantities of it: quantities.

Reeve It's excellent.

Lady B. What?

Reeve *(louder)* It's excellent.

Lady B. So sorry to make you shout; but I'm getting so deaf these days.

Reeve Did Richard Shewin drink very much, Lady Blackie?

Lady B. Did he what?

Reeve Drink very much?

Lady B. Well, it's very odd you should ask that: it was always a bit of a mystery to me. I had always been told he never drank at all. And certainly the first time he came here he never did. I remember it was a little luncheon-party I gave for him and Charlie Chaplin. Just a few friends we had in: oh ... Willie Maugham, I think, and Margot and Max, and Mr Yeats, and Sir Flinders Petrie (such a clever man! What a loss!). And I forget who else was there. Ellen Terry, I expect – she usually was. And Mr Shewin never drank at all on that occasion. But certainly he always drank a very great deal whenever he came afterwards.

Reeve Indeed?

Lady B. And very often he seemed to have drunk a very great deal before he got here. Still people are very unpredictable about drink, aren't they? One day when Mr Bernard Shaw came to luncheon, I saw him looking at a glass of Burgundy quite longingly.

Reeve Really?

Lady B. Yes. And once Mr Dylan Thomas came, and drank water.

Reeve Can you remember what Shewin used to talk about, I wonder?

Lady B. What? Oh, about friends, you know, we usually talked about our friends. He was always very nice about everybody. He did once make rather an unkind remark about Bosie, but people did, you know; and I don't think Bosie heard.

Reeve An unkind remark about *whom*, Lady Blackie?

Lady B. Bosie.

Reeve Bosie ... ?

Lady B. What?

Reeve Bosie who, Lady Blackie?

Lady B. Yes, Bosie . . . Did *you* get on with him?

Reeve I don't think I know who you –

Lady B. I'm so sorry to make you shout, Mr Reeve. Something seems to have gone wrong with my little hearing-aid. Sometimes if I shake it . . .

> (*she does so. It emits a long quiet whirr, ending in a soft musical ping*)
> There, perhaps that's better.
> (*a long silence follows*)

Yes, that's much better, I can hear you perfectly, now.

Reeve I . . .

Lady B. M'm? Sorry?

Reeve . . . .

Lady B. Oh, yes, I think so too; I did at the time. It was obvious . . . But I'm sorry you didn't like poor little Bosie.

Reeve I didn't say that, Lady Blackie. I was merely asking who he was.

Lady B. Who?

Reeve Bosie.

Lady B. I never minded at all. Of course not.

Reeve But, please forgive me, Lady Blackie, whom do you mean when you say Bosie?

Lady B. They both were. I knew all along.

Reeve You said Richard Shewin once –

Lady B. Yes, it does sometimes.

Reeve Made an unkind remark –

Lady B. At other times, it's as clear as a day in June.

> (*fade*)

Reeve We must not of course exaggerate the social element in Shewin's life. We remember that in the novel, *The Top and the Bottom*, the hero, after each of his excursions into high life, returns to the bosom of his family 'to make', as he puts it, 'a fresh start': nine times in all. It is perhaps something more than a coincidence that in our studies Shewin's own family has provided for us a number of . . . similar 'fresh starts'.

Stephen Good afternoon, Mr Reeve; who let you in?

Reeve The . . . the maid, Mr Shewin.

Stephen Yes. (*pause*) Mr Reeve.

Reeve Yes, sir?

Stephen My wife's left me, Mr Reeve.

Reeve *Left* you, Mr Shewin! Oh dear, I am sorry, sir. What a dreadful thing.

Stephen All of a piece, isn't it, Mr Reeve? It all fits. How good of you to call. The influence of a dead person can do a great deal.

Reeve I . . . I don't quite understand, Mr Shewin.

Stephen My late brother. His spirit, as you see, lingers on. In the watches of the night, Mr Reeve, I sometimes hear him mocking me with his nasty scurril.

Reeve His nasty what?

Stephen (*sharply*) Scurril. (*with a sigh*) All, all of a piece throughout. Imagine it, Mr Reeve. The empty house, the loneliness, day after day. If I even had a television machine . . .

Reeve I'm terribly sorry: is there anything I can do?

Stephen Oh, no, it was to be. I must bear it with fortitude, that's all. I hope your researches are proceeding satisfactorily, Mr Reeve. How did you get on with Miss Tablet?

Reeve Miss Tablet?

Stephen I thought I gave you her address?

Reeve No. It was the two Miss Burkleys; and very kind and helpful they were too. I am most grateful, sir. But . . . who is Miss . . .?

Stephen Tablet.

Reeve I don't think I . . .

Stephen Well, it's of no consequence. Perhaps I shouldn't have mentioned her.

Reeve But dear Mr Shewin . . .

Stephen No, it would have been better not . . . *Hilda* Tablet the name was.

Reeve *Hilda* Tablet!

Stephen Yes. The lady music-writer.

Reeve Oh! I'd no idea you meant *her*.

Stephen You know about her and Richard?

Reeve No. I didn't even know they knew each other.

Stephen (*significantly reserved*) Oh.

Reeve Perhaps . . .

Stephen He said he wanted to marry her. He swore it. Some didn't believe him, some did. He didn't always tell lies. Not that I ever liked her. *I* could never have married her, quite apart from her being a lady music-writer, and the noise that that must entail. She remains a spinster to this day.

Reeve Yes . . . I knew, of course, that she was unmarried.

Stephen Yes. (*a tiny pause*) Her daughter is said to be a very nice girl however.

Reeve Her d– (*he stops, appalled*)

Stephen I, of course, have no views on the matter.

Reeve But, Mr Shewin . . .

Stephen And what else have you been doing, I wonder, while I have been lying deserted, alone, and bereft here?

Reeve Please let me ask one question about Miss Tab–

Stephen It is a change to meet anybody so interested in the past as you are, Mr Reeve. I am devoted to the study of the past, myself; its rights and wrongs I brood a great deal over. I sometimes sit up in bed and look straight at it, Mr Reeve, with a steady gaze, fixedly. The future I disregard. One cannot have eyes in the back of one's head, can one?

Reeve (*submissively*) No.

Stephen And my late brother's literary executrix, you've seen her, of course – Miss Rich?

Reeve I'm seeing her next week. It's very difficult to make an appointment with her; she's so busy the whole time.

Stephen You will find her very interesting no doubt. My brother wrote a poem about her too.

Reeve Really! About his literary executrix?

Stephen Well, she was his secretary as well, you know. And he would have written poems about anybody.

Reeve I . . . wonder if you recall it?

Stephen Extremely well, Mr Reeve. The poem began: 'Little Miss Rich' . . . (*after a pause*) and the rest of it, Mr Reeve, I would not recite to anybody. Though it was quite short, so far as it went.

Reeve I see.

Stephen A mere distich. And whom else will you be visiting?

Reeve Well, in about a fortnight's time I hope to be able to get down to Mulset to see the other part of the Shewin family. And of course the native haunts of Shewin himself.

Stephen (*horrified*) You are going to see my other brother's widow, and all that dreadful brood of children?

Reeve Yes. Mrs Edward Shewin has kindly invited me to stay for a few days.

Stephen Then I had better accompany you.

Reeve I . . . (*very uneasily*) . . . that would be delightful, of course, but . . .

Stephen I could not dream of letting you submit yourself to such an ordeal without my protection. I hope your life is insured, Mr Reeve?

Reeve Y-yes.

Stephen Good. But I had better come all the same.

Reeve But . . .

    (*mewings begin in background*)

Stephen Oh don't thank me. The change will do me harm, no doubt, but no matter. I think I would like to be alone now, Mr Reeve.

Reeve Oh yes, of course. And thank you very . . .

Stephen And, Mr Reeve . . .

Reeve Yes?

Stephen Disregard completely what I may have said about Miss Tablet. She lives at 109 Coptic Street. I am sure I have been misinformed about her. What in goodness' name are all those cats mewing about?

Reeve I'll look. (*door*) Oh . . .

Connie (*downstairs*) Is that you, Mr Reeve? I'm so sorry I was out. I had a little shopping to do. When you've finished up there, do please come and have a cup of tea with me and pussies. It's Muffy's birthday.

Reeve (*calls back*) Thank you . . . (*baffled and embarrassed*) Mr Shewin . . .

Stephen Yes, Mr Reeve?

Reeve It's . . . it's Mrs Shewin . . .

Stephen (*indifferently*) Oh. Well, she must have come back again, I suppose, that's all. No matter.

    (*door closes: pause*)

Reeve Here was a slight dilemma. Mr Shewin had given us strong and interesting hints about Miss Hilda Tablet, the distinguished composeress. He had also, however, seemed to urge us to avoid contact with her. What were we to do? For clearly it was not a problem that would solve *itself*.

    (*piano loudly and suddenly. The music in this scene is always atonal in character. After three or four incisive bars, Elsa is heard singing a loud high passage. The words are by Schopenhauer, and run as follows:*)

'Junghahn relates that he saw in Java a plain far as the eye could reach entirely covered with skeletons; and he took it for a battlefield.'

(*Elsa – Austrian – is modest and pathetic, with a beautiful voice which she finds rather difficult to accommodate to the demands of the music. Hilda Tablet, who has written the music and is accompanying her on the piano, has a loud, jolly, warm voice*)

Elsa (*singing loudly and clearly*)
'Junghahn relates . . .
that he saw in Java . . .
a plain . . .
far as the eye could reach . . .'
(*on the sustained high note 'reach', the door opens and the maid speaks*)

Housekeeper (*loudly*) The visitor's come!

Reeve No, no, look, I can wait . . .
(*Elsa gets to the end of the note. Piano alone behind next speech*)

Hilda Come in, come in! Excuse a moment. Do sit down. She's just getting it right, must go on for just a sec. (*to Elsa*) Now!

Elsa (*singing*) 'Entirely covered with skeletons . . .'

Hilda Gooooood! Lovely!

Elsa (*slipping into 'tune'*) 'And he took it for a battlefield.'

Hilda (*breaking off*) No, Elsa, damn it. Damn it, for heaven's sake, please! I've told you before this isn't *Madame Butterfly* you're singing.

Elsa (*almost in tears*) I cannot help . . .

Hilda Of course you can help, you silly little dotty. I've told you a hundred times: throw your voice *at* the note, by all means, but for God's sake, remember to miss it.

Elsa But I cannot sing so always out of *tune* like this.

Hilda (*helplessly*) Tune. (*pause: then a low urgent prayer*) Dear God, save me from madness, amen. Welcome, Mr Reeve.

Reeve I . . .

Elsa (*pathetically*) Shall I make some tea and tost?

Hilda Yes, yes, make some tea and tost, it's all you're good for. Hello, Mr Reeve: have a cigarette?

Reeve I do hope I haven't come too early, Miss Tablet. You did say four.

Hilda Perfectly OK. Sorry about Elsa. Been rehearsing all afternoon. New piece of mine. Like what you heard of it?

Reeve Very much. Though of course it's difficult for me to judge . . .

Hilda Without the orchestra, you mean, yes. Yes. Actually it'll only be four trombones and a violin. But I agree it doesn't sound much on the piano.

Reeve Who are the words by?

Hilda Well, that bit was Schopenhauer, of course.

Reeve Ah, yes.

Hilda I've assembled the words myself from here and there: eight chunks of 'em: Isaiah, Emily Dickinson, St John of the Cross, Schopenhauer, Herrick, Cyril Connolly, Homer, and Kingsley Amis. (*shrugging*) Oh, it'll be all right, I think. It's called 'Nocturne'. You look nice.

Reeve (*disconcerted*) I . . .

Hilda You write, I think you said in your letter?

Reeve Yes, I'm –

Hilda Wouldn't like to do me a libretto on Gide's *Faux-Monnayeurs*, by any chance?

Reeve Well . . . I'm afraid it's not quite my line . . .

Hilda (*cheerfully*) Oh well, never mind. You wanted to talk about Dick Shewin?

Reeve Yes, if . . .

Hilda Sure. (*she goes a little distance away, and says*) Elsa, don't bring in the tea till I call. Mr Reeve and I don't wish to be interrupted. And don't think what you look as if you're thinking. (*she returns*) A nice girl. Mad, of course. Like her?

Reeve Y-yes, I . . .

Hilda Oh, she's all right. Good voice too, if only she didn't make everything sound like a cross between Brahms and Benjamin Britten. In so far as it's possible to distinguish between the two, of course.

Reeve She's your daughter, I suppose?

Hilda My *what*!

Reeve Your daughter.

Hilda (*a huge gusty laugh*) That's a good one. I give you nine marks for that. She's been taken for my *niece* before now by a few nice-minded people, but that's a new one on me. (*another laugh*) Well, well . . .

Reeve I'm *very* sorry if . . .

Hilda Don't give it a thought. You know, you look rather like Dick Shewin.

Reeve Look like him?

Hilda Well, no, not really. Still I'm glad you're writing a book about him. Most writer-chaps are so ugly.

Reeve I . . .

Hilda You know all about him and me, of course?

Reeve Not ...

Hilda Well, I mean you know what he did with me. (*a few notes on the piano*) I'm Madeleine in *The Head and the Heart*.

Reeve (*reverently*) I didn't know, no, Miss Tablet.

Hilda Oh, I never minded. I didn't really give him the push as hard as all that, of course. Well, there was never any question, of course. Still he did come rather a smacker over it, poor devil.

Reeve I knew that he had been in love with you, Miss Tablet.

Hilda Yes ... yes. (*gravely*) Love. Yes, he was in love with me. I was not able to return that love, Mr Breve.

Reeve (*respectfully*) No.

Hilda But I respected it. I was honoured by it. And of course I never minded about Madeleine. Good book, I thought.

Reeve Oh very. But ... forgive my mentioning it, Miss Tablet, but Madeleine, in *The Head and the Heart*, is actually dead, you know, before the book opens.

Hilda Yes, well, there you are, there it is. Or was, rather. I was quite proud, really; one always is. I regarded it as a sort of ... well *enshrinement*, that sort of *coglioni*, you know ... And after all, it was a two-way traffic. Hell, you can't get away from the soul, can you?

    (*door*)

Elsa (*at door*) Hilda, would the gentleman like one pair of boilt eggs with his tea?

Hilda (*greatly irritated*) Good heavens, no, girl. (*to Reeve in a rapid parenthesis*) Sorry. I mean you don't want one pair of boiled eggs with your tea, do you? No? No. Nò, Elsa, of course he doesn't. Go away.

Elsa (*plaintively recedes*) I shall go back to –

    (*door*)

Hilda Listen, Mr Beat. I'll tell you something about Dick Shewin I've never told anybody except Elsa, and she didn't know what I meant anyway.

Reeve It's very kind –

Hilda (*politely*) Just shut up and listen, will you? (*sincerely*) Mr Beat: in my Piano Sonata, Opus 43, the basic note-row is F, B, C-sharp, G, D, A, F-sharp, B-flat, G-sharp, E, C, D-sharp, as you probably know ... Well, old Dick Shewin and I used to talk, you know, oh, a hell of a long way into the night sometimes. Oh, it was only talk, don't get ideas. But it was good talk. Of its kind, it was the best talk I ever remember.

Reeve What was it about?

Hilda Do shut up. I'd been working on my Sonata all day, I remember. I was bogged down in it. It's such an airy sort of little thing, I expect that will surprise you. Well, don't spread it about, old cock, *but* – originally the D-sharp in my basic note-row was where the B-flat is now, and vice versa . . . Well, one night, I was seeing Dick Shewin off the premises, and I was just about to shut the front door when I noticed he was still looking up at me from the pavement . . . We stared at each other, in the half-dark for what must have been, oh, a good minute, I suppose. Then, very gently, he lifted his hand, and in that quiet, slow way of his he said: 'Good night, Hilda . . . old chap.' Then he went away. I watched him out of sight. I closed the door very gently, and suddenly . . . I knew.

Reeve . . . Knew . . . ?

Hilda Something told me.

Reeve Told you what?

Hilda I'd got to swap 'em over. In my basic note-row. D-sharp and B-flat. That's all. Makes the work, of course.

(plays D-sharp and B-flat on piano; then reverses them)

That's Dick Shewin for you, Mr Reeve. In two notes. *(rather huskily)* You may write a whole ruddy book about him, but you'll never get him expressed as briefly as that. *(more bravely)* Listen, Mr Reeve, can you turn over?

Reeve Turn over?

Hilda Music. I'll play that piece for you, so help me. Here it is. Damn it, I'll play it. I expect you'll find my writing a bit hard to follow, but just turn the pages over every time I shout out '*now*', will you?

Reeve Certainly.

Hilda Good . . . Ready? . . . Right!

(she launches into a tremendous velocissimo. After a short time she calls out . . .)

. . . Now!

(rustle of page, muffed by Reeve)

Reeve Sorry . . .

(more music. Reeve, more agitated, muffs it a second and third time)
(fade out)

Reeve (*a little sombrely*) This, to us, momentous encounter . . . was to prove the first of many highly distrac – destruc – d-delightful visits to Miss Tablet's charming flat in Coptic Street. She was to provide us with much in the way of . . . of . . . *documentation*. Yes. Yes, indeed . . . Yes . . . (*He seems to lose himself in thought for a moment or two; then he resumes with slightly artificial brightness*) Documentation is, of course, indispensable to biographical study, and we are especially grateful to Miss Eileen Rich for help on certain difficult technical points connected with our work. Miss Rich, well known for her distinguished work in the Ministry of Home Consumption, was Shewin's secretary in his later years, and during his last illness she managed to get . . . she w-was appointed his literary executrix. Shewin cherished always a warm regard for her; indeed he is known to have written at least one unpublished poem about her. As we have noted before, only the first half of this has so far come to light. It runs as follows:

'Little Miss Rich.'

(*Miss Rich is efficient, smiling, heartless, and impeccably civil*)

Miss Rich I am sorry to have kept you waiting, Mr Reeve. I have had a busy morning, and I must get back to my office in eight minutes' time.

Reeve It is most kind of you to see me.

Miss Rich You have doubtless brought a list of the questions you wish to ask?

Reeve Well, not exactly a list . . .

Miss Rich I should have remembered to ask you to do so. I usually do ask that of Mr Shewin's biographers.

Reeve Are there many others, Miss Rich?

Miss Rich What did you wish to know, Mr Reeve?

Reeve I wished first of all to ask if the manuscript of Shewin's last, unfinished novel is still in your possession?

Miss Rich It is with the bank, of course, but I have charge of it.

Reeve Do you think I might at some convenient time be allowed to see it?

Miss Rich (*very courteously*) No, I am afraid not, Mr Reeve.

Reeve I see. I wonder if you could give me an idea of when it might become available for inspection?

Miss Rich Oh yes, certainly. There is a definite date fixed. You will be able to see it any time after May 14th 1992.

Reeve   Oh, I see . . . I rather wonder if I shall still be . . . here . . . to . . .

Miss Rich (*indulgently*) We all have to ask ourselves questions like that at times, Mr Reeve.

Reeve   One can but hope.

Miss Rich Exactly.

Reeve   And . . . the legal documents in connection with the Shewin-Eversleigh lawsuit in the first world war . . . can you tell me anything about the accessibility or otherwise of those?

Miss Rich Those, Mr Reeve, will certainly be available as from February 22nd, 2017.

Reeve   (*pathetically*) AD?

Miss Rich I beg your pardon?

Reeve   May I just make a note of that date? February 22nd 2017. What a charming coincidence! It will be my hundred and third birthday.

Miss Rich Indeed? Is there anything else?

Reeve   I . . . wanted to say that various people have shown me long and rather intimate letters written to them by the late Mr Shewin. I hope you will be so kind as to allow me to quote from them.

Miss Rich I will answer that question by letter, Mr Reeve, if you will allow me . . .

Reeve   Oh, thank you.

Miss Rich So that there may be no mistake.

Reeve   Thank you. There is just one other point, Miss Little . . . I'm sorry . . . Miss Rich. It is rather a problem. I have been shown a group of letters – you have perhaps seen them yourself – they are in the nature of love-letters addressed to Shewin. They are all signed with the initial D. I wonder, if by chance, you know who 'D' was?

Miss Rich Yes, Mr Reeve, I do.

Reeve   I wonder if you would be willing to divulge her identity?

Miss Rich (*affably*) No, Mr Reeve, I am afraid not. And now, if you will forgive me, I must return to my office. Any help I can give you at any time, of course . . .

   (*fade on 'forgive'*)

Reeve   What a theme the life of such a man is! One might spend a lifetime in its pursuit. Nor would such a lifetime have been ill-spent. But when all is said and done there is one spiritual climax to such a quest, which once achieved is never quite to be repeated. We mean the first moments when we set foot in a great man's early scenes, his native heath, as it were. To travel down to Mulset for the first time would, in any event, have been a not unmoving experience; to make the journey in the company of the poet's brother was a further enrichment. Indeed, our debt to Mr Stephen Shewin at all times during our researches would be difficult to express in words.

(train noises up and hold in background)

Stephen It is costing me a great deal to make this journey with you, Mr Reeve, quite apart from the fare. I can never contemplate my brother Edward's enormous family without the extreme of revulsion, disgust and shame.

Reeve But, Mr Shewin, it was you yourself who suggested accompanying me.

Stephen Oh, I could not have let you face the whole monstrous brood unprotected. It would not have been like me.

Reeve Are there so very many of them?

Stephen Well, there's Edward's widow and twelve children, if you call *that* many . . .

Reeve Twelve. I never realised there were so many. Are you quite sure, Mr Shewin?

Stephen Quite sure, Mr Reeve.

Reeve I see . . . and how old are they?

Stephen Twenty-three, twenty-two, twenty-one, twenty, nineteen, eighteen, seventeen, sixteen, fifteen, *twelve* (my brother was away in Turkey for some time), eleven and ten. The vulgarity of it.

Reeve Well, some people like large families.

Stephen That was not their origin, Mr Reeve. It was Richard's fault.

Reeve Richard's!

Stephen You probably are unaware that my brother advertised his intention of leaving the entire fortune that his so-called literary writings brought him in equal parts to all his nephews and nieces. It was nothing more than a low spirit of competition that brought so many horrible little creatures into the world. I refused to engage in it. Which didn't of course prevent my brother from writing unseemly verses on the subject.

> The Shewin family, it seems,
> Is apt to fly to great extremes.
> While Stephen does no more than read
> Little books on How to Breed,

42

> *On the other hand my brother Ned*
> *Mistakes his home for an oyster-bed.*

The commonness of it!
  (*train noise up and out*)

Reeve And finally . . . The magic of being in leafy Mulset itself; this was the air he breathed. Here he was born, here he made his home in later years. And here, now, were we also – at Throbbing, the charming Palladian house he bought for himself, with its enchanting gardens and lawns, the house he had bequeathed to his brother Edward (alas, with us no more), and his wife and family. Here they lived still, in full proud consciousness of the reverence due to their noble inheritance.

  (*sudden and passionate burst of bird-song. Hold behind conversation.*
  Nancy Shewin, Edward's widow, is sweet, fluffy and confused)

Nancy And of course, we can't even get the National Trust to accept it now. Another cup of tea, Mr Reeve?

Reeve Thank you.

Nancy I thought you would like to have tea on the lawn. The weather is so lovely, and one gets such a pleasant view of the hills from here.

Reeve Enchanting, aren't they? This must be the scene of your boyhood also, Mr Shewin.

Stephen Yes, I entertain extreme dislike of it.

Nancy Now, Stephen dear, don't start grumbling. The landscape is very pretty at this time of year. Ah, now, there's my elder daughter Janet coming across from the paddock. I do wish she wouldn't slouch so, but of course nineteen is an awkward age, isn't it? She's at Cambridge, you know.

Reeve Yes, I think I knew that.

Nancy Come and sit down with us, Janet? May I introduce my daughter Janet, Mr Reeve.

  (*how d'you do's exchanged*)

Janet Hello, uncle Stephen.

Stephen (*despondently*) Hello.

Nancy Now, is everyone's cup full?

Stephen My cup is always full.

Nancy Mr Reeve is writing a book about Uncle Richard, Jan

Janet Good God!

Nancy Darling! What a thing to say.

Janet A whole book?

43

Reeve Well, one can hardly hope to deal with such a writer in a shorter space.

Janet Can't one? Perhaps not. At any rate you'll be able to debunk that stuff about the Poet's Novelist.

Reeve } But, Miss Shewin . . .
Nancy } Janet, *dear* . . . I suppose *you*'ve read *all* my brother-in-law's books, Mr Reeve?

Reeve Oh yes, indeed, many times.

Nancy How *very* kind of you. I haven't actually read all through any of them myself, I've hardly had the time, you know.

Stephen I don't wonder at that.

Nancy But they *are* good, aren't they, Mr Reeve? I heard they were very good, people have told me a number· of them were very nice indeed.

Reeve Well, naturally, I think they're splendid.

Nancy I'm so glad. There, Janet, Mr Reeve says they're very good, splendid was the word he used.

Janet He may have. Actually they're not.

Nancy Janet, darling, *please* don't start being unpleasant about your poor uncle's books again. It's so ungrateful.

Stephen Ingratitude is by no means uncommon in this family.

Nancy I'm sure I don't know how we should have sent you to Cambridge without them.

Janet I've never denied uncle Dick's capacity as a moneymaker. He produced a very efficient line in consumer-goods just at the moment when a rising middle class felt it was ripe for culture. Hordes of reviewers from Eton and Oxford were ready to tell them that this *was* culture; so they bought it.

Nancy Oh dear. I don't know why it is, but young people are so unjust nowadays, aren't they, Mr Reeve?

Reeve (*indulgently*) A little, perhaps . . .

Janet Actually, I can't think anyone's been at all unjust to Shewin. Shewin's early novels . . .

Nancy Dear, *don't* call your poor uncle by his surname like that. It sounds so mannish.

Janet Sorry, mother. But uncle Richard's early promise, such as it was in its completely derivative way, was actually quite fairly evaluated in a footnote in the autumn number of *Scrutiny* a couple of years after uncle died.
He was ill such a long time, Mr Reeve, but so very patient . . .

Nancy He was ill such a long time, Mr Reeve, but so very patient ...

Stephen So it is given out.

Nancy Well, Stephen dear, he *was* patient . . .

Janet I must get back. Will you excuse me, Mr Reeve?

Reeve Oh certainly, Miss Shewin.

Nancy What are you doing, dear? Can't you stay and talk to us?

Janet Sorry, mother, I must get this thing on Flaubert finished.

Reeve Are you writing about Flaubert, Miss Shewin?

Janet Yes.

Reeve An appreciation?

Janet (*darkly*) Of a kind. I think I've managed to make a *few* relevant
constatations. See you later.

Reeve I-I hope so.

Nancy (*after she has gone*) Oh dear . . . You must forgive her, Mr Reeve,
it's a difficult age, and of course she is rather plain at the moment,
though the boys are very good-looking. She doesn't always
behave like that. She's really quite playful sometimes – I know
you wouldn't think of it, but really I have known her pass the
whole evening without mentioning a single book, *or in fact
anything unpleasant*, at all.

Stephen That must be an unusual experience.

Nancy Well, I expect you would like to look round the garden, Mr
Reeve, and perhaps visit the church. The memorial tablet is very
nice, but of course every one was very upset he couldn't be
buried there, but as he had become a Roman Catholic, it was . . .

Stephen My brother could always be trusted to join any fashionable
movement, Mr Reeve.

Nancy Oh don't say that, Stephen, I am sure he meant well . . . I daresay
you'll come across some of the boys, Mr Reeve: I have rather a
houseful of them at the moment. . . .

Reeve (*to himself*) (*pause*) You'd only ever understand *him*, if, quite
triumphantly, you understood the whole family as well. How
those words of Mrs Hepple in *The Hot and the Cold* came back to
us there in Shewin's own native ambiance . . . the sunlit summer
fields he knew so well . . . his nephews and nieces with their
precious heritage, not only of his home but of his name . . .

(*behind this the noise of children playing in a field has crept in. It is
heard intermittently through what follows. The only passage fairly
distinctly heard is after Reeve says 'but of his name' when we hear
children's voices some distance away*)

Children Bowl! Come on, Humphrey, bowl!

No, Humphrey can't bowl!

Why can't Humphrey bowl?

Humphrey's too small to bowl!

I'm *not* too small to bowl!

Well, let somebody else bowl!

Well, let *me* bowl!

No, it's not your turn to bowl!

Well, let Humphrey bowl . . . !

> (*at some point after this is established, it fades behind the following dialogue*)

Brian (*aged 13*) Hello, sir. Are you Mr Reeve?

Reeve Yes, yes, I am.

Brian How do you do, sir? I'm Brian Shewin. Mother said you were coming.

Reeve How do you do?

Brian This is my brother, George Shewin, sir.

George (*aged 12*) How do you do, sir?

Reeve How do you do? You're not playing cricket with the others?

Brian Not at the moment, no, sir.

George Where did you go to after tea, Bry?

Brian I went off to the apple-room to finish my lyric.

George I wrote *two* lyrics this morning.

Brian Any good?

George No, not very. Tore 'em both up. What's yours like?

Brian I've been trying a new kind.

George Let's have a look.

Brian No – haven't polished it yet.

George Well, I might be able to help.

Brian No, thank *you*. And if it isn't any good you won't see it at all.

George You squish . . . Oh sorry, sir. But he is, rather.

Reeve Did I hear you say you were writing . . . writing . . . ?

Boys (*exactly together*) Lyrics, yes, sir.

Reeve Ah, yes . . .

George We spend a lot of time during the summer writing lyrics.

Brian Don't have much time during term, of course.

Reeve No, no, of course not . . .

Brian We aren't all that good at them yet . . .

George Would you care to glance at some of them, Mr Reeve?

Brian Oh, come off it, George, we can't expect Mr Reeve to be interested in that sort of thing.

George No, s'pose not. Sorry, sir, I forgot.

Reeve No, no, my dear chaps, I'd be delighted to see them. I might even be able to . . . place some of them for you.

Brian Place them, sir?

Reeve Well, I mean I know one or two publishers . . .

Brian Oh, I say, sir, how *jolly* nice.

George Of course, they're not much without the music.

Reeve The music?

Brian Yes, our brother Owen does the music. Would you like to go up to the house and hear some?

Reeve Very much, yes.

George Owen's music is terrific.

Reeve A composer in the family as well!

George Oh yes, we must get him to sing Brian's latest for you.

Brian (*modestly*) Oh, I dunno.

George Oh yes, sir, Brian's latest is terrific.

Brian Oh it's nothing really.

George It's *ever* so good, sir. Good title, too.

Reeve What is its title?

Brian Oh, it's just a piece called 'Don't Hurt my Heart'.

Reeve (*much struck*) Really? Ah, yes. 'Don't Hurt my Heart'.

George Shall we go up? We can go through the kitchen garden . . .
      (*fade*)

Reeve How very easily, how very lightly the young write of sorrow's touch! It seems that youthful genius has *instinctively* a knowledge of those depths which experience has not yet, thank God, led it to. One thinks at once, of course, of the youthful Leopardi, of Rimbaud, of Keats . . .

Brian (*calling*) Owen! Can we come in?

Owen (*off*) Yes, come in. What do you want?
      (*door*)

Brian Owen, this is Mr Reeve, who's writing a book about uncle Dick. This is my brother, Owen Shewin, sir.

Reeve How do you do?

Owen How do you do, sir?

George Mr Reeve wants to hear the new piece.

Brian Yes, he wants you to sing 'Don't Hurt my Heart'.

Owen You mean you want me to. Don't you take any notice of them, Mr Reeve.

Reeve No, really, I should be awfully pleased if you would play and sing for me.

Owen Well, if you really mean it, sir . . .

Brian Of course he does.

George He wants to hear 'Don't Hurt'. Come on, Owen.

Owen Well, if you're sure.

Brian Come and watch from this end of the piano, Mr Reeve: you get the full effect from here.

Owen Don't order Mr Reeve about like that, Brian.

Brian Sorry, sir. But really, it *is* best from just here.

Reeve Thank you.

Owen (*with a cough*) Well, of course, Mr Reeve, this hasn't really had the finish put on it yet, so you will bear that in mind, won't you, sir?

George Go *on*, Owen.

Owen OK. And of course, sir, it isn't really much without the band parts. Still, here goes . . .

(*the music opens with the opening bars of Beethoven's* Pathetic Sonata, *followed by a rapid and disconcerting deterioration in style*)

George Jolly good chords, aren't they, Mr Reeve?

Brian Sh-h-h!

(*Owen sings the words not too slowly – and later they are sung faster by the three boys together. The whole thing is faintly terrifying*)

> Why did you say
>   That terrible Thing?
> Can you have known
>   The wound it would bring?
> Right in the midst
>   Of that wonderful Spring,
> Baby, you made me cry.

(*refrain*)

> Baby, don't hurt my heart, baby,
> Baby, don't make me sigh.
> Baby, don't make me smart, baby.
> Baby, don't make me cry.
>
> There are just a few things
>   Since the world began,

48

> You may not think it,
>> But believe me, they can
> Hurt so that even
>> A big grown-up man,
> Baby, just has to cry.

(*refrain*)

>> Baby, don't hurt my heart, baby.
>> Baby, don't make me sigh.
>> Baby, don't make me smart, baby.
>> Baby, don't make me,
>> Baby, don't make me –
>>> (How can you bear to?
>>> How can you care to?)
>>> – Baby, Don't Make Me Cry!

(*at the end of the song Owen collapses in sobs over the piano. A tense pause*)

Brian (*reverently*) Gosh, he's super.

Reeve (*nervously*) Is he all right?

George (*whispers*) Yes, just give him half a sec. to get over it.

Owen (*cheerfully*) Well? How'd I do?

Brian It was super, Owen, terrific.

George It was jolly dee, Owen.

Reeve Very charming. I hope you are . . .

Brian Did you get real tears, Owen?

Owen Well, look! Am I wet, or am I wet?

George Gosh! Real ones.

Brian D'you see, Mr Reeve? He got real tears.

Reeve Yes, I could see he was greatly moved.

Brian He really cried! There are only five people in the world who can do that, Mr Reeve, did you know?

George And none in England.

Brian I declare my brother to be top musical genius of England!

George Let's all sing it!

Brian Yes, come on, start it again, Owen.

(*Owen starts it again, at the refrain. They join in. Fade and hold behind Reeve*)

Reeve The fire of creative genius: it does not expire. Divided it may be, but it does not expire. In a sense the best monument to Shewin's genius that can be imagined – and we are not forgetting the great bronze statue designed (but unfortunately never executed) by Mr R. Egerton Bunningfield, ARA – the best monument is in the thriving creative gifts so strikingly displayed by the Shewin nephews.

(music up briefly (not full) and down behind Reeve)

A famous phrase from Shewin's last completed work comes to one's mind, 'We live in others'. No one can read the moving passage in which it occurs without the ghost of the great novelist seeming to hover, perhaps with his familiar wry smile, over the page. Let us look at that page: it is the last scene from that final exquisite study in the ambiguity that attends all human relationships, *The Arse and the Elbow*.

Roderick, the young and dissolute airman, has died in action. Grace, the girl he has possibly ruined (though we are left intentionally unsure of this, of course) talks in her distress to Father Tippett, the uncertain priest, who has – again a beautiful ambiguity – failed to save him. The two characters utter their elegy over him. It begins with Grace's pathetic cry.

Grace　*But what shall I do, Father Tippett?*

Shewin's Prose　*She asked.*

Tippett　*Go out and look for him, my child.*

Prose　*He replied.*

Grace　*Look for him, Father Tippett! Whatever do you mean? He's dead. Roddy's dead. How can you joke about such a thing?*

Tippett　*We have all of us just died in some sense or another, my dear.*

Prose　*He said.*

Tippett　*All of us.*

Prose　*He added.*

Tippett　*All of us, and all of the time.*

Prose　*He went on.*

Tippett　*Throughout the whole of our lives . . . A great poet once said that . . . At least I suppose he was a great one . . . I wouldn't know any longer.*

Grace　*But, Father Tippett, what use is poetry to me now?*

Tippett　*This poet, my dear, was a great sinner, you might say. But he was also a little touched with sanctity. Perhaps – who knows – all great sinners are.*

Grace　*Oh, I don't understand all this, Father Tippett. I only know . . .*

Prose　*She stopped, as if she didn't quite know what it was she only knew. The rain still poured down. Father Tippett waited for her to go on –*

*you had to wait with the young, however thirsty you were – you
couldn't just send them away.*

Grace   *I don't understand.*

Prose   *She said.*

Grace   *I don't understand.*

Prose   *She repeated.*

Tippett   *None of us, except God, can understand everything, my child. And
He . . . well, it's an old commonplace – we can only pray it's a true
one – to understand all is to forgive all . . . And perhaps God forgives
all . . .*

Prose   *Wondering what more there was to say, he scratched his groin furtively,
then remembered, and stopped. He looked down at the young up-turned
face, and pity twisted his dry mouth and stomach; it doesn't matter if
they are pasty-faced so long as they're young. What a bad priest he was.*

Tippett   *Go out and look for him, my child.*

Prose   *He had said that before, but it was almost as if he wasn't saying the
words himself.*

Grace   *But where, Father Tippett? He's dead.*

Prose   *Suddenly he seemed to know what it was he had to say to her, though
he couldn't have told anybody why. He said:*

Tippett   *We live in others, my dear. And the greater we are the more we live
in them. And Roddy – Roderick – well, Roddy was perhaps a very
great man indeed.*

Prose   *THE END.*

The Private Life of Hilda Tablet

To the memory of Mary O'Farrell

The Private Life of Hilda Tablet was first broadcast on 24 May 1954. The production was by Douglas Cleverdon, with music by Donald Swann. The cast was as follows:

HERBERT REEVE	*Hugh Burden*
STEPHEN SHEWIN	*Carleton Hobbs*
CONNIE SHEWIN	*Gwen Cherrell*
HILDA TABLET	*Mary O'Farrell*
ELSA STRAUSS	*Marjorie Westbury*
NANCY SHEWIN	*Dorothy Primrose*
OWEN SHEWIN	*Denis Quilley*
JANET SHEWIN	*Gwen Cherrell*
BRIAN SHEWIN	*Wilfred Downing*
GEORGE SHEWIN	*Marjorie Westbury*
HUMPHREY SHEWIN	*Wilfred Downing*
MUFFY, MILLY, ETC.	*Vivienne Chatterton*
EVELYN BAXTER	*Colin Campbell*
MRS PITNEY	*Vivienne Chatterton*
HAROLD REITH	*Frank Duncan*
R. EGERTON BUNNINGFIELD, A.R.A.	*Norman Shelley*
ROGER CLOUD	*Deryck Guyler*
THE DUKE OF MULSET	*Frank Duncan*
THE DUCHESS OF MULSET	*Diana Maddox*
THE RECTOR OF MULL EXTRINSECA	*Deryck Guyler*
REUBEN COBB	*Carleton Hobbs*
SIR ERIC TABLET	*Norman Shelley*
LADY TABLET	*Susan Richmond*
MISS WELBECK	*Vivienne Chatterton*

Reeve Friendship. What a very rare and beautiful thing friendship is, after all, and how unpredictable are its beginnings! Not least, perhaps, among the joys that humanise the scholar's life are the personal relationships that spring up in, as it were, the suburbs of his work. Our relationship with Miss Hilda Tablet, the distinguished composeress, was one such. We were working at the time on our (alas! still uncompleted) critical biography of Richard Shewin the late novelist. It came to us as something of a surprise that Shewin and Miss Tablet had actually known each other. We might, indeed, have remained quite ignorant of this important fact, had it not been for a chance remark dropped one afternoon by the great novelist's brother, Mr Stephen Shewin, in the course of one of our many interviews with him. We recall the occasion as though it were yesterday.

Stephen *Hilda* Tablet the name was.

Reeve *Hilda* Tablet!

Stephen Yes. The lady music-writer. My brother said he wanted to marry her. He swore it. Some didn't believe him, some did – he didn't always tell lies. Not that *I* ever liked her. I have never forgiven her for the way in which she behaved at my brother's funeral.

Reeve How was that?

Stephen She was absolutely *uncontrollable*, Mr Reeve.

Reeve Well, of course, deep grief does lead some people to break down on these occasions, as we all know.

Stephen *Grief*, Mr Reeve? I noticed no manifestation of any feeling that could be called *grief* on her part. I was alluding to a form of behaviour quite other.

Reeve I . . .

Stephen In a place of worship, too. (*with relish*) You will imagine the reluctance I have to overcome in order to mention the incident, Mr Reeve, but the minute the funeral was over, Miss Hilda Tablet saw fit to make a provocative and unseemly *overture* to me in the vestry.

Reeve Oh. Oh dear . . .

Stephen A most unsavoury woman, Mr Reeve. I am not surprised that she has remained a spinster.

Reeve Yes . . . I knew, of course, that she was unmarried.

Stephen Yes. (*a tiny pause*) Her daughter is said to be a very nice girl, however.

Reeve Her d . . . (*he stops, appalled*)

Stephen I, of course, have no views on who the hapless girl's father is likely to have been.

Reeve B-b-but, Mr Shewin, are you suggesting that R-*Richard* is the . . . ?

Stephen (*interrupting*) And what else have you been doing to further your researches, Mr Reeve?

Reeve Please let me ask one question about Miss Tab . . .

Stephen It is a change to meet anybody so interested in the past as you are, Mr Reeve.

(*pause*)

Reeve It was but a few days later, after an exchange of letters, that we made our way to Miss Tablet's house in Coptic Street. With her public fame we were – as who is not? – well acquainted already. We had, in fact, heard a repeat performance of her *Three Fragments from Cnossos* only a few nights before on the ever-admirable Third Programme, and had enjoyed it . . . very, very much. We had long looked forward to the British première of her original and distinguished opera, *Emily Butter*, already acclaimed in Europe and South America, but so far unheard in its native land. We were, indeed, bold enough to sense that music, ever our second love, might prove a bond between ourselves and Miss Tablet. Little did we divine, however, as we rang at the door of 109 Coptic Street, how momentous this occasion was to be.

(*ring at the street door. It is opened by Hilda's secretary, a happy, unabashed young man, with a seductive, rather self-mocking drawl. His manner greatly disconcerts Reeve*)

Evelyn (*amiably*) Hel-*lowe* . . .

Reeve G-good afternoon.

Evelyn You Herbert Reeve?

Reeve Y-yes.

Evelyn Thought you were. Come in. (*coyly*) My *mistress* is expecting *you.*

Reeve Your m . . .?

Evelyn (*gurglingly*) Old Hilda . . . I *always* call her my mistress. Makes her *roar* with laughter.

Reeve Oh . . . oh, yes.

Evelyn I'm Evelyn.

Reeve Indeed?

Evelyn Old Hilda's secretary. Jolly good, too. Just going out shopping.

Reeve Oh . . . ah . . . yes.

Evelyn Got to match some material.

(*Hilda's housekeeper, Mrs Pitney, is heard in the distance*)

Mrs P. (*sharply*) Is that someone at the door, Evelyn?

Evelyn Hope you'll be here when I get back.

Reeve I . . . hope so.

Mrs P. (*approaching*) Really, Evelyn, must you always keep visitors standing there in the open door like that?

Evelyn We were *talk*-ing.

Mrs P. Good afternoon, sir.

Reeve Good afternoon.

Evelyn (*with loud intimacy*) This is the madwoman of Chaillot, Mr Reeve.

Mrs P. You go on with you!

Evelyn So you be careful!

Mrs P. Evelyn! Will you go about your business!

Evelyn (*receding*) G'bah-igh! (*in American*) I'm on my way!

(*door closed loudly. Music begins in the very far distance as it closes*)

Mrs P. (*briskly*) I'm so sorry; but one has to remember that the poor lad has no father.

Reeve (*sympathetically*) Oh, yes. I see. Yes.

Mrs P. Shall I take you up? The music-room is upstairs. You'll find this house a very strange one, I'm afraid.

Reeve Really?

(*a musical shriek in the distance*)

Mrs P. (*eloquently*) Well – just listen! They've been hard at it since eleven this morning.

(*music gradually nearer*)

Reeve (*nervously*) At it?

Mrs P. The rehearsaling. They're rehearsaling for Miss Tablet's next concert.

Reeve Oh, I . . . yes.

Mrs P. I get used to it, of course. I hardly notice it, except of course the quiet bits.

Reeve No, I suppose not. Perhaps I ought to wait till . . .

Mrs P. Oh, no, this could go on for hours.

Reeve Miss Tablet did say four o'clock.

Mrs P. Yes. I'll shout and tell her you're here.

Reeve Oh, but perhaps . . .

Mrs P. Oh, *she* won't mind. Why should she?

    (*switch to inside of music-room*)

Elsa (*singing*) 'Junghahn relates . . .

           That he saw in Java . . .

           A plain . . .

           Far as the eye could reach . . .'

    (*door opens on sustained note 'reach'*)

Mrs P. (*loudly*) The visitor's come!

Reeve No, no, look, I can wait . . .

Hilda Come in, come in! Excuse a moment. Do sit down. She's just getting it right, must go on for just a sec. (*to Elsa*) Now!

Elsa (*singing*) 'Entirely covered with skeletons . . .'

Hilda Gooooooood! Lovely!

Elsa 'And he took it for a battlefield.'

Hilda (*breaking off*) No, Elsa, damn it. Damn it, for heaven's sake, please!

Elsa (*almost in tears*) I cannot help . . .

Hilda Of course you can help, you silly little dotty.

Elsa (*pathetically*) Shall I make some tea and tost?

Hilda Yes, yes, make some tea and tost, it's all you're good for. Welcome, Mr Reeve: you look nice.

Reeve (*disconcerted*) I . . .

Hilda You wrote. I think you said in your letter you wanted to talk about Dick Shewin?

Reeve Yes, if . . .

Hilda Sure. ELSA!

Elsa (*off*) What is it?

Hilda (*calls*) Don't bring the tea in till I shout . . . A nice girl. Mad, of course. Like her?

Reeve Y-yes, I . . .

Hilda Oh, she's all right. Good voice, too.

Reeve She's your daughter, I suppose?

Hilda My what!

Reeve Your daughter.

Hilda (*with a gusty laugh*) That's a good one. I give you nine marks for that. She's been taken for my *niece* by a few nice-minded people, but that's a new one on me. (*another laugh*) Well, well . . .

Reeve I'm *very* sorry if . . .

Hilda Don't give it a thought. I'm glad you're writing a book about old

Dick Shewin. I knew him for years. We were kids together in the country, as I expect you know.

Reeve (*eagerly*) No, I didn't know that.

Hilda Oh, yes, he was always coming over to Tutting.

Reeve T–Tutting?

Hilda My people's place in Mulset ... You know all about him and me, of course?

Reeve Not ...

Hilda Well, I mean, you know what he did with me? I'm Madeleine in *The Head and the Heart*.

Reeve (*reverently*) I didn't know, no, Miss Tablet.

Hilda (*soberly*) Listen, Mr Beat. I'll tell you something about Dick Shewin I've never told anybody. (*sincerely*) Richard Shewin is the only man, alive or dead, who can ever have been said to have interfered with ... my basic note-row. Look, Mr Beat: can you turn over?

Reeve Turn over?

Hilda Music. There's a piece of mine I always associate with our Dick. I'll play that piece for you, so help me. Here it is. Damn it, I'll play it. I expect you'll find my writing a bit hard to follow, but just turn the pages over every time I shout out *Now*, will you?

Reeve Certainly.

Hilda Good ... Ready? ... Right.

> (*tremendous velocissimo on piano*)

Hilda Now!

> (*clumsy turnover on page*)

Reeve Sorry.

> (*music as before*)

Hilda Now!

> (*clumsy turnover again*)

Reeve Sorry.

> (*music as before*)

Hilda Now!

> (*he manages it this time, but accidentally turns two pages instead of one. This lands Hilda unexpectedly in the slow movement, a plodding adagio fugato, with single notes for each hand. After a bar or two:*)

Hilda Say: what the hell's happened?

> (*she stops playing*)

Reeve I'm so sorry, have I ... ?

Hilda (*chortles*) You turned over two pages at once, old cock. We're slap in the middle of the slow movement. Hahaha! *You* wouldn't be much good at the Royal So-called Festival Hall, now, would you? Never mind.

Elsa (*pathetically*) Hilda, the tea and tost are getting to be so *colled*.

Hilda Sorry, old girl; bring 'em in. Have some tea, Mr Beat, you deserve it.

Reeve I . . . thank you very much.

Hilda And the sooner the tea's out of the way, the sooner we can get out the gin, eh?

Reeve (*dimly*) Oh, quite . . . quite.

Elsa (*invitingly*) Cake? Tost? Honny? Cham?

Reeve Oh . . . oh, thank you. T-tost, toast, please.

Hilda Who put you on to me, Mr Beat?

Reeve Put me . . . ?

Hilda Who sent you round?

Reeve Ah, for that I am indebted to my good friend, Mr Stephen Shewin.

Hilda What! Dick's brother?

Reeve Yes.

Hilda You *do* choose peculiar friends, don't . . . Good Lord! Look here, Mr Breve, was it old Steve Shewin who tried to make out that Elsa was my daughter?

Elsa *Daughter?*

Reeve Well, he didn't exactly *say* . . .

Hilda Don't tell me: I can imagine. No actual statement, just a few nasty innuendos oozing out like reluctant vinegar. (*contemptuously*) The nasty old devil!

Elsa (*sweetly*) But you have always been like a *sort* of mother to me, Hilda.

Hilda You shut up!

Elsa (*passionately, in tears*) I shall go back to Vienna!

Hilda All right, do; go back to Vienna; you'll find the fare in the housekeeping money.

(*ad lib sobs from Elsa during the following*)

Hilda Oh God, oh God, and people expect one to create! Sorry, sorry, sorry, Mr Breve. But you touched me on the raw.

Reeve I'm so . . .

Hilda I have to make it clear that Stephen Shewin Esquire and my humble self are Not Friends. I've never forgiven him for what he did at Dick's funeral.

Reeve What was that?

Hilda (*darkly*) He chose the music.

(*loud sob from Elsa*)

And will you kindly stop those revolting *singhiozzi*, Elsa?

Elsa (*one gulp*) Yes. Shall I take away the tea-*tray*?

Hilda Kindly do. And get out the gin. Yes. He chose the music.

Reeve And you thought it . . . ?

Hilda The occasion was a calculated insult. It had been an understood thing for years that when poor Dick passed on, they should play my little dirge, written ages before, a little piece called *Funeral Baked Meats*, for two flutes, harmonium and tam-tam: oh, just a simple little elegiac sort of little piece, the second half being of course an inverted cancrizans of the first half, as you naturally expect in a piece written for a funeral . . .

Reeve Oh, yes, yes, yes, yes, yes.

Hilda And poor Dick was very fond of that piece, very fond. He said to me, 'You'll play that piece over my dead body one of these days, Hilda,' he said. So, of course, I took it as fixed. But oh, no. In marches Mr Stephen Blasted Shewin, and orders the music for the funeral himself. And do you know who every damned note was by?

Reeve I don't think I quite recall . . .

Hilda (*impressively*) Lobby Ludwig.

Reeve L-Lobby Ludwig?

Hilda Yes. So help me.

Elsa I have brought the Chin.

Hilda Ta.

Reeve But . . . who *is* Lobby Ludwig, Miss Tablet?

Hilda (*kindly*) Where were you at school, Mr Beat?

Reeve Well, the first four years I . . .

Hilda Mr Beat: have you never by any chance heard tell of one Ludwig van Beethoven?

Reeve Oh . . . I . . .

Hilda (*broodingly*) To think of poor old Dick Shewin, a good clean-living man, inserted into his final resting place to the strains of the so-called Fifth Symphony. (*sings, with passionate contempt*) Bo-bo-bo-*bom*. Bo-bo-bo-BOM!

Elsa (*continuing happily*) Ha-ha-ha-ha. Ha-ha-ha-*ha* . . . Ha –

Hilda (*sharply*) Elsa! (*sincerely*) Mr Breve: we in this world can have little conception of what difficulties that may have landed poor Dick Shewin in on the Other Side.

Reeve Oh, dear . . .

Hilda Have some gin. Yes. I have yet to settle my score with Mr Stephen Shewin. And what is more, Mr Breve, the nasty old scavenger tried to make a pass at me the minute the funeral was over.

Reeve A pass?

Hilda Yes. In the vestry. Pretended he was trying to straighten my tie for me. Never seen him since. But I *shall*. Believe you me: I shall.
　　(*fade*)

Reeve Few . . . very few of our meetings with Miss Tablet were destined to be short ones. This first one was no exception. It was only when we came to say good-bye that we realised that Miss Tablet had kindly accorded us some nine-and-a-half hours of her illuminating company. With the liberality characteristic of the creative artist the world over, she dispensed tirelessly . . . the flowing bowl, while ever and anon Miss Elsa Strauss would enter, bearing omelettes, sauerkraut, and other savoury dishes, most of which she consumed herself. It was the first time we had heard a creative artist speak intimately of his, or in this case her, aims and aspirations; and musicians, as the world well knows, are of all artists the most reluctant to discuss their own lovely art.
　　(*they are both pretty drunk by this time*)

Hilda And . . . and . . . and you *like* music, don't you, Herbert?

Reeve Indeed, yes. It has ever been my second love.

Hilda Never been what?

Reeve Ever my second love.

Hilda Really? It was my fourth, 'smatter of fact. In fact, Herbert, I'll tell you a secret about me and music . . .

Reeve Yes?

Hilda I . . . played hard-to-get. Oh yes. I never fell for music like some so-called composers I could name. No.

Reeve No?

Hilda No. It fell for me. I was flirting with architecture at the time. I have always been *mad* about architecture; well, I don't have to say it. You can tell it from the structure of Butter.

Reeve Butter?

Hilda *Emily Butter*, my opera. Say what you will, 'spretty soundly architected. I believe in architectonic in music. There's nothing like it. 'Sthe fiist thing you have to learn. (*intimately*) *I* learned it years ago, y'know . . . the first time I ever realised Purcell.

Reeve The first time you ever realised what, Hilda?

Hilda Purcell. (*confidingly*) Oh, yes, Herbert, I realised a lot of Purcell in my early days.

Reeve Sorry, Hilda, but . . . realised he was what?

Hilda What was what?

Reeve You said you realised Purcell.

Hilda Course I did. Ev'body knows that. I realised a lot of Palestrina, too, if it comes to that.

Reeve (*lost, but sympathetic*) Yes, well, of course, we all have to realise such things, when the time comes, I suppose.

Hilda Structure . . . that's the ticket. Structure, my dear old friend. Structure.

(*fade*)

Reeve This great encounter had left us with much to think of, much to be grateful for, yes, and much to puzzle over also. For it was clearly not, as yet, *quite* possible completely to reconcile Miss Tablet's views about the girl Elsa with those of Mr Stephen Shewin. It was a delicate matter, and we ventured to touch on it when we next saw Mr Shewin.

Stephen Well, Mr Reeve, and how did you get on with Miss Tablet?

Reeve Oh, very well, I think. I'm most grateful to you for mentioning her to me. She was . . . really quite forthcoming.

Stephen That I can well believe. She spoke of Richard?

Reeve Oh, most appreciatively, yes.

Stephen Yes. No doubt.

Reeve (*with a slight cough*) There is . . . just *one* thing, Mr Shewin, I think I may perhaps venture to suggest you are under a slight misapprehension about.

Stephen Indeed? And what is that?

Reeve I really think that you may perhaps have made a . . . a possible slight error . . . about the parentage of the girl Elsa.

Stephen I am not aware that I expressed any opinion on the subject, Mr Reeve.

Reeve Well, no, not exactly, perhaps . . .

Stephen (*meekly*) I *have* no opinion, Mr Reeve.

Reeve N ... no. (*after a tiny pause*) You see, sir, it's quite clear that Elsa ... is an Austrian girl.

Stephen (*politely*) Oh, yes? By which I suppose you mean she speaks with an Austrian accent.

Reeve Yes.

Stephen (*delicately*) One naturally expects people brought up in Austria to speak with an Austrian accent. I have never *personally* regarded that as *necessarily* implying Austrian parentage. But, after all, what is my opinion worth? Less than the dust. My brother once went to Austria. To broaden his mind, no doubt.

Reeve Yes, I know. His valet gave me a ... very full account of the Austrian trip.

Stephen (*with reserve*) Oh.

Reeve And he ... never ... I mean, he didn't suggest ... (*he fails*)

Stephen I heard my brother complain on many occasions that it was difficult to find a really discreet manservant. (*a brief pause*) He seems, however, to have succeeded, for once.

(*pause*)

Reeve Miss Tablet, with the easy-going generosity of the creative artist the world over, had invited us to call again. That was, indeed, our firm intention. But in the event, we did not have to make this intrusion ourselves. A very short time after, early one morning, we were engaged in ... sorting our data, when the telephone rang.

(*telephone*)

Reeve Hello.

Evelyn Hel-*lowe*. (*he adopts for the telephone the soft, voluptuous voice of a beautiful female spy*)

Reeve Who's that?

Evelyn It's Evelyn.

Reeve Oh ... good morning.

Evelyn Hel-*lowe*.

(*pause*)

Reeve Did you ... want something, Evelyn?

Evelyn (*in no hurry*) It's old Hilda: she wants to speak to you. Asked me to ring you. She'll be here in a minute.

Reeve Oh, yes ... Thank you. I'll hold on.

(*another pause*)

Evelyn (*gently*) What are you *wearing* today, Mr Reeve?

Reeve W-what? Oh . . . just an ordinary dark suit.

Evelyn Jolly pretty, I bet.

Reeve I . . . well . . .

Evelyn I've got my *jeans* on.

Hilda (*suddenly*) Hello, is that you, Bertie?

Evelyn (*eclipsed*) G'bah-igh!

Reeve B . . . This is Herbert Reeve speaking.

Hilda That's right. This is Hilda here.

Reeve Good morning. How are you?

Hilda OK, ta. Look, Bertie: what have you got on this morning?

Reeve Oh . . . just an ordinary dark suit.

Hilda Oh, don't ass about, Bertie! What are you doing at the moment?

Reeve I . . . I'm . . . sorting my data.

Hilda Doing *what*?

Reeve Sor . . . arranging my information.

Hilda Well, look, old boy, I need your help, pretty drastically. Can you come round?

Reeve Oh, yes . . . of course.

Hilda Straightaway?

Reeve Yes.

Hilda Good. See you then, then. G'bye.

 (*telephone replaced noisily*)

Reeve Needless to say, we hastened round to Coptic Street as quickly as a taxi could take us. We were received by Elsa, who was alone in the music-room . . . A little treacherously, perhaps, we seized the moment to try to bring the conversation round to . . .

 (*fade up Elsa*)

Elsa Yes, it is very nice weather this morning. But you do not always have such nice weathers in England, I find. In Vienna . . . (*rapturously*) Ah!

Reeve I suppose you often return to Vienna, Miss Strauss?

Elsa Not so often as I try to.

Reeve I expect you have your relations in Vienna?

Elsa Yes, and also very good calves' liver and –

Hilda (*distant, behind door*) Bertie! Is that you, Bertie?

Reeve (*calls back*) I . . . Yes, it's . . . I.

Hilda Come on in!

Reeve (*apprehensively*) Where *is* Hilda?

Elsa (*placidly*) She is taking her bath.

Reeve Oh, well . . . I'll wait here, shall I, till . . .

Hilda Bertie!

Reeve (*agitated*) I . . . I . . . I . . .

Elsa This is the way, please.

Reeve But . . . wouldn't it be better if I . . .

    (*cross-fade to Hilda and immense splashings. She plays the scene with irresistible energy*)

Hilda Come in, Bertie. Excuse the old bod. Don't mind, do you? *C'est sans façon, chez nous.* (*gusty laugh*) Do sit down . . . No, not on *that*, unless, of course, you prefer it. There's a stool just there. (*further splashings*)

Reeve G–good morning, Hilda.

Hilda Good morning. Now look. I want your help, desperately. Have you ever heard of a couple of chaps called Faber and Faber?

Reeve Oh, of course, I . . .

Hilda Good. Right. Well, they're both after my life.

Reeve After your *life*, Hilda? Good God!

Hilda Well, don't be so ruddy surprised, old boy. Damn it. Several publishers have asked for it. It's been quite an interesting life.

Reeve (*relieved*) Oh, I see, you mean . . .

Hilda Exactly. Well, of course, as you can well imagine, the written word is not my medium. And the money means nothing to me. I've got plenty. Sorry to boast, but I have. Now I'm going to ask you, Bertie, as an old pal . . .

    (*great watery sounds as she gets out of the bath*)

to let me put myself entirely in your hands. Just chuck us that large towel, marked H.T., will you. Thanks.

Reeve But, Hilda, I . . .

Hilda Now, it'll need a goodish bit of research, but of course you're used to that, and the book itself need only be about 350 pages.

Reeve But I . . .

Hilda The advantage is you'll easily be able to fit it in with your life of old Dick Shewin; after all, our lives crossed the hell of a lot, kids together in the country, intimate pals in later life and all that sort of *coglioni*. I should say you'd make a damned good job of it.

Reeve (*with increasing misery*) Hilda, I'm sure . . .

Hilda It won't take long. Mustn't, in fact. They want it for when my opera *Emily Butter* goes on at Covent Garden, and that's next autumn.

Reeve But, my dear Hilda, I assure you it's not at all the sort of thing I should be good at. I . . .

Hilda Now, Herbert, no false modesty, please. I hate that. Mind you, I don't want to rush you into anything. But, Bertie . . . (*with disconcerting pathos*) j-just provisionally, I want to ask you . . . not to say 'no' straight off. I . . . can't bear being snubbed.

Reeve (*miserably*) I . . . I . . .

Hilda You won't, will you, Bertie?

Reeve Won't what?

Hilda Won't . . . just snub me.

Reeve Oh, no, Hilda . . . no, no, of course not.

Hilda (*her energy revives*) Thank you, Bertie. I like you for saying that. Now will you, *whatever happens*, just open the airing-cupboard and reach me out a nice clean shirt? And then go into the music-room, and Elsa will pour you out a nice large whisky and soda.

Reeve Yes . . . I could do with one . . . ah, thank you.

Hilda And Evelyn will show you my diaries. He has them ready. They should prove invaluable to you. Elsa!

Elsa (*off*) Coming!

　　(*brief pause*)

Evelyn Hel-*lowe*. Know what you've come for.

Reeve Hilda said I might look at . . . her diaries.

Evelyn Here they are. You'll find the best bits in September and October each year.

Reeve Oh . . . really?

Evelyn She always goes to Morocco in September and October. Shall I find you some good bits?

Reeve Well, I . . . think perhaps I'd better find those as I come to them.

Evelyn Which you *will* do.

Reeve Idly, we opened the first volume to hand: 1951. How very expressive of personality the human handwriting always is! As our eye fell on the first page we opened, Hilda herself seemed to . . . spring out at us.

Hilda (*forthrightly*) April 4: Began Violin and Piano Sonata. April 5: Bogged down in Violin and Piano Sonata. April 6: Finished Violin and Piano Sonata. Sent it off to the Menuhins. Began, late in evening, Concerto for Oboe and Strings. April 7: Concerto for Oboe and Strings giving me hell. April 8: Finished Concerto for

Oboe and Strings, took shoes to be mended, and sketched out settings for first eight cantos of the *Inferno*. April 9: After much thought have decided to scrap *Inferno*, and use same sketches for setting *Swann's Way*. April 10: Began to rehearse *Swann's Way* with Elsa. April 11: Fetched Elsa back from London Airport. April 12: Fetched Elsa back from London Airport. April 13: Fetched Elsa back from London Airport. April 14: Fetched Elsa back from Northolt.

Evelyn (*dreamily*) She's jolly clever, young Elsa. But not half so clever as old Hilda.

Reeve Don't ... don't lean on my shoulder, Evelyn, there's a good chap.

Evelyn (*gently*) Ticklish?

    (*door*)

Hilda Ah, I knew you'd be hard at it already. Once a scholar, always a scholar.

Reeve You know, Hilda, I still don't think I'm the right ...

Hilda I've been wondering about the question of title. That's always important.

Reeve Yes. (*pause*) You could always call it simply *Hilda Tablet*.

Hilda I'm ... inclined to think that's a bit *bare*. I wouldn't like that.

Reeve No ... *The Life of Hilda Tablet*?

Hilda That rather suggests I'm dead.

Evelyn (*roguishly*) Call it: *Take One at Night*.

Hilda You get on with your copying.

Evelyn (*evaporating*) O ... K.

Hilda I wonder if a general sort of title might be better.

Reeve Y-yes. We might call it *Woman Composer* ... or just *Composeress*.

Evelyn And see what you *get*.

Reeve How about *Aspects of Hilda Tablet*?

Hilda That suggests I'm monumental. And ... it's my music that's monumental, really, not me. What about *The Private Life of Hilda Tablet*? How about that?

Reeve A little ... sensational, perhaps?

Hilda You think so?

Reeve I do, rather.

Hilda Right. Then we'll call it that. Good. It gives a sort of shape to the thing. It needs that. It must be soundly architected. I may be able to help a bit there. There's a great connection between architecture and music, as you probably know.

Reeve Yes. Who was it once said that architecture was frozen music?

Hilda Search me. Who was it?

Evelyn The *Daily Telegraph* once said old Hilda's music was like thawed architecture.

Hilda (*loudly*) Now, of course, Bertie, I'm not going to influence you at all, as you know. You just say what you choose. Be objective. Naturally, it'll be best if I vet the thing a bit afterwards, just in case anything has slipped in which . . . oh hell, Bertie, I hate to be sentimental, but I wouldn't like there to be anything in it that might . . . well, throw a spanner into what to me is . . . well, a very dear friendship, Bertie.

Reeve Oh, yes. No.

Hilda But, of course, you will say exactly what you choose. Be absolutely objective. I hate subjectivity. No one can say that anything I've ever written has been subjective.

(*she plays a few strikingly objective strains on the piano*)

No ruddy fear.

(*she continues playing soft chords during the next few speeches*)

Now of course, you'll want to go round and see a few people who . . . well, people who really *know* me, and know *about* me. You might start with Harold Reith.

Reeve Harold Reith?

Hilda Yes. He's done the libretto for *Emily Butter*, my opera. You'll find him easy to get on with. A good sort, Harold; and so tremendously *loyal*. Tremendously loyal, Harold Reith.

(*a final chord after this. Harold Reith is peevish and rather impassioned*)

Harold . . . But you see, the whole trouble with *Emily Butter* is you can't hear a bloody word anybody *sings*. I said so to Hilda.

Reeve And what did she say?

Harold She said '*All* librettists say that'. She seemed to think that disposed of the matter. She added that most of them ought to be jolly thankful.

Reeve Oh . . . I'm . . . I'm sure she wasn't referring to you.

Harold Yes, she was. 'Including you,' she said.

Reeve Oh, dear.

Harold You see, this opera doesn't seem to be part of *me*, at all. You can't imagine *I* wanted the thing to be an *all-woman* opera, can you? There are no men at all in it. The part I hoped Jussi Bjoerling would sing is being sung by a perishing mezzo-soprano.

Reeve Oh . . . I . . .

Harold Hilda's smashed the whole thing about. The original idea was that it should take place in the sixteenth century on a boat anchored off Rimini: it's Hilda who's altered it all to a mutiny in the bargain basement of a drapery store. (*contemptuously*) And all those passages on *film* . . .

Reeve (*firmly*) But, Mr Reith, all the reviews on the Continent say that the passages on film are *most* effective.

Harold (*indignantly*) Yes . . . but they're all on *silent* film. *Silent*. What the hell am *I* there for?

    (*further decisive chords from Hilda*)

Hilda *Tremendously* loyal, old Harold. And after that, you ought to go and see old Bunny.

Reeve Bunny?

Hilda R. Egerton Bunningfield, ARA. He painted a damned good portrait of me in 1943.

    (*fade chords behind Mr Bunningfield. He seems rather weighed down by unsuccess*)

Bunningfield Well, yes, the picture *has* been much admired, and it was very good of Miss Tablet to sit for it. I asked her to, you know. It was meant to be one of a series of great women of the time, their part in the war effort. Naturally, I wasn't quite prepared for quite all the conditions Miss Tablet imposed. I wanted her to be playing an instrument, of course, but what I had in mind was a clavichord or the like, with highlights on a brocade dress and so on. I never imagined she would insist on the instrument being a bugle, though I agree it was appropriate to a picture illustrating the war effort and that. And she also insisted on it being an open-air composition; that's the whole of the Pennine Chain in the background . . . And quite frankly, Mr Reeve, she's the kind of figure I really would have preferred to have painted *draped* . . . but no, she insisted . . .

    (*fade last words behind chords*)

Hilda Agreeable, I always found old Bunny. Receptive to new ideas. And then, there are my colleagues in the world of music. I . . . advise caution with those. There's such a thing as jealousy, God help us, even in the creative arts, Bertie.

Reeve Alas, yes. I . . . I fear so.

Hilda Still, go and see Old Roger Cloud. He's one of the best. He may insist on playing his own frightful compositions to you, but his heart is in the right place. I've known Roger since my so-called student days ...

(*fade chords behind Roger Cloud*)

Cloud Yes. Yes. Yes. I've known Tabby since we were students together. A nice woman, frightfully nice; awfully good fun at a party. Good-natured too; generous. Such a pity about ... t't.

Reeve (*gently*) About what, Mr Cloud?

Cloud It's ruined her life, of course. A tragedy, really.

Reeve (*eagerly*) Ruined her life, Mr Cloud? What has?

Cloud Oh, her music. She's a dear good-hearted girl, and awfully good fun at a party. But she insists on regarding herself as a sort of superior Schoenberg. And one had such very high hopes of her. With a few years of trouble, patience and effort, she might easily have been the Chaminade of our day, you know.

Reeve Oh, indeed?

Cloud Just as *I* might be described – and in fact have been described – as the César Franck of our day. I don't want you to think I mean, or that anyone else means by that a *pastiche* César Franck, Mr Reeve.

Reeve Oh, no ...

Cloud But I'm sure you know my *Chorale, Chorale, and Chorale* for Piano, Mr Reeve?

(*he subsides luxuriously into this. After a few bars it is resolutely ousted by Hilda on another piano*)

Hilda He's Grade A, is old Roger Cloud. As a chap, I mean. You'll like him. But finally, the real person to go and see is Betty Parborough.

Reeve Is that the ... Duchess of Mulset?

Hilda Little Betty, yes. A sweety-pie. She's known me, and known me really well, for a very long time. And Jack's all right too.

Reeve The ... Duke?

Hilda Sure thing. Betty's a musical woman herself; plays Bach quite exquisitely. She's music critic of *Vogue*, as you probably know. I'd say Betty knows more about me than any woman alive. I've always found it so easy to confide in her. I've known her well for a good ten years. A sweety-pie.

(fade chords behind the Duchess of Mulset, who is young, fluent in speech, and maddeningly wise)

Duchess Yes, yes, yes. I've known Hilda for a good fifteen years. Haven't I, Jack dear?

Duke (*youngish*) Easily, my dear.

Duchess And yet, you know, Mr Reeve, I've never known her at all.

Reeve (*a trifle disappointed*) Oh.

Duchess One never really *knows* a genius.

Duke I think my wife makes rather a good point, there.

Reeve But I rather hoped . . . Hilda said . . .

Duchess Oh, one wonders, of course . . . One is bound to wonder.

Reeve Yes.

Duchess A rather despicable part of one is bound to wonder . . .

Reeve (*invitingly*) To . . . wonder . . .?

Duchess Oh . . . the usual things one hears. About Emilio Gonzaga-Visconti, for example. Did he really kill the Princesse de Pouilly-Schlumberger on Hilda's account, and so on . . . And all that talk about Hilda and the Sheikh, in Marrakesh. Of *course* one wonders. One wonders exactly the same things about Emily Brontë.

Reeve Ah . . . yes.

Duchess And wonders . . . *quite* as ineffectually, Sir Herbert.

Reeve N-no. Just Mr.

Duke I think my wife makes a *very* good point there.

Duchess What can these things matter . . . to posterity? Or to us? The thing about Tablet is her radiant genius. Her newness, her impact. Hilda . . . is one of the great innovators, Sir Herbert. As Frescobaldi was. The great innovators.

Reeve Yes, of course; the idea of an all-woman opera . . .

Duchess Oh, that's only a tiny, infinitesimal part of it all. She must have talked to you of her larger aims?

Reeve A . . . few of them, perhaps.

Duchess (*eagerly*) She's spoken to you about the *castrati?*

Reeve C-castrati?

Duchess (*adoringly*) She's so original, so far-reaching. Of course, we've all *dreamed* of reviving the *castrati*; but it's needed Hilda to take the first practical steps towards making them a reality.

Reeve (*apprehensively*) P-practical steps?

Duchess (*devoutly*) Yes, thank God. She's drawn up a list of well-known singers who she thinks would benefit from . . . treatment. Some of them have been singing baritone or even bass for years. It's only a question of getting them to agree. There *may* be difficulties. Singers are very conservative, as you know. But I'm sure that in the end the truth will prevail.

Reeve *(reverently)* Yes. One hopes so.

Duchess But what are ideas compared with the music itself?

Duke *(profoundly)* Little. Little. Little.

Duchess As my husband says, negligible. You know the score of *Emily Butter* backwards, I'm sure, Sir Herbert.

Reeve Well, only the parts that are played backwards, of course.

Duchess The ludicrous thing is the way people think of her as being only a serialist. Why, she embraces the *whole* of music, Sir Herbert.

Reeve I . . . suppose so.

Duke Yes, I think my wife makes a very good *point*, there.

Duchess It's her superb gift – Carissimi had it too – of suddenly producing out of eternity a *melody*, yes a melody, a *tune* (to put it vulgarly) that seems to have been existing there for ever, just waiting for Hilda to . . . draw it out.

Reeve Ah, yes.

Duchess Take, for example, the passage where Emily gets locked in the lift; all those fragmentary utterances, so pathetic, and so disjointed, and then suddenly that heavenly tune which . . . ah God! . . . one seems to have known all one's life. You know the passage, of course? I *must*, oh very imperfectly, of course, but I *must* play it over to you.

> *(plays and sings Emily's pathetic and disjointed utterances. Recitative on one note in spite of accompaniment)*

So late . . . to go . . . it is . . . far . . . and . . . I have . . . and
> *(suddenly to the strains of the big theme in Tchaikovsky's D minor symphony: slowly and exquisitely)*

> It is so late and I have far to go.
> It is so late and I have far to go . . .

Isn't it almost as if one had known that melody for the *whole of one's life* . . . Lord Reeve?

> *(Hilda resumes with a few chords, less familiar)*

Reeve Somehow, it had not been easy or convenient – one is so reticent – to divulge to Mr Stephen Shewin that we had for a time set aside our biography of his brother for a more transient task. He had accompanied us to Mulset on a most profitable and engaging visit to the family of his other brother, the late Edward Shewin; we had returned, and still *The Private Life of Miss Tablet* was unmentioned. It might indeed have remained unmentioned, had it not been for a question put to us by Mrs Stephen Shewin, on the first occasion we partook of afternoon tea together after our return to London.

(*appropriate mewings of cats throughout scene*)

Connie (*fade in*) Yes, a good pussy; and how are you getting on with your book about poor Richard, Mr Reeve?

Reeve Well, I do a little from time to time, of course.

Connie How kind of you. No, pussy.

Stephen Only a little, Mr Reeve? I was under the impression it was a morbid obsession with you?

Reeve Oh, not quite, not *quite* that.

Stephen } Oh. Indeed.
Connie } And a bright pussy never has morbid obsessions, does a pussy?

Stephen What other tasks employ your leisure, Mr Reeve?

Reeve Well, it's rather odd you should mention it, but . . .

Connie (*sotto voce*) No, Muffy.

Reeve . . . but Miss Hilda Tablet has asked me to . . . (*he pauses embarrassed*)

Stephen To what, Mr Reeve? To an orgy?

Reeve } Oh, no no . . .
Connie } Stephen . . .

Stephen To what, Mr Reeve?

Muffy Miaow.

Reeve (*pause*) She has asked me to write her biography; in rather a hurry.

Connie I didn't know you knew Miss Tablet, Mr Reeve, how was she? I haven't seen her for years; but a Muffy mustn't put paw in Mr Reeve's teacup, must a Muffy?

Muffy Miaow.

Stephen How has this eventuated, Mr Reeve?

Connie A Muffy must sit quite quiet on mummy's lap, mustn't she?

Muffy Miaow.

Connie Miaow.

Muffy Miaow.

Stephen In so far as I can make myself heard, Mr Reeve, I asked how this has come about?

Reeve She invited me, Mr Shewin.

Stephen And you accepted?

Reeve Ah . . . in a sense, yes.

Muffy (*louder*) Miaow.

Stephen Well, well; the sordid seems to have a peculiar fascination for you, Mr Reeve.

Connie Stephen, dear, what a thing to say.

Stephen Still, I suppose it is as well for all of us to be faced with the darker side of life from time to time.

Connie Oh, Stephen, dear, aren't you being just a wee bit intolerant?

Muffy Miaow.

Stephen No. *Get down!*

Muffy Aaaaaaaaaach!

Connie Muffy: you'll have to go outside if you jump up again, and a Muffy won't like that, will a Muffy?

Muffy Aah!

Stephen Then I suppose you are seeing a good deal of Miss Tablet, Mr Reeve?

Reeve Well, not at the moment; she is not in England at the moment.

Connie It must be so nice to travel.

Stephen Where is she?

Reeve I had a postcard the other day; she was in Algeria.

Stephen⎱ Aaaah!
Muffy⎰ Miaow.

Reeve She will be back shortly.

Stephen Tell me of her, Mr Reeve. It must be a peculiar household. I suppose in a sense the woman's devotion to her offspring must be admired . . .

Connie (*nervously*) Stephen . . .

Reeve Really I . . . have no wish to contradict you, Mr Shewin . . . but . . .

(*pause*)

Stephen I am quite used to being contradicted, Mr Reeve.

(*pause*)

You were saying, Mr Reeve?

Connie (*helpfully*) Pussy was saying . . .

Stephen (*sharply*) You were saying, Mr Reeve?

(*pause*)

Reeve I . . . ah . . .

Stephen I hope you haven't been listening to malicious gossip about my brother Richard, Mr Reeve?

Reeve I ...

Stephen Bad as his life was ...

Connie (*pleading*) Stephen ...

Stephen Bad as his life was, one must always aim at accuracy. And my brother was often the target for much cruel gossip. That he laid himself open to it none will deny, but there is moderation in all things. (*pause: deadlily*) That he was the father of the boy Evelyn I for one have never believed.

    (*silence*)

Reeve (*strangled*) Evelyn?

Connie (*a whisper*) Pussy.

    (*silence*)

Stephen You seem surprised, Mr Reeve?

Reeve But ... but ... but ...

Connie And a dear little pussy is sometimes surprised, isn't a pussy?

Muffy Miaow.

    (*silence*)

Stephen (*nobly*) I have *never* believed it, Mr Reeve: whatever you may say, you will never persuade me of it.

Connie Have you ever been to Finland, Mr Reeve?

Reeve No, never. Mr Shewin, I never for a moment entertained even the idea that Richard Shewin was Evelyn's father.

Stephen You relieve my mind, Mr Reeve.

Reeve Or that Hilda Tablet was Evelyn's mo ...

Stephen Aaaaah!

Reeve The idea seems to me unthinkable.

Stephen Unthinkable, Mr Reeve?

Reeve (*greatly agitated*) But ... but ... Evelyn's mother ... is a widow ...

Connie And Muffy is a widow, aren't you, Muffy?

Reeve Evelyn's mother ... Mrs Baxter ... lives at Richmond. He has several times pressed me to go and visit them.

Connie (*rapidly*) Oh, do go, Mr Reeve. It's so charming, especially at this time of the year. I wonder which is the best bus to ...

Stephen (*inexorably*) Richmond, Mr Reeve?

Reeve Y-yes, Richmond.

    (*pause*)

Stephen (*quietly*) Mr Reeve; have you ever heard of such a thing as baby-farming?

Connie (*reproachfully*) Stephen ... (*in exactly the same tone of voice*) Muffy ...

Reeve No one will deny that tact is required in writing the biography of a living subject. But one cardinal advantage the biographer whose subject is happily still with him most certainly has. Difficult points, obscurities of chronology or of personal relationships, can always be cleared up by direct questioning, provided of course that there is complete frankness between author and subject, and provided the subject has a clear, logical mind. And what creative artist, the world over, has, when we really look into it, not?

Hilda (*quietly*) Where are the kids?

Reeve Evelyn and Elsa? In the next room, I think.

Hilda Good . . . (*with some difficulty*) Look, Herbert, I'm not a girl who's easily offended, and if it was simply myself I wouldn't give a damn.

Reeve (*baffled*) A damn?

Hilda I know it's easy to gossip. I never do myself, as it happens, but then, the creative artist never does . . . And I do know, of course, Bertie, that you're a very complicated sort of person.

Reeve Oh, Hilda, I really don't think so . . .

Hilda And *tremendously* clever. I say that without hesitation.

Reeve Oh, no . . . I . . .

Hilda But look, old cock – will you answer me a straight question?

Reeve Of course, Hilda, if I can.

Hilda Well, then; (*clears her throat*) Sorry . . . Look, Bertie; which of 'em is it you're after?

Reeve After?

Hilda Yes. Which?

Reeve W-which of what?

Hilda (*slowly*) Elsa or Evelyn – which?
     (*pause*)

Reeve But, but, but, but *Hilda!*

Hilda Yes?

Reeve I'm very fond of both of them . . . but . . .

Hilda (*horrified*) Both of them!

Reeve But, really, Hilda, I . . . I'm not *after* either of them; really, I can't think whatever can have . . .
     (*breaks off*)

Hilda (*darkly*) You sure?

Reeve But Hilda, you can have no reason at all for even dreaming of such a thing.

     (*pause*)

Hilda Dreaming?

Reeve Yes.

     (*pause*)

Hilda Odd you should use that word. Very odd. Bertie, last night I *had* a dream, a very vivid one. That's why I've had to speak to you like I have. I dreamed you'd been . . . *gossiping*, Bertie. I . . . didn't like that, you know.

Reeve But . . .

Hilda Please let me finish. I dreamed you'd been going around saying to people that Elsa was Evelyn's mistress. (*reproachfully*) Really, Bertie.

Reeve But, Hilda, you . . . you say you only *dreamed* this.

Hilda Only? Where were you at school, Bertie? Have you never read what Dr Freud says about dreams?

Reeve A little, yes . . .

Hilda (*severely*) And Shakespeare too, for that matter:

> But this denoted a foregone conclusion;
> 'Twas mine; 'tis his: they come not single spies,
> But monstrous regiments.

Reeve No, Hilda, I *must* protest at . . .

Hilda It's no good protesting, Bertie. I know a good deal about psychology. I've always had a strong grasp of it. Why, when Dr Joachim Pfeiffer was analysing me, he said it was much simpler if *he* lay on the sofa and did the talking, and I just sat behind him with the stop-watch . . . (They used to *use* a stop-watch in those days. It was very comforting. So I used one.) It made a new man of him, he said. So you see. That dream can only have meant you had a strong primary fixation on one of the objects you were accusing of hanky-panky.

Reeve (*lost and exhausted*) I . . . Hilda, my dear . . . oh, my God.

Hilda I agree. Still, Bertie; once these things are brought up into the conscious levels of the mind, they often vanish quite simply. The truth shall make you free, sort of. That's why I thought I'd better have it out with you. You see, I . . . naturally feel a bit responsible for Elsa and Evelyn.

Reeve Of course.

Hilda I'm not a sentimental woman, I hope. But sometimes . . . well, almost feel . . . like a mother to them.

     (*pause*)

Reeve Hilda.

Hilda Yes, Bertie?

Reeve I'd . . . like to ask you a question I've never asked you directly before.

Hilda Of course, Bertie, what is it?

Reeve Hilda; do you think I could have a very large glass of whisky without anything in it at all?

Hilda Of course, Bertie. It's over there. Bring me one too. And what I've said brings me to something else, Bertie.

Reeve Something else, Hilda?

Hilda Yeah. (*with a certain husky coyness*) Bertie – am I the . . . *first* composer you've ever known?

Reeve Well, certainly you were the *first*, Hilda.

Hilda (*a little hurt*) You mean there have been . . . others in your life since?

Reeve Well, only an embryo one.

Hilda Who?

Reeve Well, I thought you probably knew. Richard Shewin's nephew is a composer – Owen Shewin. I met him in the country a week or so ago. He played me some of his own compositions.

Hilda Any good?

Reeve I thought they were full of feeling. I . . . was greatly hoping to bring you together.

    (*pause*)

Hilda Extraordinary, isn't it?

Reeve What is, Hilda?

Hilda (*almost mystically*) The way the whole ruddy thing all fits together . . .

Reeve I don't quite understand.

Hilda Listen, Bertie. I told you there was something else I wanted to say. Now, I don't want you to be offended by it . . .

Reeve Oh, no. Hilda . . .

Hilda What I feel I must say, is this: (*slowly*) it's jolly kind of you to have offered to write this book about me, and I appreciate it very greatly.

Reeve Thank you, Hilda.

Hilda But – please don't mind my saying this – I really don't think that the complex problems of a mature woman's mind are quite exactly your ticket. There, Bertie, dear . . . I've said it. (*sincerely*) I think it had to be said.

Reeve (*a wild hope flooding his heart*) I . . . do you mean, Hilda . . . that I needn't . . . ?

Hilda You won't be upset?

Reeve (*bravely*) No, Hilda, I won't be upset.

Hilda I like you for saying that. Thank you, Bertie. (*expansively*) Therefore, what I propose we do, is drop the idea of *The Private Life of Hilda Tablet*. Instead I'm going to let you concentrate for the present on a separate *preliminary* volume called *The Early Life of Hilda T.*, devoted solely to my youth, my childhood and whatnot. The original work we planned we can easily return to after you've finished the *Early Life*. The good thing is it will take us all down to the country. We all need a bit of fresh air, and in dear old Mulset you'll be able to work on me in peace and quiet. And I can meet this young man Owen Shewin you think so highly of. It all fits in, doesn't it? Almost a touch of Divine Providence about it, when you think. So that what I suggest is we all go down to Tutting next week. OK?

Reeve (*meekly*) O . . . OK, Hilda.

Reeve Mulset: how permanent and certain and unchanging are the moods and emotions of that lovely country. Tutting, the Elizabethan home of the Tablets, seemed, to an English eye, even fairer than Throbbing, the Palladian home of the Shewins some twenty miles south-west. On our first afternoon there, we were conducted round the little nearby church of Mull Extrinseca by Mr Bellingham, the rector. Hilda had left us alone with him that we might collect impressions. Pump him, she had said in her simple, unaffected way.

Rector (*sunny, light and soaring in voice*) Oh, yes. Dear Miss Tablet, yes, we're proud of her, yes, very proud of Hilda we are.

Reeve Yes, I'm sure.

Rector Very proud of Hilda. She's done so much for us, you know? The organ, you know. She mended it herself for us, very clever that, you know?

Reeve Yes, indeed.

Rector Clever, I thought, clever girl. And all those hymn-books, gave us all those, you know; very useful, never know when they might come in handy, a thoughtful gift? Oh, yes. That's the tomb of her great ancestor in Richard the Second's time, Sir

Tablet de Fitztablet Tablet. Yes, the family goes back a long way, you know, goes back a long long way.

Reeve (*reverently*) O, yes, of course, I knew that.

Rector And it comes forward a long way as well: that's the memorial tablet to Sir Willoughby Tablet-Tablet, a big figure in the A.R.P. round here. Hilda wrote an anthem for his funeral, you know; oh, yes, she's written a lot of pieces for us. The choir find them a bit difficult, a little bit difficult, but we rub along, you know, we rub along.

Reeve Oh, yes, I expect . . .

Rector We rub along somehow. And that's the new altar screen she gave us; the subject's a bit unusual for a church, as you can see, rather unusual. Artistic, of course, but rather unusual.

Reeve My word, yes, it is, rather.

Rector Rather unusual for a *church*. And if you step outside again for a minute you can see the two new finials she gave us for the porch . . .

(*outside*)

Very generous: devoted to good works. There they are, finials, fine finials . . .

Reeve There . . . there seems to be only one of them?

Rector Oh, the other's there, lying there, next to the tomb of Sir Howard Tablet. It fell off, you know, quite soon after they were put up. Of course the rain has washed the blood off, by now.

Reeve The . . . blood?

Rector Oh, yes, right off, washed it right off. It fell on Mrs Midgley.

Reeve Did it hurt her?

Rector Oh, I think so, yes. Yes, I think it hurt her; I think it did.

Reeve Will it be put back?

Rector Well . . . of course, Mrs Midgley might be a little vexed, though it was rather unkind of her to suggest that Hilda actually *pushed* it on to her. I don't think there was anything of that, you know. You see, there'd hardly be room for Hilda up there, would there? (*pause*) Well, I suppose, I suppose there *might* be . . .

Reeve Oh, I'm sure Hilda would *never* . . .

Rector (*intimately*) No, I don't think she would either, not really. And she's so fond of the old church, you know. She's promised us her feet.

Reeve Her *feet?*

Rector Yes. It was my wife's idea.

Reeve I don't quite understand. Promised you her feet?

Rector Oh, yes, she used to play the organ here when she was a girl, you know, quite famous as an organist she was, locally.

Reeve But I . . .

Rector She was very good on the pedals, they say. Diddle-iddle-iddle, you know, up and down? And my wife thought we might one day perhaps have Hilda's feet. In a casket.

Reeve (*faintly*) You . . . you mean . . . after . . .

Rector (*seriously*) Oh, yes, *after,* of course, oh yes. It would be quite simple, my wife says. Good sharp knife. Good clean cut. It was very good of Hilda to agree, we thought, very good. Embalmed, we thought, embalming would be a good idea . . . (*fade*)

> *In the next scene there are sudden startling pauses. Whenever Reuben speaks he does so in unintelligible spurts, of which the words given below are merely a suggestion. Only those italicised are clearly distinguishable.*

Reeve (*fade in*) And I suppose, Mr Cobb, that you will remember Hilda as quite a small girl.

Reuben (*enquiringly*) Dü?

Reeve I said I suppose you will remember Hilda when she was quite a small girl.

Reuben (*as before*) Beeee . . . ?

Reeve I said I suppose you will remember Miss Hilda . . .

Reuben (*suddenly and rapidly*) Ay, Miss Ilda, there were rare chettlin' shail-an-wamble whene'er Miss Ilda were dü forbye i' th'evenin' *be Magna.*

    (*silence*)

Reeve You mean she . . . ?

Reuben Ay.

Reeve You mean that when she was a girl . . . ?

Reuben Ay. (*after a pause; reminiscently*) Ay, 'twere.

Reeve I'm afraid I didn't quite catch . . .

Reuben (*enthusiastically*) For do ee see, sir, as 'twere rale praaper larrupen as twere to dü whensome'er the gert feymell shorthorn as us kep' up be Mulbry Magna i' the springtime were wi' ut again, an' us *didden allus know what to dü be un, dü ee see, sir?*

Reeve N-not quite, perhaps.

Reuben Ay. An biden' wi' ut too. (*thoughtfully, after a pause*) Thicky.

Reeve You . . . ?

Reuben Proper bucken an' varten!

Reeve V-varten?

Reuben (*firmly*) No. Twadden.

    (*pause*)

Reeve I wonder if . . .

Reuben (*loquaciously and proudly*) An' us tried to mizzle an' putten by-forrards, us adden no time for to bodge en in, an' us coulden a-try for to vettle she, and twadden no-some use neether for gert nor small be *us* to try düen, and Farmer, ee tried düen, and his brother-law, ee tried düen, though Mr Perkins be the parsonage ee woulden try düen (*for ee did say twere again the religion*) but twadden no-some use, there were on'y one on us could düen and daze me if tweren't lil missy: (*slower*) for ee mus' unnerstand, sir, as *Miss Ilda were hall-ways a bit of a tom-boy.*

Reeve How permanent, as we have said, how certain and unchanging seemed the emotions and moods of the place. On our first evening as we sat at dinner, the Tablet family portraits looking down upon us (approvingly, as we liked to think), the six of us – Sir Eric and Lady Tablet, Hilda, Elsa, Evelyn and ourself – seemed part of some richer, older, finer, more excellently-rooted and permanent part of our national life. It was an occasion when all that is said seems of the best and finest.

Lady Tablet (*solemnly*) That, Mr Reeve, is the faith I was brought up in; it is the faith I shall die in. I believe it to be the only faith.

Reeve (*reverently*) Yes, Lady Tablet.

Lady T. And I am convinced that I shall see that faith triumph once more in the hearts of men. Not of course that in their heart of hearts men have ever really abandoned that faith. And I am convinced that within twenty-five years from now a liberal candidate will be returned to parliament in every constituency in the British Isles. If we can get proportional representation in the near future the time may be shorter still.

Sir Eric (*dimly*) Well said. I think that's very well said, my dear. Bravo. Bravo. Jolly good. Bravo.

Lady T. The fight is a hard one, as you know, Mr Reeve.

Reeve Yes, indeed.

Lady T. But it will not be a losing fight so long as we liberals try to maintain a healthy perspective and keep abreast of our target.

Sir Eric And that's frightfully difficult in Mulset, you know, Reeve.

Lady T. What we need above all is public support and financial backing, both of which are somewhat lacking.

Evelyn Ooooh! *Poetry!*

Hilda Shut up, Evelyn.

Evelyn Sorry.

Lady T. And, dear Mr Reeve, you can imagine how proud we are to think that possibly after the very next election you may be representing North Mulset in the House of Commons.

Reeve (*horrified*) But, Lady Tablet, I am in no way a political man, I'm afraid.

Hilda No, mums, I'm bound to say I've never heard Bertie utter a word about politics.

Sir Eric (*genially*) Oh, but we're all politicians nowadays, Reeve.

Evelyn (*sedately*) I'm labour.

Hilda Do be quiet, Evelyn.

Lady T. (*tolerantly and wisely*) Yes, you are labour, Mr Baxter. You are also very young.

Evelyn (*complacently*) Yes.

Lady T. When you are older, you will not be labour.

Evelyn (*complacently*) No.

Lady T. And now, perhaps, we might go into the drawing-room, Miss Strauss?

Elsa (*appreciatively*) Yes. It is a so pretty room. And what a good dinner we have had. Such a lot of food.

Lady T. Hilda, dear, will you come with us, or do you want to stay in here with ... ?

Hilda No, I want to try something out on the piano with Elsa. I'll come with you.

Lady T. And ... Mr Baxter?

Evelyn I'll come into the drawing-room too, if I may, please. 'Cause I don't smoke and I don't drink and I don't like rude stories and I've left my sewing in the drawing-room anyway.

Lady T. (*suppressing a sigh*) Then let us go ... Don't be too long, will you, Eric?

Sir Eric No, dear, just one glass.

Lady T. Mr Baxter, do you think I might call you Evelyn?

Evelyn Oooh, *please.*

(*door: pause*)

Sir Eric Well, m'm, yes ... Port?

Reeve Oh, thank you.

Sir Eric We'll join the women in a few minutes, shall we? It's a ... bit embarrassing for you, all this, I know.

Reeve (*innocently*) Embarrassing?

Sir Eric (*genially*) Bit embarrassing for me too, y'know, ha-ha.

Reeve Oh ... oh, I hope not, Sir Eric.

Sir Eric Well, doesn't often happen, after all, does it? Cigar?

Reeve Thank you.

Sir Eric And ... and I'm very *glad* about it all, y'know, Reeve.

Reeve Gl ... ?

Sir Eric I don't mind telling you we were getting a bit worried at the thought of poor old Hilda being left on the shelf.

Reeve The shelf?

Sir Eric Well, I mean, that was what it was getting to look like, you know.

Reeve I ...

Sir Eric Of course, it took her a damn long while to get over that swine, Richard Shewin.

Reeve S-*swine*, Sir Eric?

Sir Eric (*unemphatically*) A rotter. A rotter, pure and simple. I ... you've *heard* of Richard Shewin, haven't you?

Reeve Oh, yes ... I ... I ...

Sir Eric Well, of course, the blackguard simply ditched the poor girl. (*mildly*) I'd like to have thrashed him. Still, the best thing was to let Hilda get over it. She was very young, of course. And she said very little about it at the time, even to my wife. Has she mentioned it to you?

Reeve (*swallowing hard*) Y-yes. After a fashion.

Sir Eric Yes, well, I'm glad. She might easily not have. She's shy, you know, Hilda is, very shy, a shy girl. Still, there 'tis. I'm very glad. Let's take the port into the drawing-room shall we?

Reeve (*still lost*) Yes. Shall I carry the ... ?

Sir Eric And ... before we go ... oh, I – well (*much moved*) dammit, old man, please let me just shake you very sincerely by the hand.

Reeve Y-yes, of course, sir, if you ...

Sir Eric And let me say that I hope you and Hilda will both be ... *very happy.*

(*pause. The slight smash of a glass*)

Reeve (*horrified*) *Happy,* Sir Eric?

(*long pause*)

(light noise of breakfast things. Fade in conversation)

Lady T. More marmalade, Miss Strauss?

Elsa (*greedily*) Yes, thank you. Thank you so much; in London, we do not have such powerful breakfasts.

Lady T. Toast, Mr Reeve? (*pause*) Toast, Mr Reeve?

Reeve Oh . . . I . . . no, thank you.

Evelyn You look jolly pale, Mr Reeve.

Reeve (*wanly*) Do I, Evelyn? Yes, I suppose I do.

Evelyn He looks jolly pale, doesn't he, Elsa?

Elsa (*mouth full*) Yes, very pale. (*clear*) Oll-most white.

Evelyn Jolly pale. Too many late nights, I bet.

Reeve No . . . I just haven't been out of doors much lately.

Lady T. We must hope the air of Mulset will restore your colour, Mr Reeve.

Reeve Oh, I'm sure it will.

Elsa (*eating*) And good country food is good for the colour, also.

Evelyn (*helpfully*) And you can always try putting a bit of slap on.

Lady T. Slap, Evelyn? What is slap?

Hilda (*suddenly*) Bertie, have you finished breakfast?

Reeve Yes, Hilda, I have.

Hilda Then, if the others will excuse us, we'll take a turn round the garden.

Reeve Y-yes.

Hilda Come on. We'll go through the french windows . . .

(fade up rooks)

Reeve A wonderful view from here, isn't it? A . . . fine prospect.

Hilda Not bad. Look, Herbert, I've got to talk to you.

Reeve Yes?

Hilda It's difficult for me to say it, but there's one thing you ought to get clear. I . . . don't want to hurt anybody's feelings: I remember poor old Dick Shewin too well. But I must ask you to remember that I'm . . . just not the marrying sort of girl, that's all.

Reeve Oh, no, Hilda . . . I mean I . . . I had no intention of . . .

Hilda (*after a brief pause*) You sure?

Reeve Oh, quite.

Hilda Are you the marrying sort of man?

Reeve Well, I . . . of course I . . . (*with a ghastly effort at lightness*) I'm always waiting for Miss Right, and so on.

Hilda Miss Wright? Who's she? You've never mentioned her before
. . . have you?

Reeve I was speaking metaphorically.

Hilda I don't get it, Bertie.

Reeve (*dreadfully embarrassed*) Well, you know. There's a Miss Right
and a Miss Wrong, I suppose.

Hilda (*a little severely*) Two of them? You're not . . . *promiscuous*,
I hope, Herbert?

Reeve Oh, no, no, please, I . . .

Hilda (*a bit huffily*) Well, it's none of my business; though I'm bound to say
I'm a bit surprised. But I just wanted you to be quite clear you mustn't
expect any . . . funny business, so to speak, between you and me.

Reeve Please, Hilda . . . I never . . .

Hilda Good. So long as it's understood. I don't mind the odd kiss, of
course, now and then. But . . . let's keep it just friends, shall we?

Reeve I hope we shall always be . . .

Hilda Good. Let's walk back to the house together . . . You know,
Bertie, I've been thinking about this volume you suggested on
the early life of my humble self. You know . . . I don't think it
will work.

Reeve (*with a faintly dawning hope*) No, Hilda? You mean you think – ?

Reeve I'm convinced it won't work . . . not as it stands, that is. You see,
Bertie, a creative artist's early years are almost the most important
part of her life. What I think we ought to begin to consider is
planning out the *Early Life* in two volumes, not one. And I'm
more and more convinced that the first of these ought really to
contain a consideration of my . . . *pre-natal* existence, which is
always very important in . . .

Reeve (*incoherently*) But . . . Hilda . . . I . . . oh . . .

Hilda Now, my *mother* ought to be able to help you a good deal with
that. It means approaching the old darling rather carefully, but
I feel sure you can do it. Try it this afternoon.

Reeve But, Hilda, we were going to the Shewins' this afternoon.

Hilda Were we? What for?

Reeve I promised Owen that you would hear some of his music.

Hilda Oh, damn.

Reeve I am very anxious to bring you together. Two generations of
composers . . . I thought it might be . . . very interesting.

Hilda What?

Reeve Two generations . . . I thought . . . ?

(pause)

Hilda (*pensively*) Yes. M'm. Odd you should say that.

Reeve (*apprehensively*) Why, Hilda? (*silence*) Did you say anything, Hilda?

Hilda No, I was just thinking ... I'll tell you later ... Yes, yes, of course we'll go. Get Evelyn to ring 'em up and say we'll be there for tea. Only, we must shoot off straight after, don't forget. We must be at Berivale by eight.

Reeve Berivale, Hilda? What is Berivale?

Hilda (*hurt*) My dear Bertie! I sometimes wonder if your memory is failing. Why do you suppose I'm wearing this appalling tie?

Reeve I ... I don't know, Hilda.

Hilda It's my old school-tie. I told you weeks ago. I promised to go and address the senior girls this evening after supper. You'll find it pretty helpful, too, seeing the old school. It'll help with the atmosphere for volume two. Pity we have to go to the Shewins' first ... (*thoughtfully*) Still, that may come in useful too; you never know. (*fade*)

(*Fade up a vivacious concerto of how d'you do's, Nancy being, as it were, the solo violin. There are present: Reeve, Hilda, Elsa, Nancy, Evelyn, Brian, George and Owen*)

All (*syncopated*) How do you do? How do you do? How do you do? (*etc. about a dozen times; Evelyn's 'Hel-lowe' is also heard*)

Nancy (*with the above*) So very good of you. My son Brian. So very good of you. My son Owen. So very good of you. My son George. So very good of you. How do you do? (*then: solo*). So very kind of you to come all this way to hear Owen's music, Miss Tablet.

Hilda A pleasure, a pleasure. (*laughs*) Let's hope.

Nancy A little professional encouragement means so much.

Hilda 'Fraid it does, yes.

Nancy And so good of you, Mr Reeve, to bring Miss Tablet. And so good of you to do so much about the boys' lyrics.

Brian Yes, it was jolly kind of you to show our lyrics to the Littry Editor of *The Listener*, Mr Reeve.

George Jolly kind.

Brian Yes. He hasn't actually printed any of them yet, but he says we can send him anything we write.

George So of course, we do. We sent him thirty last week.

Elsa Such big, delicious muffins ...

Evelyn Now, don't get hiccups again, baby.

Nancy I'm sorry my daughter Janet isn't here to meet you, Miss Tablet. She's in bed with a boil.

Hilda Ah, that's bad; poor girl. I've had 'em, myself, I know what they're like. Not that they've ever interfered with me much – I can always work standing up.

Evelyn I didn't know girls *had* boils.

Nancy Oh yes, very bad ones. I thought it best to keep her in bed.

Janet But, mother, I'm not *in* bed.

Nancy (*startled*) What? Oh, darling, I didn't see you. I'm so sorry. You must have got up. Miss Tablet, this is my . . .

Owen (*loudly*) Good Lord, look at Humphrey!

(*silence*)

The Shewins } Humphrey!
Nancy } Humphrey! What *have* you been doing?

Humphrey (*aged ten: a strong character*) Keeping goal.

Nancy But why is your face so black?

Humphrey I fell on it.

Nancy Oh, dear . . . hadn't you better go and wash, darling?

Humphrey (*stolidly*) I want my tea.

Nancy Well, you'll promise to go and wash afterwards, won't you?

Humphrey No.

Reeve (*tactfully*) And what is the new work you are going to play and sing for us, Owen?

Owen Well, it's partly a choral number, this one. It's about the moon.

Reeve (*sentimentally*) Ah, yes. A good old subject.

Brian } (*politely, but a little hurt*) Old, sir?
George }

Reeve Well, I mean (*benevolently*) there have been several great lyric effusions about the moon, you know.

Brian } (*firmly*) But not since 1951, sir.
George }

Evelyn And *that* was pretty dud.

Owen I think you'll find that's right, sir.

Elsa (*exuberantly*) Ah, I so love pieces about the moon for singing. I would like so always to sing from the moon. Have you been to Vienna, Mrs Shayvin?

Nancy Not to Vienna, no, I'm sorry to say, Miss Strauss. But I have been to Zurich.

Elsa (*affably*) It is not the same. There is not so much food in Zurich.

89

Brian We've written two pieces about Vienna.

Elsa Aaaah! (*rapturously begins to vocalise the Wienerwald Waltz*).

Hilda (*sharply*) Elsa! (*Elsa stops abruptly*)

Elsa (*a mutinous murmur*) I shall go back to . . .

Hilda And how about hearing this piece of yours, Mr Shewin?

Owen Well, it's very kind of you, Miss Tablet. (*nicely*) Of course, I'm afraid if you only like Beethoven, this may not appeal to you very much.

Hilda (*genially*) Oh, I wouldn't let that worry you.

Brian (*receding*) Come on, chaps, let's open the piano.

(*preparatory noises in background*)

Nancy (*intimately*) And we do hope you'll let us hear some of your own pieces, Miss Tablet. I adore music. I often feel I could almost write it, if only I were able to play some sort of instrument.

Hilda (*sympathetically*) Yes, a lot of people feel that way.

George (*distant*) We've been practising this one up for you, Miss Tablet.

Hilda That's the spirit. I hate under-rehearsal, *don't I*, Elsa?

Elsa (*mouth full*) Yes. Sometimes we never eat.

Nancy And, Humphrey, darling, you will keep quite quiet, won't you?

Humphrey Some of the time.

(*song with piano*)

Owen (*solo*)

Moonlight over Naples,
All over that lovely bay;
Quiet the noise of the traffic,
Vanished the lovely day;
But moonlight stealing everywhere,
And trying to steal away.

(*refrain*)

Oh, moon, don't go!
Oh, moon, just stay in place.
Oh, moon, go slow;
Don't slip off this beautiful face before me.
Just for a time just linger here,
Just for a time don't disappear.
Oh, moon, just stay . . .

Owen
Brian } (*an urgent, panting moan*)
George
Oh, moon: don't.
Oh, moon: don't.

90

Don't, moon, no, don't.
Don'-go-way-like-that.
Don't . . . don't . . . don't . . .

Owen (*solo*)
Just for a time just linger here,
    Just for a time don't disappear.
Oh, moon, just stay in place.

All three (*sadly*) *I ask you . . .*

Owen (*solo*)
Moonlight is a magic,
    They call it an alchemy.
Just look at those lovely glimmers
    All over the isle of Ca-pree.
But it's you who enchant the moonlight, my dear,
    And make it a magic for me . . .

Owen (*solo*)
Oh, moon, don't go!

George ⎱
Brian ⎰ *Don't go . . .*

Owen (*solo*)
Oh, moon, just stay in place.

George ⎱
Brian ⎰ *Moon: do . . .*

Owen (*solo*)
Oh, moon, go slow.

George ⎱
Brian ⎰ *Please . . .*

Owen (*solo*)
Don't slip off this beautiful face before me.

George ⎱
Brian ⎰ *Don't do that thing!*

Owen (*solo*)
You are my chance of happiness,
    Please don't turn it into distress.
Oh, moon, just stay . . .

All three *Five minutes longer,*
Four minutes,
Three minutes longer,
Two minutes,

One minute.
Oh! Oh!
No, moon, don'-go-way-like-that!
Oh, moon, just stay in place!

(a long pause)

Hilda *(interested)* How does it go on?

Owen Well, actually, that's the end.
  (discreet applause)

Humphrey *(suddenly bursts into uncontrollable weeping)*

Nancy Humphrey, darling! Whatever is the matter?

Humphrey I feel so *sadly.* *(he continues to weep)*

Nancy No, darling, don't, don't. It didn't mean anything.

Brian Oh, I say, mother!

Nancy Humphrey's so sensitive, you know.

Hilda Clearly. Cheer up, old cock, come on.

Elsa Give him a piece of cake, why not?

Evelyn I know just how he feels.
  (Humphrey's weeping gradually subsides behind talk)

Hilda It's really frightfully interesting. One thing puzzled me – what exactly was he up to? The chap who's supposed to sing it, I mean.

Owen Well, it's meant to be a . . . sort of picture of . . . romantic sort of thing, well about . . .

Brian *(helpfully, his voice cracking on the word)* Love.

Hilda What?

Brian Love.

Nancy Oh, *dear* . . .

Hilda Ah, yes, I see.

George With a lady.

Owen Yes, that's the sort of thing.

Brian Or, of course, with a gentleman, if a lady sings it.

Hilda Ah, yes.

Elsa *(passionately)* I would *love* to sing it. I would like to take a copy away with me.

Owen Oh, I say, that is nice of you, Miss Strauss.

Brian Shall we do it again? You could join in, Miss Strauss.

Nancy No, dear, *please*. Not that one again, with Humphrey feeling so sensitive. And we ought to ask Miss Tablet.

Owen Oh, yes, please, Miss Tab . . . Hilda. I do hope you'll oblige us with one of your own numbers.

Brian
George } *Please . . .*

Hilda Well . . . yes, why not? Elsa?

Elsa (*mouth full*) One moment . . .

Nancy And you'll try to be very controlled, won't you, Humphrey?

Humphrey (*with a final gulp*) Yes.

Brian Shhhhh . . . everybody . . .

(*Hilda thoughtfully plays an opening chord*)

Hilda (*to Elsa*) We'll give 'em *Deduke men a salanna*, Elsa, shall we?

Elsa (*with a sigh*) Yes.

Hilda Perhaps I'd better explain that our own little . . . number . . . is also about the moon. The words are in Greek. They were written centuries ago by a great woman whose name I won't bother you with.

Evelyn As if we didn't know.

Hilda The words mean, very briefly: The moon has set, so have the Pleiads. It is midnight, later in fact. I am off to bed by myself. (*quietly*) Elsa, please put that bun down.

Elsa (*quietly, but seriously*) It's not a bun, it is a cake.

Hilda (*quietly*) I don't care what it is; put it down.

Nancy (*pleasantly*) My husband was British Consul in Athens for a time.

(*Hilda plays. Elsa sings*)

Elsa
>Deduke men a salanna
>kai Pleiades, mesai de
>nuktes, para d'erkhet ora,
>ego de mona kateudo.

(*no one knows when it finishes. A pause*)

Hilda (*modestly*) Well; that's it . . .

(*the briefest pause, and . . .*)

Humphrey (*suddenly bursts into uncontrollable laughter*)

Nancy (*through it, horrified*) Humphrey! Humphrey! What is it?

Humphrey (*continues to roar with mirth*)

Nancy Humphrey! Humphrey! Oh, dear! I'm so sorry. (*desperately*) He's so highly strung, you know . . . Humphrey, dear . . .

(*the others endeavour, not with complete success, to drown Humphrey's mirth with applause and compliments: 'Superb', 'Awfully good', 'Jolly good rhythm', etc. Fade right out*)

Reeve (*levelly*) On the road from Throbbing Mulbury to Mulminster Berivale, where Hilda's old school was, and is, situated, there is an inn called the Meredith Arms. Defoe is said to have stayed there on his tour of the West Country. What he thought of it is not recorded. But to us it will always have special memories. It was here that we paused for supper on our way to the school.

Hilda You're not drinking, Bertie. Why not? This is some of the best Burgundy I've ever tasted.

Reeve B-but do you think you *ought* to drink quite so much before speaking at the school, Hilda?

Hilda Ought? Of course I ought. Must. Why, my dear Bertie, I'm nervous.

Reeve Nervous? You, Hilda?

Hilda My dear boy; I could, I assure you, address a large audience at the Royal So-called College of Music with calm and equanimity. The thought of talking to me dear old school reduces me to a jelly. Well, you can see. The only thing is to drink a very great deal of good red wine beforehand. Let's order another bottle.

Reeve Well, Hilda, if you insist . . .

Hilda (*seriously*) It's all very well for you, Herbert Reeve.

Reeve I . . . what do you mean?

Hilda (*eloquently*) *You* can be calm; *you* can be confident. It's all right for you.

Reeve I don't understand, Hilda.

Hilda You can relax there; knowing . . . knowing you've won.

Reeve Won?

Hilda Yes. Knowing you've won. I . . . (*meekly*) I give in, Herbert.

Reeve (*suspiciously*) Give in over what, Hilda?

Hilda Very moved I was, this afternoon, Bertie. Very moved. It was exactly what you'd said: the two generations. Made me feel quite old. Still, I saw why you took me there. In the end, I saw what you had in mind.

Reeve (*frightened*) In mind?

Hilda I have to hand it to you, Bertie. It needed a brain like yours to see it. What a brilliant conception! And moving; very moving.

Reeve *What is?*

Hilda I hope I'm worthy of it. God knows I hope that, Bertie.

Reeve Worthy of what, Hilda?

Hilda I suppose you were half-laughing at me. I hope not. I . . . I've tried my best. But there was I, thinking of my Life . . . as a thing that could be dealt with by a couple of preliminary volumes here, a couple more there, one in the middle, one at the end, and so on.

Reeve *Of what are you thinking, Hilda?*

Hilda You make me realise – oh, so very humbly, Bertie – that though I may be an artist, I am also a woman. I think in small terms, immediate projects. Well, I don't have to say. It needed you, Bertie, a man, to see that the whole thing must be bigger, bigger, bigger than I could conceive. It needed you to see the whole thing must have . . . epip spoke. (*a pause*) Epic scope, I should have said.

Reeve (*with slow horror*) Epic scope, Hilda?

Hilda I see now why you took me to Throbbing. It was for . . . guidance from the spirit of Richard Shewin, wasn't it?

Reeve That was not *quite* what I had in m . . .

Hilda (*nobly*) Never mind, Bertie. You win. You shall . . . have your twelve volumes.

Reeve Twel . . . !

Hilda (*pleadingly*) But not *more* than twelve, Bertie, I beg you. For the love of God, no more than that. It was enough for Gibbon, it was enough for Proust. Let it be enough for you, Bertie.

Reeve It . . . *will* be, Hilda.

Hilda (*gravely*) I like you for saying that. Thank you. And I don't mind telling you, Bertie, what you have done today gives me courage for tonight. Now, I can go forward and face these fine young *jeunes filles en fleurs* at me old school. What they will hear from me tonight, Bertie, what you will hear too, is a Statement of Faith. And you . . . have given me the courage to make it. I thought only Burgundy would see me through. But it is you, Bertie, not the Burgundy . . . Still, there'd be no harm in having another bottle, would there?

(*fade*)

(*fade up light applause, which subsides*)

Miss Welbeck Girls. This is a very special occasion this evening, and it is not my intention to occupy your time for very long. You see quite enough of me during the daytime.

(*light amusement from girls*)

Hilda (*emits a dutiful guffaw, and adds quietly to herself*) I bet they do . . .

Miss W. This evening it is Miss Tablet who claims our attention. And Miss Tablet is that rare thing, a creative artist. Now the works of a creative artist are not always easy for their first audiences to understand.

Hilda (*mumbles privately*) Yes, they are.

Miss W. But – if those audiences are intelligent and sincere and anxious to learn ...

Hilda (*as before*) Which they never are ...

Miss W. They will regard it as their bounden duty ...

Hilda No, they won't.

Miss W. ... to listen to everything, whatever it may sound like to begin with, in a spirit of fair play.

Hilda I know.

Miss W. It is for this reason that I have asked Miss Tablet kindly to cast her talk to us this evening in the form of a little illustrated lecture-recital centring upon her own work.

Hilda Oh dear.

Miss W. And I feel sure that Miss Tablet, who knows how proud we all are to have her with us this evening, will ... let us down lightly ... Miss Tablet.

(*applause*)

Hilda (*rises creakily*) Well ... thank you, girls. And thank *you*, Miss Welbeck, especially for that last rather mysterious remark.

(*slight tittering from girls*)

Well, girls, as Miss Welbeck has said, I propose to cast my remarks this evening in the form of a little ... a ... m'm ... (*to Miss Welbeck*) What was it you called it?

Miss W. A little illustrated lecture-recital.

Hilda Yes. I see. So be it. Well, girls (*cheerfully and very fluently*) it's very kind of you all to roll up and listen to it, whatever it is; jolly kind, and just what I'd have expected from dear old Berivale, the only school from which I was never expelled.

(*reaction of admiration from girls*)

I had been ... *removed*, not ungladly, from some five or six similar establishments before I got silted up here. But I remember Miss Egmont, the headmistress at the time, saying to my father: 'We will take *any* child of yours, Sir Eric.' We never knew quite what she meant, especially as I was the only one. But she was an agreeable little body, on the surface, and certainly you don't see headmistresses like her these days.

Jane (*from the audience*) Hear, hear.

Girls Shhh!

Miss W. Was that Jane Williams?

Jane Yes, Miss Welbeck. I'm sorry, Miss Welbeck.

Miss W. (*coldly*) Thank you.

    Hilda Well, so much for Miss Egmont. And the very thought of that dear, good woman reminds me that here I am, years later, on the very brink of delivering to you a . . . a little . . .

        (*brief pause: then, very politely to Miss Welbeck*)

    what was it again?

Miss W. A little illustrated lecture-recital.

    Hilda Yes, that was it. Now, girls. Let us face one fact, all of us. We *are*, all of us, you, me, Miss Welbeck, the late Miss Egmont and myself, all of the same sex, with all that that implies. And all of us, some of us dimly, some of us obscurely, some of us hesitantly maybe, and some of us even dimly, must all of us, in whatever way – (*rapidly*) obscurely, in some cases, dimly, hesitantly or dimly in others – fully realise, girls! our own (*crescendo, aggressively*) inner: intrinsic: intimate: ineluctable . . . *fragility!*

    (*silence. Then one girl claps, absorbedly*)

  Others (*a terrified reproachful whisper*) Jane Williams!!!

    Hilda Thank you, Jane Williams. (*continues rapidly*) And when I say fragility, I mean not what *you*, perhaps, or *you*, or *you*, or that girl there, or (*pauses briefly, obviously a little surprised at what she sees*) or even the one next to her, may mean by fragility: I mean (and I think it must be abundantly clear by now what I mean) that we are, all of us, just as God made us. And by *all* of us, I mean, of course, *most* of us. And I think I can best illustrate this point, in what after all is only . . . a . . . (*to Miss Welbeck, thoughtfully*) what was it?

Miss W. (*with commendable restraint*) A little illustrated lecture-recital.

    Hilda You heard that, girls? By taking the case of one of my own early works, my opus 70 . . . A *large* number, for an early work, some of you may reasonably opine. But I must make it clear that while some of my opuses have no number, because I've never got around to numbering the blighters, some of the actual opus numbers have, on the other hand, little or no music attached to them at all: a former habit of mine much plagiarised by dear old Anton Webern; though I'm bound to say he was frightfully good fun at a party. I shall return to this point later. Now the opening of my opus 70 runs as follows . . . (*to Miss Welbeck*) You don't mind if I just have a use of your piano, do you, dear?

Miss W. Oh, please, Miss Tablet. It is there for you.

    Hilda What make is it?

Miss W. A Glueckheimer.

Hilda (*reservedly*) Ah, yes ... it always was, I remember. Well, girls, this is the opening of the little number I referred to.

(*piano, briefly*)

Now, girls, if you were asked for an opinion on that ... 'little phrase', as dear old Marcel Proust, though I never actually met him, might have called it, you'd probably and justifiably describe it as a *haunting little tune*. Now let me just run over it once again.

(*she does so. Fade behind Reeve*)

Reeve We shall always recall, and never without emotion, the faces of Hilda's eager young audience that night in the gymnasium of her old school – the 'crush-bar', as Hilda herself so affectionately referred to that large old lofty apartment, so splendidly equipped. It was a moving occasion, and doubly moving perhaps for ourselves; for this was a ... Statement of Faith, made by the great artist who was permitting us to devote years and years of our life, years and years and years or our life, in fact, years and years and years and ...

(*fade behind Hilda*)

Hilda (*euphorically*) Years later! Years later, in fact only last year, you will find that simple little phrase used in another work of mine, and it is part of the inner pith and marrow of this little electro-plate – No. (*to Miss Welbeck*) Sorry. Say it again?

Miss W. L-little electrustrated-electure-ecital.

Hilda Exactly ... to explain how this comes about. The work I refer to is my recent Quintet for Eight Instruments. Now, my dear girls, eight instruments may seem to you rather a *lot* of instruments for a quintet. And it *is* a lot, I freely grant you. But the only condition under which the Consolidated Instrumentalists' Union would allow this quintet to be performed was if eight performers were paid for. They didn't all play, of course. I beg you not to think that. *Five* of them played. The other three sat around, or collected cups of tea for those who were actually playing. In the recording of this work I shall now play for you, if you listen carefully you will hear the chink of teacups quite distinctly. Now, would this be a gramophone, Miss Welbeck, or (*roguishly*) is it just the school cocktail-cabinet?

(*girls' laughter behind Reeve*)

Reeve (*fade in*) and years and years and years of our life we might happily devote to this work. Not only this year and next; but other years. Years and years of them. How happy we felt, at the thought of those years. Let us put it another way: we could devote year after year after year after year after year after year ...

    (*there is no excitement in his voice. Fade behind Hilda*)

Hilda And before I conclude this little ... m'm ... yum ... this little thing that Miss Welbeck keeps on about, there is one most significant episode in my own life I'd like to tell you about. It's this. In 1947 they asked me to go to Russia.

    (*a small burst of applause from a section of the audience*)

    (*a bit disconcerted, to Miss Welbeck*) What's that? Did I say something?

Miss W. I think Miss Tablet would prefer us to reserve our applause to the end of her ... (*the next words afford her some slight difficulty*) lecture-recital, girls.

Hilda No, no, I don't mind. Let 'em go on, by all means.

    (*silence*)

Ah, Miss Welbeck, you killed something there. Never mind. Well, Russia, I was saying. I went there. And, girls, it was an experience that spoke volumes to me. (*profoundly*) Girls, it spoke *volumes* ...

    (*cross-fade to Reeve*)

Reeve (*hypnotised*) Volume one, volume two, volume three, volume four, volume five, volume six, volume seven, volume eight, volume nine, volume ten, volume eleven, volume twelve.

Hilda (*fade in*) And it showed me as plain as Miss Welbeck here that you can compose your so-called great soaring heart-easing *melodies* (*there is much contempt in this last word*) and the week-end journals will be taking the mickey out of them before the last note dies away. But not even the music-critics of the *Observer* and the *Sunday Times* and that other one they have now, can really muster the confidence to try and sit on a girl's basic note-row. Or at any rate, not all three at once. (*earnestly*) I want you girls, when you go from here tonight, to think over that point very carefully ... Yes, well, that's all for now, ta. Thank you girls, and thank *you*, Miss Welbeck, for so kindly listening to my ... No, no, Miss Welbeck, I can manage, thank you ... my (*easily and triumphantly*) little illustrated lecture-recital. (*quietly to herself, as she sits down*) I should shay sho.

(great applause)

Miss W. Thank you, Miss Tablet, very much. I am sure you have given us a great deal to think about.

Hilda *(absently)* Oh, shucks it was nothing really . . .

Miss W. Now, though it is getting rather late, girls, Miss Tablet has kindly consented to answer any questions that anyone may like to put to her.

    (pause)

Olga *(from the hall)* I would like to ask a question, please, Miss Welbeck.

Miss W. Yes, Olga? This is our head girl, Miss Tablet – Olga Peacock.

Hilda Olga what?

Miss W. Olga Peacock.

Hilda Ah, yes.

Olga I would like to ask Miss Tablet, please, did she say the tune she played to us first was a haunting little tune, or a halting little tune?

Miss W. Miss Tablet?

Hilda I . . . *(rapidly)* I was rather hoping someone would ask that question, because as a matter of fact there were two girls called Peacock at the school when I was here – Grace and Lucy. Lucy, oddly enough, married a Red Indian and had seven children in five years; nice-looking kids they were too, though of course with their father being a Red Indian, you see, they naturally looked rather as if they were blushing the whole time . . . Interesting effect. Thank you.

Miss W. Does . . . does that answer your question, Olga?

Olga Yes, thank you, Miss Welbeck. Thank you, Miss Tablet.

Petal *(deep-voiced)* Please, Miss Welbeck . . .

Miss W. Yes, Petal Mullins?

Petal I would like to ask Miss Tablet, please: who is her favourite living composer?

Hilda *(promptly)* Yes . . . well . . . the answer to that on the whole, I think, is that it was a *haunting* little tune. *Very* haunting.

Petal Thank you, Miss Tablet . . .

Rosabelle Miss Welbeck.

Miss W. Yes, Rosabelle Spinney?

Rosabelle I would like to ask Miss Tablet, please, if she would be willing to sign some of our autograph books, please?

Hilda Certainly, certainly, of course I will. And you'd better have my telephone number as well, in case any of you want to ring me up any time . . .

(*fade into applause*)

Reeve What a moving occasion! As we watched the eager young faces,
surging round Hilda, pressing their eager young autograph books
upon her, we recalled the beautiful lines:

> *Alas! that Spring should vanish with the Rose,*
> *And Youth's sweet-scented Manuscript should close.*

So it might. So indeed it would. (*no pause*)
(*sedately in the background the girls begin to chant: 'For she's a jolly
good fellow'. This continues until the end*)

Youth's sweet-scented manuscript *would* close. But we knew of
another manuscript not likely to do so with such rapidity. Yes.
No. We were very happy at this thought, very happy, happy at
the thought of a task that would occupy so many of our years: all
of them probably. It made us happy. Happy we felt. It was the
thought of the years that made us happy, the years and years of it.
That thought had sustained us this evening. It would sustain us
through many months in Hilda's company, through a long
journey with her to Marrakesh, a further journey to Vienna,
other and briefer journeys to London Airport in search of
rebellious Elsa, journeys to Mulset, journeys, journeys, journeys,
right up to the great opening night of Hilda's opera, *Emily Butter*,
(*with controlled emotion*) when Hilda, wearing our own tails-jacket,
her baton raised, her fine figure silhouetted against the soft glow
of the orchestra lights, hurled herself upon her greatest triumph.
What a climax! It gave us a sense of great *happiness*.

  With the generosity of the creative artist the world over, Hilda
had already made ourself very, very happy, and we knew that at
this very moment she was making others very happy too. Their
happiness might not last so long as ours. But ours would last a
very long time. For us, there would be years. And years and years.
Of happiness. Yes, indeed.

A Hedge, Backwards

To Carleton Hobbs

A Hedge, Backwards was first broadcast on 29 February 1956. The production was by Douglas Cleverdon, with music by Donald Swann. The cast was as follows:

HERBERT REEVE	*Hugh Burden*
STEPHEN SHEWIN	*Carleton Hobbs*
CONNIE SHEWIN	*Gwen Cherrell*
HILDA TABLET	*Mary O'Farrell*
ELSA STRAUSS	*Marjorie Westbury*
NANCY SHEWIN	*Dorothy Primrose*
OWEN SHEWIN	*Denis Quilley*
BRIAN SHEWIN	*Wilfred Downing*
GEORGE SHEWIN	*Marjorie Westbury*
MUFFY, MILLY, ETC.	*Vivienne Chatterton*
GENERAL GLAND	*Deryck Guyler*
NEVILLE PIKELET	*Allan McClelland*
HÉLÈNE	*Cecile Chevreau*
RICHARD SHEWIN'S PROSE	*Frank Duncan*

Characters in Richard Shewin's works:

PETER	*Michael Meacham*
PAUL	*Denis Quilley*
MRS BANNISTER	*Vivienne Chatterton*
ROGER	*Michael Meacham*
BILLY	*Frank Duncan*
JENNY	*Janette Richer*
ROGER'S MOTHER (DAISY TREDDLE)	*Vivienne Chatterton*

Reeve We had been ordered to *rest* a great deal. It had been well said that rest was what we needed. And indeed, the time seemed not unpropitious for rest. We had had temporarily to lay aside our work on the biography, in two volumes, of the late novelist Richard Shewin, in order temporarily to embark on the biography, in twelve, of the well-known composeress Hilda Tablet, happily still with us. We had all but begun the second of these tasks when a brief respite seemed to offer itself: Miss Tablet, in the company of her young singer, Miss Elsa Strauss, was departing for her annual holiday in North Africa. On the beautiful airport terrace, she had given us our final instructions.

(*public noises in background*)

Hilda And Bertie . . .

Reeve Yes, Hilda?

Hilda Don't overwork. Just do as much of it as you can every day. But don't overwork. See? You've got a clear run ahead of you, haven't you?

Reeve Run, Hilda?

Hilda Time, I mean. You've got plenty of time.

Reeve Well, actually, Hilda, there *was* just one thing . . .

Hilda Good. Elsa! What have you been buying all those packets of sandwiches for? We shall be having lunch the minute we're in the air.

Elsa These are for between lunch and tea.

Hilda Save me from madness. . . . Were you saying something, Bertie?

Reeve Well, it was just that . . . I hope you don't mind, Hilda, but there is just one little point in my work on Richard Shewin that I thought I might perhaps try to clear up while you were away.

Hilda (*coldly*) Really, Bertie? The minute my back's turned?

Reeve Well, it was just something that . . .

Hilda Look at me, Bertie.

Reeve Yes, Hilda?

Hilda I hope you're not planning to do anything *dishonourable*, are you?

Reeve No, no, Hilda, please don't think that.

Hilda Well, it's a very strange world, I must say. People upsetting people, just as they're about to start off on a brief and (as I had

hoped) well-earned holiday. A bit . . . *shabby*, I'd have thought.
I may be wrong.

Reeve No, Hilda, I do assure you . . .

Hilda (*dismissively*) All right. Come on, Elsa. (*stiffly*) Good-bye, Herbert.

Reeve G-good-bye, Hilda.

Elsa (*warmly*) Good-bye, Mr Reeve. And please, don't overwork.

Reeve No, Elsa. Thank you. *Bon voyage!*

    (*pause*)

Reeve Dishonourable? Shabby? No, we . . . we ardently trusted not.
Nevertheless, on our way back from the airport, we could not
wholly suppress a spasm of guilt when we recalled that we had
failed to disclose the fact that we were about to call on Mr Stephen
Shewin, the late novelist's brother, that same afternoon. Alas for
conscience! – our guilt was quickly eclipsed by the prospect of
resuming, if only so briefly, those pleasant afternoons of calm
and illuminating discourse, leisurely, human, and cheering.

Stephen I suffered *greatly*, Mr Reeve.

Reeve Yes, I . . . I'm sure, Mr Shewin. I am very sorry.

Stephen I have often suffered greatly, Mr Reeve.

Reeve Yes.

Stephen Yes.

    (*brief pause*)

Reeve Mr Shewin: I wonder if your late brother . . .

Stephen Mr Reeve: you are a man of very wide literary cognisance. Have
you ever encountered the expression: 'It was like being pulled
through a hedge, backwards'?

Reeve Oh, yes, indeed . . . very . . . (haha) . . . very racy.

Stephen Have you ever felt like that yourself?

Reeve Well, sometimes, perhaps.

Stephen I suppose Miss Hilda Tablet makes you feel like that?

Reeve (*loyally*) Oh, no, I wouldn't say that.

Stephen Mr Reeve: on the occasions when, as you put it, you have felt as
though you were being pulled through a hedge, backwards, have
you ever meditated for a moment on what it might feel like . . .
to be the *hedge*? The hedge itself?

Reeve No . . . haha . . . no.

Stephen It is no matter for mirth, Mr Reeve. I will tell you something.
(*pause*) *I* . . . am a hedge, Mr Reeve. Yes, a hedge. Many people,

and many things, have been pulled backwards through me; and if my foliage seems a little wantonly ravaged here and there, it is solely due to that. My life has been a very sad one, Mr Reeve. Not, of course, that it has been sadly borne. I think I may claim to have always commanded some small smack of fortitude. All the same, Mr Reeve, had my character ever become blighted, darkened, umbrageous or despondent . . . who could have cast the first stone at me?

Reeve *(sympathetically)* Yes. Who, indeed?

Stephen Why, my *wife*, of course, Mr Reeve. She. My wife. Of all my graver misfortunes the shameless architectress . . . Ah, here she is . . .

> *(the door has opened to admit Connie, a tea-tray, and a fair number of cats)*

Connie Now, down a good pussy. Down, there's a darling. I'm sorry tea is so late, Mr Reeve, but I had to get it myself. Here we are.

Pussy Miaow.

Reeve Let me help you with the tray. You really ought not to have bothered.

Connie Oh, it was no trouble (down, pussy!) . . . It's just that we have somebody's little birthday in the house today, haven't we, Snowdove? And I had to send the girl to the shops before they close, to get some nice H.A.L.I.B.U.T. for P.U. double S.I.E.S.

Pussy Miaow.

Stephen A hedge, backwards.

Connie There. We'll have tea by the fire.

Reeve Oh, thank you, Mrs Shewin.

Stephen A hedge.

Pussy *(loudly)* Miaow.

Connie What did you say, dear?

Pussy ⎫ Miaow.
Stephen ⎭ A hedge. Get *down!*

Pussy Pssssssst!

Connie Stephen!

Stephen *(with passion)* Have you ever played darts, Mr Reeve?

Reeve I . . .

Stephen *(vehemently)* Because I am also a dartboard, Mr Reeve! I am not only a hedge! I am one of nature's dartboards. Like Saint Sebastian.

Pussy Miaow.

(brief pause)

Connie   Now, let's have some nice tea, shall we, then we shall all feel better. I do hope you like these cakes, Mr Reeve. Our new girl made them. She's French. She's over here to learn English.

Reeve   Oh, really? Is she getting on well at it?

Connie   Well, of course, it's *still* better if we speak in French. But she *is* picking up a little, yes. Just a little. Now, how do you like your tea? I'll . . . *(a sudden ripple of laughter)* Oh, no, no, no, how ridiculous!

Stephen   What?

Connie   I've forgotten to put any tea in the pot! I'm just pouring out hot water. Oh, *dear*, how funny!

Reeve   Haha . . . !

Stephen   *(sombrely)* I foresaw this.

Connie   *(pleased)* Now I wonder what it *means?*

Stephen   Means? It means that in your unconscious mind you wished Mr Reeve hadn't come to tea.

Reeve   Oh, I do hope . . .

Connie   Don't be silly, Stephen. It means either a telegram or a registered letter. It's one or the other, I'm sure. I shall look it up in my book. Do forgive me, Mr Reeve. I'll go and make some fresh. And we'll put a lot of lovely real tea in the pottikins, won't we, a bright pussy? Yes.

    (she departs, closing the door)

Stephen   *(meekly)* I'm sorry my wife makes you so unwelcome, Mr Reeve.

Reeve   Oh, I'm sure she didn't mean . . .

Stephen   But it's all of a piece, isn't it? We are very lucky to have shamed her into making amends. I have sometimes had to make do with hot water instead of tea for months on end.

Reeve   Oh, dear. Perhaps . . .

Stephen   I only wish I had my health and strength back, Mr Reeve. I would have made you a *very* nice cup of tea. Indian tea, or China tea: you could have had whichever you preferred.

Reeve   Oh . . . thank you, Mr Shewin.

Stephen   Don't mention it.

    (fade on last lines. Cats heard softly behind)

Reeve   How pleasant it was to be back here! – to feel oneself once more sitting here so intimately with the brother of Richard Shewin. How easy, natural and inevitable it was to recall the charming

idylls of brotherhood which abound in the Shewin novels. It was
so clear to us, now, where they had had their fount and origin.

Shewin's Prose *There, by the familiar shining stream, in that glade as verdant and fresh
as the groves of Avalon, Peter looked at Paul. It was as though he were
seeing him for the first time. Or no, not seeing him for the first time, but
for the first time realising, realising like some slowly delicious, slowly
flickering delicious flame, that Paul . . . was his brother. The words
flamed in his thought like some utterance from Holy Writ: THOU
ART MY BROTHER. Peter had never known it so innerly until he
had seen Paul there by the stream, in tears, his thin young nakedness
shivering in the intense heat: Thou art my brother. And suddenly, he
had said it aloud:*

Peter Th'art maï bruther.

Prose *And Paul looked at him. They looked at each other. Paul sniffed, and
stared hard downstream, unseeing, and said, in his still unbroken voice:*

Paul They can bloody choke theirsens, for all I bloody care. Bloody wenches,
I dunna give a piss for none on 'em.

Prose *His young distress had made him more eloquent than Peter had ever
known him. A lump rose in his throat. There seemed only one thing left
to say.*

Peter Paul.

Paul Ay?

Peter (fraternally) Th'art maï bruther, Paul Stilt; and so long as th'art maï
bruther an Aï'm thaïne . . . well, tha knows what. (pause) Dussent?

Paul Ay. Reckon Ah do.

Prose *It was as though some deep-flowing, deep loud uterine cry were crying
between them. No, by God, he would never abandon Paul! Moving
across the green space between them, he laid his arm awkwardly across
the thin bare shoulders, and said gently:*

Peter So be it, Paul, lad. Get tha breeches on, then. Hastn't forgot, hast, Paul?

Paul Forgot what?

Peter Why, Paul lad – we'm got jam for tea!

Prose END OF BOOK THE FIRST.

Stephen What are you thinking about, Mr Reeve?

Reeve Oh . . . a passage from one of your brother's books, Mr Shewin.

Connie Oh, how kind of you, Mr Reeve. No, pussy.

Stephen Brother, indeed! I may say, Mr Reeve, that my brother frequently
cast the most painful doubts upon our relationship. 'You are a

bastard, Steve', he used to say. 'You are a bastard, Steve, and you
know it.' I quote his words verbatim, Mr Reeve.

Connie (*plaintively*) Oh, dear . . .

Reeve (*cheerfully*) Oh, but Mr Shewin, that expression is quite often used
. . . almost as a term of endearment.

Stephen You must move among persons of a very peculiar affection,
Mr Reeve.

Connie No, *please*, dear . . . Oh, is that someone at the door? No, come
back, Muffy. Come in, Hélène, *entrez*. It's our girl from France,
Mr Reeve. *Entrez!* (*door*) Did you want something, Hélène?
Vous voulez quelque chose, dear?

Stephen A hedge, backwards.

Hélène (*in distinct, faultless English*) Excuse me, Mrs Shewin . . .

Connie Do come in. *Entrez. Fermez la porte, s'il vous plaît*, dear, if you
wouldn't mind. *Merci. Parceque de Monsieur Shewin's mauvaise
épaule, vous savez*. Thank you.

Stephen A dartboard.

Muffy Miaow.

Connie *Non*, pussy, *non! Bas! Bas*, pussy. What was it, Hélène?

Hélène The postman has just called, Mrs Shewin . . .

Connie Oh, *oui? Quelquechose pour moi?*

Hélène He has delivered a telegram and an enregistered letter. I thought
you would wish to have them at once.

Connie There! I said so!

Stephen A dartb– (*sharply*) What! What monstrous nonstrance!

Connie (*triumphantly*) I said so! *J'ai dit!*

Stephen (*passionately*) This house is *riddled* with superstition, Mr Reeve,
riddled with it!

Connie (*likewise*) Stephen dear, *s'il vous plaît! Je sais que c'est très extra-
ordinaire, peut-être, mais ce n'est pas la superstition, vous savez que ce
n'est pas* . . .

Stephen (*outraged*) Constance Shewin! Will you, if shout at me you must
kindly shout at me in the language you have shouted at me in
for the past twenty-seven years!

Connie (*collapses*) Oh. Oh, I'm so sorry. *Je suis si confusée*. Please forgive
me. Down, pussy. Hélène, *permettez que j'introduce Monsieur Reeve*.
Mr Reeve, this is Mademoiselle Moutier.

Reeve (*breathless*) En . . . *enchanté de vous* . . . de . . . de . . .

Hélène How do you do?

Reeve M-*merci*. Thank you very much. *Oui*.

Connie I must just open the telegram, if you'll forg . . . Why! How wonderful! It's from my brother Arthur!

Stephen Good God!

Connie Oh, please, Stephen dear, you know you're really very fond of him. And he of you. Yes. It's my brother Arthur, Mr Reeve. General Gland. He's back from the East. Isn't it splendid news?

Stephen No.

Reeve Oh, excellent! I have often heard you mention him. I . . . have always hoped I might have the honour of meeting him.

Stephen A hedge.

Connie But of course! You may find him very useful. He and Richard were devoted to each other.

Stephen (*vibrantly*) A hedge. A bare ruined choir, Mr Reeve, where late the sweet birds sang.

(*pause*)

Reeve This afternoon clearly marked a turning-point in our researches. We had long hoped for a meeting with Mrs Shewin's brother, General Gland, though we were well conscious that the occasion might prove an embarrassing one. We need not blink the fact. The question we wished to put to the General . . . concerned his sister's honour. It was a problem that had long obsessed us. For, as we have said elsewhere, within five minutes of our first meeting, months before, Mr Stephen Shewin had hinted at something of which we had till that moment been totally unaware – a . . . a sad enough tale, in all conscience . . .

Stephen My wife, Mr Reeve, my own wife. With my own brother. I would find them in this very chamber, Mr Reeve. My own bedroom. I was *gravely* displeased.

Reeve This relevation, though to some it must appear shocking, was not altogether baffling in itself. Yet it was clear that Mrs Shewin had a different recollection of the occasion.

Connie You know, Mr Reeve, my husband is really a very simple man, quite transparent. I hope you didn't get the idea that Stephen . . . *seduced* Richard's wife?

Reeve No . . . I . . . Mr Shewin said nothing that even made me suspect such a thing . . .

Connie Oh, no, I'm afraid it was Richard's wife who led Stephen astray. Poor Richard was very upset. He would never enter this house, you know. (*fade*)

Reeve Though it was not impossible to reconcile these two assertions, we could not avoid a sense of uncertainty. So that the question, all intemperately, remained: 'Who did what, when, and with whom?' That problem, abhorrent as it may squeam to the seemish ... I ... y ... *that problem* we were determined to solve. Our time was short. And there are moments when the scholar, normally a patient beast, feels he must be more down-right, more devil-may-care, more earthy even, than is his wont. It was in such a mood that we called on General Arthur Dowd Wilbraham Dowd Corke Gland, in his Bayswater hotel, and resolutely rang the bell.

Bell (*flatly*) Tink. (*pause*) Tink.
Gland (*mildly*) M'm? What's that?
Bell Tink.
Gland Eh?
Bell Tink.
Gland M'm?
Bell Tink.
Gland Well, do come in. Come in, come in. Why not try that, eh? Anybody there? (*door*) Oh, hello, good morning. Come in.
Reeve I'm so sorry, sir; the bell doesn't seem to ring.
Gland Oh, yes. Yes-yes-yes. I heard it.
Reeve Oh. I ... thought it didn't seem to sound.
Gland (*interested*) Oh, yes, I think so. Lessee. This it? Did yer press the tit, or anything?
Reeve Wha ... ? Oh, yes, I'm afraid I pressed it some five times in all.
Gland Well, I heard it five times. Funny. Less try it again, shall we? You do it. I'll go over there and listen. (*pause*) Now. Ready?
Reeve Y-yes.
Gland (*searches for a word*) I ... ah ... ym ... *Fire!*
Bell (*flatly*) Tink.
(*pause*)
Gland (*thoughtfully*) Do it again.
Bell Tink.

Gland Yes, well, yes, I heard that perfectly all right. That makes seven. Very good, really ... But come in, old boy, do come in. I'm so glad you came. Breadful weather, isn't it, breadful? So muggy.

Reeve Well, actually it has begun to ... to snow a little.

Gland Breadful. Might be Rangoon, almost. (*genially*) Still, haha, weather means sweet damn all to you, doesn't it, Colonel?

Reeve Oh, no, really. I ... I am no colonel, General.

Gland Say?

Reeve I ... I said, 'I am not Colonel Reeve', sir.

Gland Didyer? Why was that?

Reeve (*humbly*) Well, I ... I am not, that's all, I'm afraid. I am not *Colonel* Reeve.

Gland (*concerned*) Oh, dear. But I thought you were old Bimbo Reeve who made out so marvellous splendid at Tobruk. No?

Reeve No, alas. I'm afraid I have no claim to any kind of military distinction whatever.

Gland Why, what *were* yer?

Reeve When?

Gland Jawring the war, man: the late conflict. What service were you in?

Reeve I ... I'm afraid I wasn't in the armed forces at all, General Gland. I was let o ... ah, exempted, on medical grounds.

Gland Why?

Reeve (*embarrassed*) Well, sir, I'm afraid ... they discovered that I had flat feet.

(*a very long pause*)

Gland Flat feet?

Reeve Yes ... I ... fear so.

Gland (*politely*) Lessee.

Reeve See, General?

Gland (*gently*) Go on: show uncle.

Reeve Well, certainly, sir, if you wish. But, of course, nothing very much shows, I'm afraid, sir.

Gland (*dispiritedly*) Doesn't it? Oh, well, don't bother then. No, no, man, lace it up. Lace it up ... Flat feet ... T't.

Reeve So ... I'm afraid they wouldn't have me in the armed forces.

Gland No?

Reeve No.

Gland Well ... (*generously*) It's all right by me, you know, old boy.
I believe every man has a right to his personal beliefs.

Reeve No, no, it wasn't a question of ... I have *got* flat feet. They said it
was absolutely ...

Gland I'm the very last person in the world, I hope, to override a
fellow's religious convictions, provided they're sincerely held.
Dammit, that was what we were fighting for. They said.

Reeve But, sir, I ...

Gland No, no, *please*, Mr Reeve. Every sincere thinking man asks himself these questions. Ought to ask 'em, by Golly. Yes, by Golly,
I've asked 'em meself. Put the question often. In the watches of
the night and so on. Oh, yes. Always been forced to answer 'no',
of course, but there it is.

Reeve But I thought I ...

Gland There it is. You know I heard that bell as clearly as I hear you.
Tink. Breadfully faint of course. If it isn't rude, Mr Reeve, how
long did they put you in for?

Reeve In?

Gland Don't think I'm unsympathetic, Mr Reeve, I know the lavatories
in some of these places are in a shocking state. Not that they were
up to much in the jungle, if it comes to that. Breadful it was, you
know ... Still, the past's past. It's ... it's been nice mulling over
old times, hasn't it?

Reeve Oh, yes, v-very.

Gland I've enjoyed it, personally, very much. Was there anything else
you came about?

Reeve Well, I really came in connection with a rather delicate question
concerning your brother-in-law, Richard Shewin.

Gland Ah, yes, really? Old Dick? Splendid feller. He wrote books, you
know. (Or they *say* he did, it may be just hearsay, I s'pose.) But
you know, he was splendid, really *splendid*. He made out bril-
liantly in the fort'n-eight'n thing, you know. Got the DSO.

Reeve Oh, but ... forgive me, sir, but Richard Shewin never partici-
pated in the ... the Great War.

Gland Say?

Reeve He had severe mastoid, and was never allowed to ...

Gland Oh, come-come-come, Mr Reeve, please. I've told you I have
every respect for *your* feelings, but you mustn't try to foist 'em of
on to old Dick. *Please* leave poor old Dick Shewin to his glory
Come, come.

Reeve I...

Gland Why, mentioned in every dispatch there ever was, he was, pretty well. Ah, well. *Tink.* Look, Mr Reeve.

Reeve Yes, sir?

Gland Have you ever met my sister Connie?

Reeve Why, yes, it was she who wrote to you suggesting I should call.

Gland Did she really? Good for her. Well, do you know her husband, old Stephen Shewin?

Reeve Yes, of course...I...

Gland Well, look, Mr Reeve, there's something I've always wondered about. It's a breadfully delicate question; I hope you won't mind my putting it?

Reeve Of course not, sir.

Gland Well, you must have had a lot of experience of odd types in wherever it was they put you, but listen – can you tell me *this* – I won't let it go any further, of course.

Reeve Sir?

Gland 'Sthis: (*slowly and earnestly*) in your candid opinion, which would you say it was: did old Connie drive old *Steve* dotty? Or did old Steve drive *Connie?* It's a problem I can't get off my mind. Because you see, there's never been anything of that kind on *our* side of the family... *Tink, tink*, it said; *tink, tink, tink, tink, tink...*

   (*fade on last line*)

Stephen Well, Mr Reeve, I gather you saw my brother-in-law the other day?

Reeve Yes.

Connie Oh, did you, Mr Reeve?

Reeve Yes, indeed. A most agreeable encounter.

Connie Was he as you expected?

Reeve Oh, yes, exactly. I feel no doubt now that he is the original of Colonel Thyroid in *The Bang and the Whimper.*

Connie How charming.

Stephen He also appears in a slightly less idealised form as William Acorn, the English keeper of a Japanese tea-house in *The Back and the Front.*

Connie ⎱ Stephen!
Reeve ⎰ Oh, I can hardly believe that!

Stephen And, as you are doubtless aware, he figures in my brother's will as the legatee of all the less seemly pictures in my brother's collection.

Connie Oh, Stephen dear, I don't think we ought to bring up Richard's will again. Do you, Mr Reeve? Such a painful document.

Stephen Pain, I personally have never flinched at. I was well prepared, Mr Reeve. As I have mentioned before, my brother Richard made it quite clear that he intended to leave the whole of his vulgar fortune to the unsavoury brood of children begotten by my other brother Edward upon Nancy, his imbecile spouse.

Connie Stephen, I really *don't* think you should refer to poor Nancy like that.

Stephen (*coldly*) My dear: isn't it about time you went and made Mr Reeve a nice pot of hot water?

Connie Oh, I'm so sorry: yes, of course: I'll ask Hélène to put the kettle on.
(*pause as she departs*)

Stephen The final words of my brother's testament are burned in letters of fire on my brain, Mr Reeve.

Reeve Yes . . . I . . . yes.

Stephen The spitefulness of it! (*excitedly*) 'And to my dear brother Stephen Shewin I bequeath all my real estate in London and the Home Counties, my aeroplanes, my Shakespeare first folios, my medicine-cupboard and the performing rights in all my dramatic works.' Why, Mr Reeve, the only tangible object in the whole farrago was the medicine-cupboard! And even *The Times* could not refrain from pointing out that my brother had never possessed any real estate in London *or* any aeroplanes *or* any Shakespeare first folios, to leave to anyone.

Reeve (*sympathetically*) Or, of course, any dramatic works.

(*pause*)

Stephen Well, there perhaps you are slightly in error, Mr Reeve.

Reeve But, Mr Shewin, I had always understood that your brother had no interest in the drama.

Stephen (*politely*) Had you, Mr Reeve?

Reeve Yes.

Stephen Oh. (*a pause*) Oh.

Reeve But d-d-do you mean that . . . (*he breaks off*)

Stephen Mr Reeve, since you press me so hard, perhaps I should confess to you one of our darker family secrets: my brother did indeed leave one play behind him – alas.

Reeve But, Mr Shewin, this is a literary fact of very great moment!

Stephen Possibly, Mr Reeve, very possibly.

Reeve Does the work still exist?

Stephen I fear so, Mr Reeve. I am afraid I could not undertake the responsibility of showing it to you. (There is such a thing as family piety, after all.) I dare say my brother Edward's widow, down in Mulset, might be less discreet. But I hope not.

Reeve But . . . you know, this is splendid news, Mr Shewin!

Stephen You would, I fear, think it less splendid, had you conned the manuscript and acquainted yourself with the theme of the work.

Reeve (*tentatively*) Mr Shewin: what would the theme of the work . . . be?

Stephen The play deals very frankly . . . with a Certain Subject, Mr Reeve. Alas.

Reeve W-what subject, Mr Shewin?

Stephen Mr Reeve: as you have gathered, the aspect of himself that my brother presented to the world was but a simulacrum. In your forthright way you have penetrated beyond that, and who shall say you nay? But beyond that there was far more. *Far* more, Mr Reeve.

Reeve H-how far, Mr Shewin?

Stephen (*mildly*) My brother's interests and habits were very far-ranging, Mr Reeve: they were not *simply* confined to seduction, adultery, fornication and rape.

Reeve (*faintly*) N-no?

Stephen (*a mere coo*) Oh, no. Far from it. *Far* from it.

    (*fade slightly on last line*)

Reeve So, once again, as so often before, we were lured down to leafy Mulset, the scene of so much of Shewin's life and art. There, at Throbbing, the graceful home he had left them, surely Nancy Shewin and her bright offspring would give us unstintingly of their aid. So would Mulset itself, that incomparable landscape, clear-rivered, tree-crowded, bird-haunted . . .

    (*fade in. Tea-things*)

Nancy I know we have the play somewhere or other, Mr Reeve. I'm sure we have. I don't think the children destroyed it.

Reeve (*anxiously*) Oh, I hope not.

Owen Oh, don't worry, Mr Reeve, it'll turn up. We'll all have a good hunt for it.

Reeve Oh, thank you, Owen.

Nancy It *must* be somewhere, because I remember we used it only last Christmas for something else.

Reeve Something else?

Nancy Yes, you see it's only typed on one side of the paper, so we used the blank sides for playing heads-bodies-and-legs, I remember.

Reeve (*murmurs*) Great God!

Owen Oh, of course, so we did.

Nancy And some of them were so funny we felt we couldn't throw them away immediately. You know how ridiculously one hoards such things.

Reeve I – I hope so.

Owen Look, I've finished my tea. I'll go and round up George and Brian, and we'll instigate a mammoth search. I can see Mr Reeve's rather nervous.

Reeve Oh, no, no, no, Owen. It's only that . . .

Owen (*receding*) Don't worry. See you later.

Reeve How very kind of him.

Nancy Well, it's very kind of *you* to take all this interest in dear Richard, Mr Reeve. I'm sure he would have appreciated it. He was so gentle and sweet. He was more like a woman than a man in some ways, I often thought.

Reeve (*with a slight gulp*) Y-yes.

Nancy I suppose Stephen and Connie will have told you a great deal about him?

Reeve Yes, they have been most kind and explicit. There are still one or two points in his personal relationships that continue to baffle me. In fact, Mrs Shew –

Nancy It's *so* horrid when things prey on the mind, isn't it? I have my own problems too.

Reeve Oh, I'm very sorry to hear that.

Nancy Well, of course, it's little Humphrey really. He *has* rather a strong character, as I expect you've noticed. But he's a very sincere boy, and I know he genuinely means it when he says he wants to become a j.d.

Reeve A j.d?

Nancy Yes, a juvenile delinquent. I . . . I wonder if you could help me a little with him?

Reeve Well . . . I could *talk* to him and try to dissuade him, perhaps.

Nancy No, I don't want him to be dissuaded. It may be only a passing craze, but I do think he should be allowed to work his way naturally through it.

Reeve Well . . . that is a point, of course.

Nancy (*dimly*) Yes, I felt it was rather a point. I . . . I felt that.

Reeve (*gently, after a pause*) Mrs Shewin: there is one question concerning Richard Shewin, which I feel sure you could help me about.

Nancy Well, of course, if I can, of course.

Reeve I expect you are aware that there is one side of Richard's domestic relationships that the great world so far knows nothing at all about?

Nancy Well, yes, I . . . yes, I suppose they don't.

Reeve I hope to be the first to tell the world the truth.

Nancy Yes. I see. (*gently, after a pause*) Mr Reeve: what I've been wondering is whether you'd be willing to have Humphrey with you in London for a time?

Reeve Humphrey! In London?

Nancy Yes. You see, there is very little scope for a juvenile delinquent in the country; and I thought you might know some select little gang he might go around with for a time.

Reeve (*appalled*) But, Mrs Shewin, you don't want Humphrey to go round with a . . . a-a-a- *cosh*, do you? Assaulting old people.

Nancy (*slightly embarrassed*) Well, actually, Mr Reeve, he *has* a cosh. Oh, only a very *little* one. We gave it him for Christmas. But I feel sure he'd only use it on people smaller than himself. And he has grown lately, as I expect you'll notice.

Reeve (*bewildered*) Well, Mrs Shewin . . . I can only say I shall have to . . . to think, very deeply, about the matter.

Nancy Thank you. It's so kind of you.

Reeve (*gently, but firmly*) Mrs Shewin: forgive my reverting to the matter. But it has been very strongly hinted to me that all was not quite as it has hitherto been supposed to have been, between Richard Shewin and his brother's wife.

Nancy (*faintly*) No. No . . . of course not.

Reeve I have had two conflicting accounts. One from Stephen; one from Mrs Stephen. Now, dear Mrs Shewin, I wonder if you would be willing to help me to . . . the real truth? I do hope you are not offended at my mentioning all this?

Nancy No, no. I ... I felt you were ... bound to mention it sooner or later.

Reeve I am only anxious to discover the truth.

Nancy (*after a pause*) Mr Reeve. I will *tell* you the truth. I hope you will believe it.

Reeve But of course.

Nancy I don't know how much the others have said. But it was one Christmas. Richard was down here by himself. The place was his, of course, in those days. And he'd asked myself and the children here for Christmas. There were only eight of them at the time; or nine perhaps, I can't quite remember. He was so good to them.

Reeve Oh, of course.

Nancy Well, anyhow, there he was. Rather sad, I thought he seemed, that Christmas. And it was while my husband was away in Turkey. And Richard and I were both ... well, rather lonely, that was what it was, I suppose. I remember we used to walk round the park together ... rather like the two people in that poem:

> *Dans le vieux parc solitaire et glacé,*
> *Deux spectres ont évoqué le passé.*

I ... I went to a finishing school in France, you know. Near Bougival. I did want to send my daughter Janet there, but we decided against it in the end. They finish young girls in such strange ways nowadays, don't they?

Reeve Yes, I ... suppose they do ... but ... ?

Nancy Very strange.

    (*pause*)

Reeve You were about to say something, Mrs Shewin.

Nancy Oh. Well, only that that was how it happened. I was terribly sorry afterwards, of course. After all, I was chairman of the Women's Institute that year, and there was the choir, and one has one's obligations, but ... well, Richard was lonely, and I was lonely, and ... there it was. It ... it didn't seem such a very serious thing at the time.

Reeve (*deeply shaken*) M-Mrs Shewin: you ... mean ... you ... ?

Nancy And it *wasn't* serious, really. I don't know what the others have told you, Mr Reeve. In fact, until you said so, I never realised they knew. But I do give you my solemn word of honour ... (*with great delicacy*) that it was only the *once*.

Reeve (*dully*) The once.

Nancy Oh, yes. That I could swear to.

(*pause*)

Reeve 'Even bravest heart may swell.' That has been well said, and it may well be added that even bravest heart may on occasion contract. This was perhaps such a moment. It did indeed seem to us that, though we had just unearthed a new and arresting fact, it was not a fact that solved our earlier problem. Rather, indeed, did it complicate it. Perhaps, we were tempted to put it to ourselves, we might do better for the moment to let these deep waters simmer gently in our mind, and to turn our attention to the purely literary problem that confronted us: Shewin's unknown play. Rarely can a temptation more beguiling have advanced to meet a humble scholar.

(*the boys are heard approaching*)

George (*singing*) We've found it, we've found it!
Brian We've found Uncle Richard's play!
Owen It's a bit battered and tattered, I'm afraid, Mr Reeve, but you're a fan of Uncle's, you won't mind that.
Reeve Of course not.
George It's a jolly *good* play!
Owen And I hope you won't mind about the heads-bodies-and-legs on the backs of some of the pages.
Reeve No. no. Thank goodness it survives.
Owen I think most of it's there . . .
Reeve M-most?
Owen Yes, I don't think there's much of it missing.
Brian And it's ever such an *interesting* play, Mr Reeve.
(*fade on last line*)

Reeve Here, then, it was. It had not been difficult to come by, after all. Only a title-page was lacking. We perused it – ay, and reperused it – that same night, in our room. It did not perhaps very greatly resemble any of those novels that have earned for Shewin the title of the poet's novelist. But how should it? This was not a novel, but a play. And ah, heavens! how moving the experience! – to see from the very first page how complete a master Shewin had made himself of the technique of the lovely art of drama. As we conned the opening moments of act one, we could, instantaneously and unescapably, conjure up . . . the theatric image. *(rather tremulously)* Act One . . .

Shewin's Prose *(precisely)* Act . . . One. *The drawing-room of Roger Waterson's flat in Cavendish Square. Tastefully furnished. Grand piano back left, Picasso Harlequin in frame over it. Large window in middle of left wall. Downstage of this, door to dining-room. Door to corridor, back centre. Between this and right wall, low book-case; over it reproduction of Correggio's Ganymede. Fireplace in centre of right wall. Sofa left centre. Near piano, small table with telephone. At rise of curtain: discovered: Mrs Bannister, the daily help, on knees, tidying grate. After a few moments telephone rings. She gets up, crosses upstage, and lifts receiver.*

Mrs Bannister Hello. Yes it is . . . Who is that, please?

Prose *(grimly)*

Mrs B. Oh, it's you again, is it? . . . What I say: it's you again . . . Well, is it or isn't it? . . . Well, keep a civil tongue, if you've got one . . . No, I'm not . . . No, he's not . . . No, we're none of us not . . . What? No, he isn't . . . I couldn't say . . . You could always leave a message . . . No . . . Kindly don't refer to Mr Waterson like that in my presence . . . No, and it's as well for you you're not . . . You know what I . . . Oh, sir!

Prose *(Roger Waterson has just entered from corridor, back centre. He has his hat and coat on; his features are weary and unshaven, as though he had not been to bed. As soon as she sees him, Mrs Bannister claps hand over telephone)*

Roger Who is it, Mrs Bannister?

Mrs B. Oh, sir . . . it's him *again*.

Prose *(pause)*

Roger I see.

Mrs B. What shall I say, sir?

Prose *(pause)*

Roger Say I am not at home.

Mrs B. Mr Waterson is not at home . . . What?

Prose *(whispers loudly)*

Mrs B. Oh, sir. He says he heard you.

Roger I see.

Prose *(crosses L. and takes telephone from Mrs Bannister)*

Roger Thank you, Mrs Bannister. Perhaps you could get me some tea?

Mrs B. Yes, sir. And oh, sir, I am so sorry.

Roger That's all right, thank you.

Prose Mrs Bannister *crosses downstage R., turns at door, shakes head, and exits.*

Roger Hello. Yes. I thought we agreed that you were not to ring up again? . . . Of course I meant it . . . I'm very sorry, I can't help that . . . I'm afraid not . . . I'm afraid not . . .

Prose (*firmly*)

Roger I'm afraid not . . . I should have thought *you* knew *why* . . .

Prose (*between his teeth*)

Roger Good-bye.

Prose (*replaces receiver*).
     (*receiver replaced*)

Reeve (*respectfully*) A phrase we had somewhere heard or **read** came into our mind: 'sense of theatre': a phrase which somehow or other we had hitherto found it difficult to pin any particular meaning to. But now we understood, fully, what a fine, sensitive, expressive phrase it was. 'Sense of theatre.' Yes, indeed.

Brian Did you like uncle's play, Mr Reeve?

Reeve Very much, Brian, thank you.

Brian It's a jolly *interesting* play, isn't it?

Reeve Oh, very.

Brian Pity there aren't any girls in it, though, isn't it?

Reeve Well, that . . . *might* be a criticism, yes.

Brian Well, I mean, it's not much like Shakespeare, is it?

Reeve No, Brian, that's quite true; it isn't greatly like Shakespeare.

Owen Well, there are *songs* in Shakespeare, just like in this.

Reeve Songs, Owen? I didn't notice any songs.

Owen Yes, there's one in act two. May I show you . . .
     (*rustle*)

Brian Old Owen's written a tune for it.

Owen Yes. There. There it is.

Reeve Oh, I . . . well, that isn't actually meant to be set to music, Owen. You see, it just says: 'Roger reads aloud from book'.

Owen (*regretfully*) Yes, I see. Pity.

Brian Still, you'd like to hear old Owen's setting, wouldn't you, Mr Reeve?

Reeve Oh, rather, yes.

Owen I thought it ought to have an accompaniment on this thing. (*plonk of guitar*) Quite a lot of actors can play them.

Reeve Yes, I suppose so.

Owen Would you mind reading out the words for me, Mr Reeve, please, just to jog my memory?

Reeve Certainly: 'Roger reads aloud from book':

> There once was a garden where we used to play,
>> But the flowers bloom there no more,
> There are no bright faces at the windows,
>> And the weeds grow up to the door.

'Unable to go on, Roger gets up and puts book aside.'

Owen Yes, I didn't actually set that last bit; only the lyric. This is how I thought it might be treated.

> *(sings with guitar)*
> There once was a garden, where we used to play,
>> But the flowers . . . they don' bloom there no more.
> There are no bright faces at dem ole windows,
>> *(Not as I kin see, bawss)*
>> And the weeds grows up to the door.
> Yeah, boss,
> Dem weeds
> Grow ride up'n ole home-door.
> Yeah, boss,
> Dem ole weeds,
> Dey gone ride uppon
>> *(sa–ad)*
> Dat ole home-door.
> *(after a pause)* . . . Boss.

Reeve Yes. I see. Yes. Thank you, Owen.

Owen Nostalgic, really.

Reeve Yes, very.

Owen Of course, you have to be very careful with that type of lyric. It can be done, of course, but you have to be very careful with it.
   (fade)

Reeve As Mr Shewin had observed, the play did unquestionably deal with a Certain Subject. Perhaps that was why its author had withheld it from the world. The play *was*, at first blush . . . at first sight, far better suited to a small limited printed edition, to be published, let us say, in Amsterdam.

   (pause)

Stephen Yes, Mr Reeve, it is perhaps as well that you should have read it. Though I am glad it was my sister-in-law, and not myself, who placed the disillusioning document in your hands.

Reeve (*cheerfully*) Oh, I'm in no way disillusioned, Mr Shewin, I think it's a splendid play.

Stephen I mean your disillusionment about my brother's true character.

Reeve Oh, but . . . I . . . I know the play deals very sympathetically with . . . a Certain Subject; but I can't regard it in any way as autobiographical.

Stephen (*politely*) Can you not, Mr Reeve?

Reeve N–no.

Stephen Oh. (*pause*) Tell me, Mr Reeve, is your biography of Miss Hilda Tablet to be equally evasive?

Reeve (*stung*) I . . . I don't know quite what you mean, Mr Shewin.

Stephen I suppose not. (*after a pause; reminiscently*) I suppose it all began, as these things are often said to begin, at our public-school. Who can say?

Reeve B–but Charterborough is said to have a most healthy reputation.

Stephen In the year 1893 it had indeed, Mr Reeve. My brother did not go there until the autumn of 1894. By January 1895, the cities of the plain were as an herbaceous border in compare. I was the only boy in the school to remain untouched by the disastrous infection.

Reeve But, Mr Shewin . . . we all know that . . . with boys shut away from the company of . . .

Stephen Yes, Mr Reeve?

Reeve . . . the normal contacts of life, it is only natural that they should . . .

Stephen Yes, Mr Reeve?

Reeve Well, form attachments of a romantic nature, sometimes amounting to . . . well . . .

Stephen Amounting to what, Mr Reeve?

Reeve Well, to . . . considerable affection, almost. But . . . (*he wilts*)

Stephen You speak of the subject with a certain warmth, Mr Reeve.

Reeve No, I do beg you to . . .

Stephen I can well understand your enthusiasm for my brother's play, Mr Reeve.

Reeve But, Mr Shewin, my enthusiasm for it is purely aesthetic . . . purely artistic.

Stephen (*conclusively*) Indeed? Well, let us dismiss the topic, shall we? (*amiably, after a brief pause*) My brother-in-law, General Gland, was telling us you had been in prison for a brief period, Mr Reeve.

Reeve What!

Stephen Oh, please, Mr Reeve, don't think I hold it against you; it might perhaps have been easier for my dear wife and myself, had we had the confession from your own lips; but we all have our reticences.

Reeve But Mr Shewin, I . . . I'm horrified to think that you . . . G–God *bless* my soul!

   (*door. Enter Connie. Mewings*)

Connie Ah, Mr Reeve! Welcome back!

Reeve Oh, thank you. Good afternoon.

Connie *Kathise, psipsina.* I do hope you don't mind having coffee for tea, Mr Reeve?

Stephen A hedge, backwards. A dartboard.

Connie Our French girl left us, you know, and we have a Greek girl, from Greece, at the moment. She's very nice, of course, and of course my Greek is improving a great deal, but she won't let us drink tea, she insists on our drinking *oh*-such a lot of coffee, and *oh*-so strong and black. *Kato, psipsina.* We hardly sleep at all. Her name is Medea.

Reeve Ah, a good classical name.

Connie (*earnestly*) Oh, *very*. And how was Mulset, Mr Reeve?

Reeve Oh, charming as ever, delightful.

Connie I had a letter from Nancy this morning. She says you've invited Humphrey to stay in London with you.

Stephen (*much interested*) Aaah?

Connie So very kind of you, Mr Reeve. And how very like you.

Stephen Yes.

Reeve Well, Mrs Shewin, I'm afraid she is exaggerating a little there. I do assure you that I would find it quite impossible to cope with Humphrey, either in Mulset or in London.

Connie Oh, I'm sure you'll get used to him. *Kato, psipsina!*

   (*pause*)

Reeve It may be thought by some that we behaved ungratefully in refusing, at any rate for the moment, to further little Humphrey's legitimate ambitions. But life was beginning to close in on us again; only that afternoon, when we returned home, we found a message awaiting us, in an unmistakable handwriting.

Hilda (*in bursts*) Dearest Bertie. *Back.* Longing to see you. Come for supper tomorrow, Thursday, six thirty. Bring my life with you.

Longing to see you. Neville Pikelet also coming. All love, etcetera. Tablet.

Reeve Thus it was that we found ourself repairing on the following evening to the familiar flat in Coptic Street. Hilda ... was a splendid colour.

Hilda Bertie, old son! (*gusty laugh*) Well, well, well, lovely to see you.

Reeve Lovely to see *you*, Hilda.

Hilda You're still looking a bit pale, Bertie. Mustn't do that, you know. Dangerous. Haha. Well, old boy, how's my Life? Brought it with you?

Reeve Yes, it's in my ... my satchel, here.

Hilda Let's have a dekko at it before old Neville Pikelet gets here, shall we? Thanks. (*pause*) Bertie, old duck! Is this all you've done?

Reeve I ... I work rather slowly these days, Hilda.

Hilda Clearly. I shall have to think of getting someone else at this rate!

Reeve (*stirred by hope*) Do–do you think so, Hilda?

Hilda (*consolingly*) No, no, old son, I was only joking. Don't you worry.

Reeve Ah.

(*Elsa is heard singing*)

Hilda Elsa! Stop that, and come and get Bertie a drink. Have a drink, Bertie, while I take this into a corner, and calmly face up to Truth about Humble Self.

Elsa (*entering*) Ah, Mr Reeve. How nice to see you. I hope you did not overwork?

Hilda No. He didn't.

Elsa Good. Haha. Chin? With tonic? And lemon? And ice?

Reeve Thank you. I hope you enjoyed Marrakesh, Elsa?

Elsa It had for and against ... Have you ever eaten roast hump of camel and custard, Mr Reeve?

Reeve No. It sounds ... very filling.

Elsa (*seriously*) Yes, it is filling if you can keep it *down*. But only *if*.

Reeve Elsa: excuse my ignorance, but who is Mr Pikelet? Hilda says he's coming this evening?

Elsa But you remember him! He produced for me my opera, *Emily Butter*.

Reeve Oh, of course, how stupid of me. Yes. Are ... are he and Hilda friends again, then?

Elsa Boozom.

Reeve What?

Elsa Boozom. This. (*faint pat*)

Reeve Oh, of course. Good.

Elsa Yes, he is going to produce the *Antony and Cleopatra* of Shakespeare, with loud music from Hilda.

Reeve Oh, excellent.

Hilda (*from a distance, quietly*) Herbert.

Reeve Yes, Hilda?

Hilda Will you come here a moment, Herbert. (*pause*) Look, Herbert. I . . . I've been writing music now for some thirty-two years. And like every independent musician, I am quite used to having my work sent up.

Reeve S-sent up, Hilda?

Hilda That was what I said, Herbert.

Reeve Sent up where, Hilda?

Hilda Sent up. That's all.

Reeve For . . . some sort of prize, do you mean?

Hilda *Please*, Herbert, don't joke about this. Kindly allow me to read you your opening sentence, 'In the sphere of music, female composition is a recent development, and a healthy one to boot.'

Reeve Let me see. Oh, no, no, no, no, Hilda. A comma has got left out.

Hilda Comma? Where?

Reeve There. It should read: 'Female composition is a recent development, and a healthy one, comma, to boot.'

Hilda You sure?

Reeve Of course, Hilda.

Hilda Oh. Well, let's hope the rest of it's a bit more careful. Have you been doing any more about old Dick Shewin?

Reeve A little, Hilda. A very little.

Hilda Haven't been mousing round old Stephen Shewin again, I hope?

Reeve I have seen him on occasion, yes.

Hilda Nasty old alligator.

Reeve Hilda: did you know that Richard Shewin wrote a play?

Hilda Play? Old Dick? Good Lord. He *hated* the theatre, he always said.

Reeve (*with modest pride*) So the world believes, Hilda. But he did write one play. I . . . have been privileged to see a copy.

Hilda Do I come in it?

Reeve I think not, Hilda. No.

Hilda I expect I do really. Got it on you?

Reeve Yes, it's in my satchel. Would you care to glance at it?

Hilda Course.

Reeve Here it is. (*rustle*)

Hilda (*musing on it*) Well, well, fancy old Dick writing a play. Any music called for in it?

Reeve Well, yes and no.

Hilda Good. I'll set it. (*suddenly, troubled*) Bertie: has anything been happening to you lately?

Reeve I think not, Hilda. Why?

Hilda Well, just look at all these damn silly drawings you've done on the backs of the pages. Really, Bertie!

Reeve But, Hilda! You surely don't believe that *I*...

(*door*)

Hilda I sometimes feel you have little bouts of instability, Bertie; am I right? Who's that?

Mrs P. Mr Pikelet has arrived, Miss Tablet.

Hilda Oh thank you, Mrs P.

Neville (*advancing*) Hilda, my dear!

Hilda Ah, dear old Neville! So glad you made it. Mind my tie. (*kiss*) Now, you know Bertie Reeve, of course, don't you?

Neville Oh, yes, of course. Lovely to see you again.

Reeve How do you do?

Hilda (*off*) What'll you drink, Neville?

Neville Whisky, dear, please. And lots and lots of water.

Reeve Elsa tells me you are about to embark on *Antony and Cleopatra*, Mr Pikelet.

Neville God, yes. (*moans*) Oh, Hilda darling, I've had such a terrible day.

Hilda Who with?

Neville The management. They don't want Pug.

Hilda I don't think I remember who Pug is, do I, Neville?

Neville Oh, of *course* you do, darling. Pug Judder.

Hilda I'm still a bit blank, dear. (*cheerfully*) Stupid girl, really. Who is he?

Neville He's my Antony, dear. If we can get him.

Hilda Wouldn't ... what's-his-name ... Olivier, do?

Neville Only over my dead body, darling. I've told you before, an English Antony's out of the question. We *must* have an American; and we must have Pug Judder.

Hilda (*genially*) I see.

Neville He's big, and he's large, and he has the obvious advantage of having only been in musicals so far. It means he comes to it fresh.

Hilda Ah, yes.

Neville And not only does he come to it fresh; he brings to it what it's already got. (*profoundly*) You see, lovey, in this day and age, *Mark Antony has got to be played butch.* Don't you agree, um . . . m . . . Bertie?

Reeve W-what was the word you used?

Neville Butch. The costumes will help with all that, of course. We're dating the thing forward to round about 1805. It makes the whole thing more universal, and of course it also brings out the parallel with Nelson and Lady Hamilton.

Reeve (*feebly*) Yes . . . I . . . I suppose it would.

Neville One has to try and wipe out all memories of previous productions completely.

Hilda (*modestly*) I think my music may help a bit there, Neville.

Neville But of course, darling! The opening's going to be marvellous. Pitch darkness. And then the Sphinx's opening monologue suddenly *booming out* (you know?) with the music in the background.

Hilda (*alertly*) I thought you said the music was going to be in the foreground?

Neville Well, it'll actually be everywhere, really (you know?). The Sphinx's voice'll suddenly come *booming out* of it. We open with that speech about the *thing*:

> '*The poop she sat on, like a burnished poop,*
> *Burned on the water. The sails were beaten gold,*
> *And o'er the files and musters of the war,*
> *Glowed like a strumpet's poop: and so on.*'

Reeve I . . . w . . . yes.

Hilda I may say the music is going to be a pretty sharp smack on the you-know-what for the Consolidated Instrumentalists' so-called Union.

Reeve How have you managed that?

Hilda Conkers.

Reeve C . . . conkers, Hilda?

Hilda *Musique concrète.* Concrete music. You know about it?

Reeve No.

Hilda You tape it.

Reeve Tape it?

Hilda And dub it to disc after. (*instructively*) Of course, most of the johnnies who do it rely on pure sound, amplified and speeded up and reversed and so on. Needless to say, I have my own little line on the thing. For one thing, I think the discerning listener could probably tell you almost at once that my *musique concrète* is very much louder than anybody else's.

Reeve Is it really?

Hilda Oh, yes, quite a bit. Also, for fair measure I clamp in a few simple little haunting tunes of my own, repeated, over and over. That's why my own brand is called *musique concrète renforcée*; reinforced concrete music. Like to hear the block I've done for *Antony and Cleopatra*?

Reeve Very much.

Hilda You mind hearing it again, Neville?

Neville Of course not. I have to get used to it.

Hilda The opening section is very largely based on Elsa's zip.

Reeve Zip?

Hilda Yep. *(calls)* Elsa! Come in here! I'll show you how we started.

Elsa *(approaching)* What is it, Hilda? What do you want?

Hilda Elsa: are you eating?

Elsa A little.

Hilda What have you got in your hand?

Elsa It is a small calf's kidney.

Hilda But, Elsa, you disgusting girl, it's not cooked!

Elsa They are very good and delicious raw also.

Hilda Save me, dear God. Kindly turn round. Now, Bertie, you see this zip-fastener. Now, note the sound it makes when I pull it sharply down. Like this. *(zip)*

Elsa *(winces loudly)* Oooh!

Hilda *(mildly)* Elsa! Don't be silly. Now the sound it makes when pulled up is quite perceptibly different. So. *(zip)*

Elsa Oooh!

Hilda *(patiently)* Elsa. Do you mind? Thank you.

Elsa *(mutters)* I shall go back . . .

Hilda Hear the difference, Neville?

Neville Not quite. Could you do 'em again?

Hilda OK. Listen. *(zip)*

Elsa Oooh!

Hilda Now up again. Listen. *(zip)*

Elsa Olppph! *(she produces, in succession, a squeak, a choke, a loud gulp, and the kidney)* Aaaaach! I have nearly swallowed this kidney whole *sale!*

Hilda (*indignantly*) Well, don't *show* it to people, you silly little dotty! Take the beastly thing into the kitchen.

Elsa (*retiring in loud grief*) I am at my end of the tethers! I shall go back on the first train to Vienna!

(*door, loudly*)

Hilda (*sighs*) Those kidneys were for our supper, boys, believe it or not. Where was I? Yes. Now that zip was invaluable in suggesting a certain effect – wind, whipping across desert sand. Of course. I 'treated' it. I'll put on the first fragment for you. This is how the play opens.

(*music begins. Hold, very loud, and continue behind speech*)

Hilda (*shouts*) Nice, isn't it?

Neville (*shouts*) Yes, very!

Hilda (*shouts*) Like it, Bertie?

Reeve (*shouts*) Yes, very much.

Hilda (*shouts*) Stimulating.

(*music eventually finishes*)

Hilda ... This is a quieter bit.

Reeve Yes.

Hilda More thoughtful.

Reeve Yes.

(*music alone*)

Reeve Hilda; what is that sort of 'glub–glub' sound I hear?

Hilda Ah, I'm glad you noticed that ... It's my housekeeper's heart ... It's rather dicky.

(*music*)

That's her husband's. His is all right.

(*music up, hold, and out*)

Connie We haven't seen much of you lately, Mr Reeve. But I expect you're busy with your book on dear Richard. Down, darling.

Reeve I ... I make but scant progress, I fear.

Stephen I expect you are kept pretty well to heel by Miss Tablet?

Reeve Well, that isn't quite how I like to think of it.

Stephen How *do* you like to think of it, Mr Reeve?

Reeve It ... would be difficult to say exactly.

Stephen Does she inflict her Bohemian friends upon you, Mr Reeve?

Reeve Not ... not really. I did meet the theatrical producer, Mr Neville Pikelet, there recently.

Stephen Ah, yes, of course. Mr Pikelet. Did he divulge to you his astonishing theatrical project?

Reeve Oh, yes, in some detail. I . . . suppose *Antony and Cleopatra* in Napoleonic dress *might* be interesting. One has to be . . . broad-minded in these things.

Stephen You will have to be even more broad-minded than that, Mr Reeve. Mr Pikelet has abandoned *Antony and Cleopatra*. He has been unable to secure the services of an American impersonator named, if I recall it aright, Hog Kidder.

Reeve (*surprised*) But . . . may I ask how you know this, Mr Shewin?

Stephen He wrote and told me.

Reeve Oh, I didn't know you knew him.

Stephen I don't, Mr Reeve. But he intends a presentation of my brother's play, so dear to your heart, in lieu of Shakespeare's tragedy.

Reeve What!

Connie Isn't it delightful news, Mr Reeve? And we have you to thank for it.

Reeve Me?

Stephen It appears that Miss Tablet passed on the manuscript you pressed upon her, to Mr Pikelet; with the result I have indicated.

Reeve (*dismayed*) Well, this is all very surprising, of course. But I hardly think he will be allowed to do it.

Connie Why ever not, Mr Reeve?

Reeve The . . . the play deals with a Certain Subject, Mrs Shewin.

Stephen Mr Pikelet seems undeterred by that.

Reeve But Mr Shewin, do you really . . . think that the play *should* be done?

Stephen Why not, Mr Reeve?

Reeve I . . . was thinking of Richard's reputation.

Stephen Who are we to blind the eyes of posterity, Mr Reeve? I would rather have the truth, Mr Reeve, than a coronet of rubies.

Reeve Yes. Yes, it *is* better. I see that.

Connie (*earnestly*) And besides, you see, Mr Reeve, if the play *is* done, my husband will get all the money for it.

Stephen (*sharply*) Constance!

    (*a brief pause*)

Reeve Oh yes, I recall. Yes. The terms of Shewin's will would cover that, of course. Yes, I see.

Connie And you see, Mr Reeve, it would be such a *very* great help to us. We might be able to afford a real, permanent *English* maid, then.

Our foreign ones never seem to stay. We have a girl from Green-
land at present, a Miss Øbj. She does her very best. She reroofed
the whole of the house, singlehanded, almost the minute she came
here. But the fact remains that she will, apparently, expect to be
allowed to sleep all through the winter months. Of course, the
pussies love to snuggle up to her – she does give off a surprising
amount of warmth – but nothing is *ever* quite ideal, is it? And it
would be such a help, if Richard's play did bring us in a few
pounds.

Stephen I may say that any squalid moneys that accrued from the work
I should promptly assign to one of my numerous favourite
charities.

Reeve Yes, I see . . . I see . . .

  (*fade up Hilda playing on the piano*)

Neville Well, the play simply must be done! It's wonderful! Of course,
there'll have to be a few pretty drastic rewrites. But that's never
difficult, once a play's in rehearsal.

  (*piano out*)

Hilda You and I could do those, Bertie.

Reeve B–but do you mean you would . . . *alter Shewin's text?*

Neville Well, my dear, let's face it, nobody's going to stand for a play on
that subject having a happy ending. Well, I mean, the thought of
(*he drops his voice*) the two of them living happily ever after; you
can't possibly suggest that. Take that big scene between Roger
and Billy; let's face it, no one's going to get away with *that* as it
stands, are they? Well, look at it, and imagine how it would
sound. (*on fade*) You know?

Billy (*fade in*) *No, please, Roj. Don't turn me out again, Roj. I dunno
what'd 'appen to me if you was to turn me out again, Roj.*

Roger (*gloomily*) *Much what happened last time, I expect.*

Billy *Don't frow that at me, Roj. We could be very 'appy 'ere. Why, we
could transform this flat, Roj: we could do it up. I've always wanted to
try my 'and at the interior decorating; (sniffs) only nobody's ever let me.
When I tried to paint me and Sid's bedroom at 'ome, Dad created
somefink dreadful; took 'is belt to me, and . . .*

Roger (*sharply*) *Don't, don't!*

Billy *We could be ever so 'appy 'ere, Roj. You've said yourself 'ow clean I am
about the place. And we could ask a few friends in sometimes.*

Roger I'm not aware that I have any friends any longer.

Billy You got me, Roj. I wouldn't go off on the loose. I promise. You never known me break a promise, 'ave you, Roj? (pause) Roj. (pause) Do say somefink, Roj.

Neville You're not going to get away with that on *any* stage, are you?

Reeve But in that case, I don't see how the play can be done at all. You wouldn't suggest . . . making the ending a *sad* one, would you?

Neville Lord, no. No, it's quite simple. You just turn Billy into a girl – you know?

Reeve Into a girl!

Neville Yes. Scrap the accent, make Billy a girl, called, say, Jenny, and it hardly needs touching. Well, look, I mean, it's obvious . . . (*fade*)

Jenny (fade in: very well-bred voice) *We could be very happy here, Roj. You've said yourself how clean I am about the place. And we could ask a few friends in sometimes.*

Roger I'm not aware that I have any friends any longer.

Jenny You got me, Roj. I wouldn't go off on the loose. I promise. You never known me break a promise, have you, Roj? (pause) Roj. (pause) Do say something, Roj.

Roger There's nothing to say. Perhaps there never has been.

Jenny But, Roj, the only reason I ever went with that other bloke . . . well, it wasn't really going with him, he was younger than what I was anyway, and I've never really liked blokes younger than what I am, but I've always fell for the flattery, Roj. And he kept on giving me a new five-pound note, and saying how much he admired my chest-expansion; and any girl would have been a bit took in by that, Roj. Straight, they would, Roj.

(*fade*)

Neville I swear to you, Bertie, make Billy a girl, tidy it up a bit, and it'll work like a charm. Of course we shall want your help.

Hilda (*enthusiastically*) I think the three of us can make the whole thing a splended collaboration. After all, my *Antony and Cleopatra* music will fit into pretty well any play.

Neville (*politely*) Y-yes, possibly. We'll have to see.

Hilda I've set the song already. Elsa! Did it as a sort of act of homage to old Dick. Never thought it'd be wanted quite so soon. Come on, Elsa! What have you been doing?

Elsa (*rebelliously*) I have been packing my bags.

Hilda Silly girl. There's lobster for lunch. Come and let's give 'em that song I wrote last night. You boys *do* want to hear it, I take it?

The Men Yes, rather. Certainly.

> (*song. Elsa and piano*)
>> *There once was a garden where we used to play,*
>>> *But the flowers bloom there no more,*
>> *There are no bright faces at the windows,*
>>> *And the weeds grow up to the door.* (*sustain last note*)

Hilda Elsa! Get off that note!

Neville ⎱ Yes. Yes. I see.
Reeve ⎰ Yes, thank you, Hilda.

Hilda Nostalgic, really.

Both Yes. Very. Yes.

Elsa (*a polite undertone*) Is it to be hot lobster, or cold, Hilda?

Hilda Hot.

Elsa (*gratified*) Gut.

Neville (*thoughtfully*) You know, I had rather a brilliant idea about that song, last night. I think we should give it to Roger's mother; she could sing it at the piano on the stage by herself; and Roger could come in halfway through, and stand there, terribly moved, watching her. You know?

Hilda Who would you cast for it? It's quite a difficult piece.

Neville I've had an idea for that, too. I've been dying to have old Daisy Treddle in something for ages. I'm terribly fond of the old girl; and she could be a terrific draw, even now.

Hilda Daisy Treddle! Why, she was singing in damn silly musical comedies when I was in short pants.

Neville Maybe, darling, but she's still got what it takes.

Hilda (*glumly*) Well, I can't think where she can have put it, in that case.

Neville What I suggest you do, Hilda, is straighten the song out a bit on paper, and put it into E flat . . .

Hilda (*in horror*) E flat! Does that thing still *exist*?

Neville And I swear to you that old Daisy Treddle will make it come out just like Elsa does it. She's always been good at sliding a bit off-key. You know?

Hilda (*gravely*) Neville, my dear; I do love you, don't think I don't. But I sometimes begin to think that the sort of things some people sometimes say to me are the sort of things you'd hardly think anybody would ever say to anybody.

Neville What did you say, Hilda?

Hilda I said that I sometimes begin to think that the sort of things some people . . . (*etc. Fade before end*)

Reeve Our grave doubts about the advisability of presenting Shewin's play did for a time persist; curiously enough, they remained undispelled by the admittedly skilful, but at times almost ortho-paedic, manipulations imposed upon the text by Mr Pikelet, by Hilda, by the leading actor, Mr Michael Pebble, and Miss Daisy Treddle (though we should in fairness state that Miss Treddle did not begin any large-scale emendation of the text until the night after the dress-rehearsal). It came as a surprise to hear ourself sometimes congratulated on these changes. But let it not be thought by the library pedant that the presentation of a play is a simple matter. The literary purist, hugging his cherished author's text, may have his views. But others have theirs also. We were to hear a number.

Stephen I assure you, Mr Reeve, I shall raise no finger against my brother's play. Let him be known for what he was. 'Truth shall be truth alway.'

Reeve But, you see, Mr Shewin, that is not quite the point. The play is being very gravely modified as rehearsals go on. The Certain Subject, for example, has become a rather uncertain one.

Stephen I am sure Mr Pikelet is more experienced in these matters than my brother ever was, Mr Reeve. Or, indeed, than yourself. Richard was a dilettante in all that he set his hand to.

Reeve But, Mr Shewin . . .

Stephen Let them go their way, Mr Reeve. It is not our world . . .

Reeve Our doubts were further undermined by a recurrent *leitmotiv* in the converse of Mrs Stephen Shewin.

Connie It's so exciting, isn't it, Mr Reeve? I'm sure the first night will be delightful. I'm lining a special basket for pussies, because . . . Mr Pikelet has promised us a box. He says provided they're quiet, it will be all right for them to come. And they've promised. And, oh, Mr Reeve, we've heard of such a good maid. *English*, from Stratford-upon-Avon. We daren't definitely engage her yet; but *oh*-what bliss if we could, wouldn't it be, pussies? But of course, it all depends on Richard's play . . .

Reeve Doubt we had also expressed to Mrs Nancy Shewin when she came up to London one day, with a number of her sons.

Nancy Yes, it is exciting, isn't it? I'm so delighted. I never read the play myself; I have so little time. But you said in your letter, Mr Reeve, that you were rather sorry it was being done. Why was that?

Reeve Well, it becomes increasingly difficult to say.

Nancy (*quietly*) Mr Reeve: you . . . you don't mean the play says anything . . . about what I told you? About myself and Richard.

Reeve Well, certainly it didn't to start with, and I very much doubt if it does now.

Nancy I'm so glad. Ah, here's Owen.

Owen Hello, Mr Reeve. How do you do?

Reeve Hello, Owen.

Nancy It is wonderful about Owen, isn't it? Mr Pikelet has let him set those very pretty words to music.

Owen It's not the actual setting I sang to you, of course, Mr Reeve. For one thing Miss Treddle can't play the guitar.

Nancy Though I'm sure Owen would have been very happy to play it for her.

Owen So I've written a new one. Faintly period flavour, you know. Rather nostalgic. It was jolly nice of Miss Tablet to stand down, wasn't it?

Reeve Yes, very. They are, of course, using her music in the intervals.

Owen Yes. She said she'd stop at nothing to see the play had the best possible starting conditions. You know, that's a jolly decent spirit, Mr Reeve.

Nancy (*ecstatically*) How lovely it all is! I'm so glad you came down and unearthed the play. And how glad *you* must be too!

Reeve Yes, our thoughts and opinions had much that was selfish in them, it appeared, when we compared them with those of all the people who depended so much upon the success of Shewin's play. We needed a more objective view. But where to turn for it? Suddenly a thought struck us: we would repair once more to Shewin's old friend, General Arthur Gland, happily still back from the east. He had spoken as Shewin's friend before. We would try to persuade him to do so again.

Gland (*faded in*) 'Course, I remember you. Splendid face. Reeve, isn't it? Yes. That's right: Reeve. I was terribly sorry for you. Breadful thing, almost wrote to the papers about it. Nice to see you. When did they let you out again?

Reeve Out?

Gland I absolutely loathe *any* form of persecution. Hate it. Was there anything special you came about, or was it just for a drink?

Reeve I wondered if you would mind my calling to chat once more about Richard Shewin?

Gland (*cautiously*) Well, certainly. Only you will be careful what you say about him this time, won't you, Reeve? He was a great friend of mine; I don't like to hear him run down the whole time.

Reeve No, no, I have no intention of doing so.

Gland (*with sudden glee*) I say, do you remember that bell?

Reeve Bell?

Gland DING-DONG, DING-DONG, DING-DONG, it kept going. Tremendous loud peals, I recall. Well, well.

Reeve What I wanted to ask you was if you knew that a play by Richard Shewin was about to be presented in Shaftesbury Avenue?

Gland No, really! Well, well, by Golly, that's splendid. Oh, I am so glad. I love the theatre; I could go every night. It's a great power for good, did you know that? We used to do a lot of theatricals out in the east. I took off Portia in *The Merchant of Venice*, a few years ago. Of course, I don't know how good I was. Not very, I expect. I'd like to have another try at it sometime. Still. DING-DONG, DING-DONG, DING-DONG. It's spanking good news about old Dick. There's nothing like the theatre for a man with a good message. Have you seen a play called *Sailor Beware*?

Reeve No. Not yet.

Gland Well, I saw it the other night, and, do you know, Reeve, I was appalled, *appalled*, at the way people just sat and laughed at it. It must have been very upsetting for the author. Has old Dick Shewin's play got a good message?

Reeve It was about that that I came to see you, sir.

Gland Oh, ah? (*pause*)

Reeve You see, sir, I am, personally, of the opinion that Shewin's play should not be performed.

(*pause*)

Gland (*soberly*) Reeve: I am very, very sorry to hear you say that. I like you very much personally, always have; and I know what you've been through. But my dear good man, for God's sake *don't let it warp you*. Here's Dick Shewin, a splendid fellow, secure in his glory. There's old Dick; there's his glory. And what do you do to his glory, Reeve, pardon me for saying so? Why, at every turn you try to undermine it. Don't do it, Reeve, it's not worth it. It's not worth it. When a man has glory, we should try to add to that glory (ding-dong). (*moved*) Why, I . . . I loved old Dick; and I have to say it, it does gall me to hear the way, every time you come here, you try to take the mickey out of him. No, no, let's leave him alone with his glory, like Sir John Moore at Corunna, with whom he had so much in common. Let us say no more about it.

Reeve (*defeated*) No. No, very well.

Gland I hope you don't mind my speaking so plainly.

Reeve No, no. It . . . it was rather what I hoped to hear.

Gland Well, so long as I've helped in any way, that's all that matters. DING-DONG. If you're free, we might walk across the park together?

Reeve Yes, I should like it very much.

Gland Have to go to a bespoke bootmaker's just off the bottom of Park Lane. You might like to accompany me. Always have to get my shoes made specially, you know. Breadful expense, of course, but ever since I was a child I've suffered terribly from flat feet. A martyr to them, in a very real sense.

(*pause: Hilda's music heard*)

Reeve The first night of Shewin's play has now passed into theatrical history. There were those who declared that there had been nothing like it since the first night of *Emily Butter*, a year earlier, at Covent Garden. Such a comparison serves little purpose, and we do but mention it; though it may well have been suggested by the intermittent presence of Hilda's music, precipitated about the auditorium by means of loudspeakers. Our own part in the preparations had been, after all, a very small one. Yet we had a gratifying sense of feeling needed . . .

Stephen Mr Reeve. There is one thing I would ask you carefully to look into.

Reeve Well, naturally, anything I can do . . .

Stephen It is simply this, Mr Reeve. I know that Miss Tablet is having much to do with the work, and that you are her all but inseparable friend. But if my health should spare me to attend the initial performance, I do hope you will see that she is not allowed to molest me in any way.

Reeve No. I will do my best.

Stephen I am but a hedge, Mr Reeve, unprotected and untended. And sometimes a dartboard also.

Reeve Hilda's own sentiments about a possible meeting were scarcely less ardent.

Hilda And, look, Bertie; if old Stephen Shewin rears his ugly head on the first night, just you stuff him in your overcoat pocket, and leave him in the cloaks; get a ticket for him, and then, if possible, lose it. See?

Reeve Yes, Hilda.

Hilda Thank you.

Reeve We ourself sat with Hilda and Mr Pikelet in one of the upper boxes. Our struggles and arguments were over; the strain of rehearsal was no more. The play had been transferred from us into the devoted guardianship of the cast. And one and all, the cast was giving of its splendid best.

　　(*fade in Roger*)

Roger ... *Only, you see, Jenny, there* were *sometimes moments, during the war, when I ... sort of* did *wonder. A bit.*

Jenny *Oh, Roger, wasn't that a bit awful on me?*

Roger *Yes, I know it was. I'm sorry. Only, sometimes, when you were five thousand feet up there, suddenly, you sometimes felt a ... a sort of vast uncertainty all round you.*

Jenny *I don't think I understand.*

Roger *It was rather as if ... oh, damn it, Jenny, I'm no damn good at putting things into words. I'm not one of those poet chaps. Sometimes wish I was.*

Jenny *Oh, no, Roger. I like you much better as you are. You're more reliable.*

Roger *You didn't think that last night.*

　　(the audience expresses mirth)

Jenny *Do go on.*

Roger *You see, Jenny, poetry does help in these matters; I ...*

Jenny *I didn't know I came round here for a poetry lesson, Roger. Perhaps I ought to have brought a notebook?*

　　(the audience expresses mirth)

Roger *No, Jenny, this is frightfully important. You see, there was a chap I knew in the RAF – he was my rear gunner for a time. He used to write poetry. We all liked him. He was obviously frightfully miserable a lot of the time, but he cheered us all up somehow.*

Jenny (coldly) *Do go on.*

Roger *I remember every time we crossed the German coast on the way out, how he used to grin and say: 'Christ, Roger, I'm bloody frightened'.*

Jenny *I hate cowards. I believe God hates them too.*

Roger *Well, I dunno, Jenny. I believe perhaps He understands them.*

Jenny *Well, I don't. So there.*

Roger (after a brief pause) *You know you're . . . pretty hard, sometimes, aren't you, Jenny?*

Jenny *I don't think so. Do go on.*

Roger (with sudden warmth) *But, Jenny darling, old Nicky wasn't a coward!*

Jenny *He sounds like one.*

Roger (quietly) *Jenny: cowards don't die in action firing a 4.5 machine-gun.*

Jenny (horrified at herself) *Oh, Roger . . . I'm so sorry.*

Roger (from a slight distance, thickly) *That's all right, Jenny.*

Jenny *No, come back, Roger. Come and sit here.* (shyly) *You know, Roger, you're a bit of a poet yourself sometimes.*

Roger *Do you really think so, Jenny?*

Jenny *Well, sort of. I mean the way – oh, it's silly really . . .*

Roger *Do go on.*

Jenny *Well, I mean the way when you're frightfully eager about something, the way your hair falls over your forehead.*

Roger *Oh, damn, that means I need a haircut.*

    (the audience expresses mirth)

Jenny *Do go on about Nicky; he sounds nice.*

Roger *He was the sincerest man I ever knew, apart from my father and mother. Well, what I meant to say was that one morning when we were coming back after knocking Hamburg about a bit, just as we crossed the coast on to the home ground, he looked down and said, 'By God, those folks down there are damned splendid, aren't they?' And of course, I thought about you being down there too, and somehow I found myself telling him about you and me. I know I oughtn't to have, but . . .*

Jenny *Do go on.*

Roger *I . . . sort of explained to him how we hardly ever saw each other, and how it was somehow . . . natural for a jealous bastard like me to wonder if somebody else mightn't step in while I was away . . . and he said, 'Roger. It mustn't ever make any difference to you, even if there is anyone else.'*

Jenny (quietly) *Nicky said that?*

Roger *Yes. I knew he was a poet. But up to then he'd never spouted any of his own stuff at me. And suddenly ... he began to. He said, 'It mustn't make any difference at all, Roger. Mark my words, he said:* (recites slowly)

> *... Love is not love,*
> *Which alters, when it alteration finds,*
> *Or bends with the remover to remove.*
> *Oh, no!*

Jenny *Oh, no! It is an ever-fixéd mark,*
> *That looks on tempests, and is never shaken.*
> *It is the star to every wandering bark.*

(in tears) *Oh, Roger ...*

Roger *You ... you mean ... you* knew *old Nicky?*

(*the audience expresses mirth. Across this the telephone rings. Fade behind*)

Neville You know, Bertie.
Reeve Yes?
Neville They're all loving it.
Reeve Are they? Oh.
Neville Especially the stalls.
Reeve Ah, yes.
Neville D'you know what I think?
Reeve What?
Neville If we're not very careful, we're going to have a success on our hands.
Reeve Oh. Yes.
Neville It all depends.

Reeve Certainly, after act two, there could be no doubt of the mounting excitement of the audience. The evening has, of course, passed into theatrical history, and will be forgotten by none who were present. We ourself cherish few warmer recollections than of that moment in act three when, in the fading dusk and a strong spotlight, Miss Daisy Treddle entered: that Miss Treddle who had already enchanted two generations of playgoers, and was now proceeding to enchant a fourth. First-night accidents are well known in the theatre; but with what ready art Miss Treddle turned even these to account! When, after a skilfully prolonged navigation of the full stage from up right to down left, she gracefully subsided not onto the piano-stool, but somewhat to the left of it, onto the beautiful Indian carpet, none will have guessed that this was not a calculated artifice. With what an admirable expression of baffled maternal sadness, she gazed searchingly round the stalls, dragged herself slowly up from the floor, onto the piano-stool, and addressed herself to the instrument . . . which had (and how much it contributed to the magic of the scene!) already been playing for a little over a minute.

Daisy (clears her throat slightly, and sings)
  There once was a garden where we used to play,
    But the flowers bloom there no more.
  There are no bright faces at those dear windows,
  There is no smoke rising from those dear chimneys,
    And where are the roses round the door
    — My sweetheart —
    Where are the roses round the door?
Roger Mother!
Daisy Shhh! One moment! (sings softly)
    Ah, where are the roses round the door?
Roger Mother! . . . mother!
Daisy William, my son! Do you know what has been in my thoughts all this night, my dear child?
Roger I . . . can guess, mother.

Reeve Neville, why on earth did she call him William?
Neville Oh, that was just a fluff. Don't say anything to her about it. We don't want to undermine her sense of security.
Reeve No . . . I suppose not. She has got one, has she?
Neville Oh, stupendous, yes. (*fade on last line*)

Roger You . . . make me feel very ashamed, mother.
Daisy Who is this young girl who's got such a grip on you, Harry?
    (*fade*)

Reeve The great climax of act three held the audience spellbound, by content and manner alike. How one felt it strike home! It was clearly the first time for many, many years that an English audience had heard such language in the theatre.

Jenny But, Roger, my dear, it would never work. It just . . . wouldn't work, Roger.

Roger (quietly) *We'd make it work, Jenny.*

Jenny *No, Roger. You see . . . I'm . . . frightened.*

Roger *Frightened of what? Of me?*

Jenny *I'm just frightened we might hurt each other . . . terribly. People do.*

Roger *But not us, Jenny.*

Jenny *Yes, Roger, even us.*

Roger (passionately) *Well, what if we did?*

Jenny *Oh, no, Roger, it would be terrible. I don't think I could bear it.*

Roger *I could.*

Jenny *You're a man. I'm . . .*

Roger *That doesn't matter, Jenny. Jenny! It's not really me you're frightened of; is it?*

Jenny (in distress) *No. I don't know. I don't think so.*

Roger *And it's not yourself.*

Jenny (in tears) *I don't know, Roger, I just don't know!*

Roger *No, Jenny! It's life itself you're frightened of! Life itself. And that's the thing we must never be frightened of. Life! Come and look out of the window, Jenny. Come and see all those people down there, rushing about, fretful, anxious, worried, nervous, jumpy! And all of them, frightened of life! You mustn't be like them, Jenny; nor must I. It would be the great betrayal, Jenny!* (a big statement) *The law may be against us, Jenny; but ordinary people aren't!*

(telephone rings)

Reeve I thought we'd taken that line out?

Neville We did, but he asked if he could put it back. He said he found it helped him.

Reeve How?

Neville With the build, dear boy.

(telephone)

Roger *No, Jenny! Don't answer it! Let it ring!*
(it does so. Pause)

Roger *Let it ring, Jenny!*
(telephone)

Jenny (radiantly) *Let it ring!*

Roger *Jenny! Thank God!*

Jenny (piously) *Oh, my dear! Thank God!*
(telephone. Swoosh of curtain. Immense swelling applause)

Reeve The immense popular success of the play is now of course a matter of theatrical history. We were not quite to know how certain a . . . a 'draw' it would be, for a few days yet. But during the splendid party given in the beautiful stalls bar after the performance, there was already that unmistakable sense of accomplishment, of success, of . . . of happy collaboration, brought to fruition.

Roger (*rapid rage*) Neville! Who the hell was supposed to be on the book in act three? Was she there?

Neville (*soothingly*) Yes, dear boy.

Roger (*unsoothed*) Well, sack the silly bitch tomorrow. I couldn't hear a word she said.

Neville Yes, dear boy.

Roger And get rid of old crazy Daisy as well: tumbling about the bloody stage like a bloody old lush. What the hell was I supposed to do?

Neville Yes, dear boy.

Roger God!

Neville Yes, dear boy.

      (*fade on last line*)

Reeve Yes. Tomorrow, and in the succeeding days, we would also know how well the play had 'gone down' with the critics, that helpful body. *The Times* reviewed the play at length and spoke knowledgeably of Shewin's novels. The *Daily Telegraph*, under the headline 'Novelist's Play in Verse', said that it would be of special interest to Shewin's devoted band of readers. The *News Chronicle* said that it was, fatally, a novelist's play. The *Daily Mail* said that it was, like most novelists' plays, a novelist's play. The *Daily Express*, under the headline 'No Business Like Shewin Business', gave some interesting details of the advance booking and of Miss Daisy Treddle's recent divorce. The *Manchester Guardian* said, 'It suffers a little from being written by a novelist – unlike most plays, which suffer from being written by dramatists.' The *Daily Mirror* said, 'I laughed till the tears came, but am still not sure if this is what novelist Shewin intended.' The *Observer* had a long and thoughtful review under the headline, 'Half-Brecht House'. The *Sunday Times* said, 'It was, thank God, a novelist's play'. The *Evening Standard* said, 'If I had to choose between this and "Salad Days", it would be a hard choice for me', and reproduced a photograph of Miss Daisy Treddle. The *Evening News* said that it was a thumping bad play by a thumping bad novelist, and reproduced a photograph, also thought at first to be Miss Daisy Treddle, but later identified as the dramatic critic himself...

But this... was for the future, albeit the near future. At the moment we could but simply and relievedly enjoy ourselves there in the beautiful stalls bar.

(*hubbub up and down*)

Nancy It's been so nice, so *very* nice. And how nice everyone has been to Owen! I'm so pleased, Mr Reeve.

Brian That old lady sang Owen's song a fair treat, didn't she, Mr Reeve? And he's going to play it for us in a minute. They've asked him to.

Connie And pussies were *so* good. We managed to catch Muffy again, after all. She was at the back of the gallery.

Gland I thought that telephone was absolutely marvellous, you know: brrrrrp, brrrrrp! brrrrrp! brrrrrp! And such a splendid message, too.

Connie And, oh, Mr Reeve, it *is* so wonderful. I've spoken to the booking manager, and he says he's *very* hopeful.

Gland Brrrrrp, brrrrrrp!

Reeve Only one fear momently assailed us in this happy gathering: lest we should betray our trust to Mr Stephen Shewin and to Hilda. They must, we knew, not meet. Imagine then our horror, when we suddenly looked up to see them... fixedly regarding each other from a distance of but twenty feet. Nay more, they were approaching each other (*he breaks off in horror*)

Nancy If only dear Richard could have been here himself. Let's hope he *knows* about it. I'm sure he must do. What are you looking at, Mr Reeve?

Reeve Oh, please... pl... I... stop... Good G... excuse me, I must ...I...I...I...

(*deadly pause*)

Stephen (*with overpowering geniality*) Well, well! My dear Miss Tablet, how enchanting to see you again after all these years!

Hilda (*ditto*) Stephen, my dear! I do take that a bit hard. *Miss* Tablet, indeed!

Stephen (*affectionately*) Oh dear, oh dear: you have me there, Hilda. Hilda, my dear girl, Hilda, Hilda!

Hilda (*warmly*) Steve! After all these years! Do we kiss?

Stephen Of course we kiss, Hilda, of course we do. (*kiss*)

Reeve (*suddenly*) We were present on this occasion.

Hilda Eh-eh-eh! Careful, Stephen, dear. Mind my tie.

Stephen Oh, I'm so sorry, Hilda; and it's a very *pretty* tie, my dear.

Hilda Like it? I ran it up myself. It's chiffon. You don't think it looks a bit sissy or anything, do you?

Stephen (*gallantly*) Nothing could look sissy on you, Hilda.

Hilda *Dear* old Steve! I *must* give you another kiss. To hell with reputation.

Stephen And *you* mind *my* tie, this time, Hilda dear.

(*they both laugh roguishly. Creep in piano behind*)

Reeve Beauty. The beauty of reconciliation. The most beautiful thing in the world; and we are never to know where it will break out next.

Hilda (*gaily*) Look, Steve, I tell you what. Those boys and girls over there are all going to sing that God-awful song in a minute. How about you and me joining in, eh?

Stephen Why, certainly, Hilda. I love a damned good sing-song.

(*brief pause*)

Hilda Steve.

Stephen Hilda?

Hilda Forgive me if I say it, Steve, but you ... looked a bit like old Dick as you said that.

Stephen (*pleased*) Really, Hilda?

Hilda Really, Steve.

Stephen Oh, Hilda. How nice of you to say it. It makes me feel really proud. I still miss him, you know – dear old Dick ... my dear, dear, brother.

(*the song, with the whole party gradually joining in, has begun faintly in the background. Bring slowly up to full*)

All   There once was a garden where we used to play,
    But the flowers bloom there no more,
    There are no bright faces at those dear windows,
    There is no smoke rising from those dear chimneys,
    And where are the roses round the door,
        My sweetheart,
    Where are the roses round the door?

The Primal Scene, as it were . . .

To Deryck Guyler

The Primal Scene, as it were . . . was first broadcast on 11 March 1958. The production was by Douglas Cleverdon, with music by Donald Swann. The cast was as follows:

HERBERT REEVE	*Hugh Burden*
STEPHEN SHEWIN	*Carleton Hobbs*
CONNIE SHEWIN	*Gwen Cherrell*
HILDA TABLET	*Mary O'Farrell*
ELSA STRAUSS	*Marjorie Westbury*
NANCY SHEWIN	*Dorothy Primrose*
OWEN SHEWIN	*Denis Quilley*
JANET SHEWIN	*Gwen Cherrell*
BRIAN SHEWIN	*Wilfred Downing*
GEORGE SHEWIN	*Marjorie Westbury*
EVELYN BAXTER	*Colin Campbell*
GENERAL GLAND	*Deryck Guyler*
CAPTAIN SMITHERS	*Frank Duncan*
MUFFY, MILLY, ETC.	*Vivienne Chatterton*
VENETIAN WAITER	*Frank Duncan*
AESCHYLUS APHANISIS	*Harold Lang*
PLANKTON	*Frank Duncan*

Reeve In the last analysis, everyone would, we think, agree that there are certain moments in the lives of all of us that we later realise to have been unobserved turning-points in our destiny. If *that* had not happened *then*, we may well ask ourself, would *this* be happening *now?* . . . No, we may well answer, it would not. In the . . . last analysis, we ourself may well say that the most momentous such turning-point in our own life occurred one afternoon last spring. We had, as so often, proceeded to 109 Coptic Street in order to 'report progress' to our friend Hilda Tablet about the biography of herself she had so very kindly allowed us to embark on some years earlier. The progress we had to report was, we confess, scant indeed. Nonetheless, we were about to report it. Much to our surprise, the door was opened to us by Hilda's former secretary, Mr Evelyn Baxter. It was some two years since we had last seen him, during which time he had, like so many, been gallantly serving his term in the army. We could see at once that the experience had left its mark on him.

(*door opens*)

Evelyn Hel-*lowe* . . .

Reeve (*surprised and pleased*) Why, hullo, Evelyn!

Evelyn '*lowe* . . .

Reeve How nice to see you. Are you on leave?

Evelyn No, Mr Reeve, they've let me out.

Reeve You mean you . . . ?

Evelyn Yes, Mr Reeve; I'm back in Civvy Street.

Reeve Are you . . . are you glad?

Evelyn (*expressively*) Oooooooooooh!

Reeve Well, it's splendid news, Evelyn. I hope we shall be seeing a lot of you.

Evelyn Thank you, Mr Reeve.

Hilda (*calls*) Is that you, Bertie?

Reeve (*calls back*) Yes, Hilda, it's . . . it's I.

Hilda (*nearer*) Well, can't you bring Bertie in, Evelyn? What do you think you're doing?

Evelyn Mr Reeve and I were having a touching reunion. (*to Reeve, kindly*) Come on, dear, the girls can't wait.

Hilda Excuse the silly young chump, Bertie, he's only just been de-mobbed. He's over-excited.

Reeve (*benignly*) Oh, naturally.

Hilda Nice to see him back, isn't it? Think it's altered him?

Reeve Well . . .

Evelyn (*sedately*) Don't be afraid to *say*, Mr Reeve.

Reeve Well . . . a little, perhaps.

Evelyn It made a *man* of me.

Hilda Ha!

Evelyn Well, it did while I was in, I mean. I'm out, now.

Hilda Come along and have some tea, Bertie.

Elsa (*approaching*) Ah, Mr Reeve, how nice, you come on a day of good news. First, we have Evelyn *zurückgekommen*, and then we have the yaCHt.

Reeve The . . . ?

Evelyn Don't spoil it, dear.

Hilda No, dammit, Elsa, I said I was to be the one who told Bertie.

Reeve G-good news?

Hilda Hahaha! I should shay sho. Bertie, regard this simple missive.

Reeve It's a cable, Hilda.

Hilda Read it, Bertie.

Elsa Read it *loudly*, Mr Reeve.

Hilda Yes, read it out.

Evelyn If you can.

Reeve I . . . (*reading*) *Overwhelmed by bitter memories* . . . Oh, d-do you really want me to read this, Hilda?

Hilda Sure. Only for bitter read butter. Throughout.

Reeve *Overwhelmed by b* . . . *butter memories letter follows insist you make me similar bi* . . . *butter but hellish theme letter follows happy place yatch* . . . Yatch?

Elsa For yatch read yaCHt. Throughout.

Reeve Oh yes . . . *happy place yacht at your disposal letter follows theme must repeat must be hellish and better than b* . . . *butter but the same sort aeschylus letter follows aeschylus.*

Hilda (*after a slight pause*) Well, Bertie?

Reeve S-someone's going to send you a letter, Hilda.

Hilda They have, Bertie, they have.

Reeve But . . . *who*, exactly, Hilda?

Hilda Does the name Aeschylus mean nothing to you, Bertie?

Reeve Of course, Hilda! The *Oresteia* is one of my . . .

Hilda Bertie, *dear:* be your age. Have you never heard of one Aeschylus Aphanisis?

Reeve The . . . the Greek multimillionaire?

Hilda (*modestly*) The same, Bertie, the same.

Reeve Oh, but how splendid, Hilda! I didn't know you knew him.

Hilda There is much about my life that you are unaware of, Bertie.

Reeve (*guiltily*) Yes, Hilda.

Elsa We met him at a banquet. (*recalling it*) Ah!

Reeve I don't understand all these references to butter, Hilda.

Hilda (*remotely*) You've not by any chance heard of a little operatic entertainment I once had a hand in?

Reeve Oh. *Emily Butter*, Hilda!

Hilda The same, Bertie, the same.

Reeve You . . . you mean he wants you to write another one?

Hilda You're getting it, Bertie, gradually.

Reeve (*puzzled*) On a . . . 'hellish theme' it says . . .

Hilda For hellish read hellenic. Throughout.

Evelyn (*helpfully*) I expect you could make it pretty hellish, as well, dear, if you tried.

Elsa And isn't it so very *nice*, Mr Reeve, we shall all be going on the yaCHt together.

Reeve (*apprehensively*) All?

Hilda (*affectionately*) Well, my dear old Bertie, you don't think I'd leave you out, do you? Here's Aeschylus's letter, bless his old heart. He says, 'I know that creative is a work very hard to do. I *should* know, I created sixty-three million dollars last year, and I could never have done that without the constant sympathy of my friends. So bring anyone along you think would be useful to you. Make a happy party of it.' He's a deeply understanding man, as you see.

Elsa Oh, yes. At the banquet he gave most of his own food to me. And such a beautiful round chin. Quite quite purple.

Evelyn Lovely colour for a lampshade.

Hilda So you see, Bertie, I can take whoever I want. I thought we might perhaps take those nice young Shewin kids from Mulset with us – I'm really very fond of them, you know. And of course poor old Nancy . . . And there'll be you, and Elsa, and Evelyn.

Evelyn *And* my mum.

Hilda (*uneasily*) Well, I haven't definitely promised that yet, Evelyn . . .

Evelyn (*firmly*) And my mum, dear.

Hilda We . . . we must see. And – largely on your account, Bertie – I shall ask old General Gland along.

Reeve General Gland!

Hilda We shall find him invaluable when we get to Greece. After all, he's a superb classical scholar.

Reeve Is he?

Hilda Oh, yes, he's in the great soldier-scholar tradition.

Reeve How . . . how do you *know*, Hilda?

Hilda (*lightly*) He told me . . . There is *one* difficulty, of course, about taking him.

Reeve Only one, Hilda?

Hilda You see, as he's Connie Shewin's brother, it means we really ought to take Connie and Stephen as well. That's a bit of a facer, isn't it? Still, I'm not really a girl to leave anybody out of anything I think they ought to be in on . . . (*fade*)

(*Fade in the bells of Algeciras. They are heard from time to time behind Reeve*)

Reeve We . . . we are sorry to have to mention it so early, but the still admirable Third Programme has in recent times been rudely truncated. We shall return to this point later. We mention it now merely to explain why we must move hurriedly forward to the first happy day when we all assembled at the beautiful and romantic port of Algeciras, in Southern Spain, to join Mr Aphanisis's splendid yacht, the *Jokasta*. We all fell in love with her almost without knowing it. What a radiant vision she was, white and gleaming from her topsails to . . . her lower ones. There was no sign so far of Mr Aphanisis, our generous host. But Hilda was there, looking especially imposing in her dazzling white p-pea jacket, slacks and . . . and cap. How warmly and affectionately she greeted everyone!

(*bells very faint. Seagulls*)

Hilda General Gland! Welcome aboard, General!

Gland Well, I *am* glad to see you again, Miss Tablet, very very glad indeed.

Hilda Thanks. Same here.

Gland Say?

Hilda Same here.

Gland Same here, yes, rather. Very pleasant. And isn't this a lovely spot? Listen to those church bells in the harbour.

Hilda (*sympathetically*) Awful, aren't they?

Gland Yes. A beautiful sound. Oh, I have looked forward to this. (*kindly*)

And Reeve tells me you're thinking of trying yer hand at a bit of music, Miss Tablet?

Hilda (*cheerfully*) Did he? Well, well, you chaps will gossip, I know.

Gland (*seriously*) Oh, please don't think that, Miss Tablet. There was nothing of that on my part. And you can trust me not to let it go any further.

Hilda Well, thanks.

Gland (*remorsefully*) I'm very sorry if I've unwittingly trespassed on some intimate secret, very sorry indeed. We all have our finer feelings. (*with meaning*) Haven't we, Reeve?

Reeve (*amiably*) Yes, indeed. Most certainly.

Gland Some of us, at any rate. I'm deeply sorry if I've offended you, Miss Tablet. (Reeve, don't move away. Just stand there, by that piece of rope.)

Reeve Yes, of course.

Gland And don't mumble, man. I've spoken to you about it before. Breadful it is, the way he keeps on chuntering away to himself the whole time.

Hilda Oh, come, General Gland, come, come, old thing.

Gland Say?

Hilda Well, I won't have old Bertie bullied, damn it.

Gland Why? Why not?

Hilda Well, damn it.

Gland Yes, but he's no call to go spreading rumours like that about a lady. Damn *that*, if it come to it. I'm very disappointed with him. Said you were thinking of taking up music.

Hilda Well, it has crossed my mind as a matter of fact.

Gland Really? Have you ever tried it before?

Hilda I . . . have been known to jot down the odd bar or two from time to time.

Gland (*with dawning pleasure*) Have you really?

Hilda Sure.

Gland Oh, I say, how jolly spanking splendid! (All right, Reeve, yer can move now.) I *am* delighted to hear that, Miss Tablet.

Hilda Oh, shucks, it's nothing really.

Gland Oh but by Golly it is, by Golly Even if it never comes to anything you'll always be able to tell yourself you've tried your best.

Hilda Yes, that's true.

Gland Yes, by Golly. Will it be the (*delicately*) jazz or the . . . classical?

Hilda Well, ah . . .

Gland (*quietly*) I quite understand, yes. (Reeve, just move down the deck for a few moments will you?) You can have the utmost confidence in me, Miss Tablet. I won't tell a soul.

Hilda Well, ta very much.

Gland And I'll see Reeve keeps his mouth shut in future. He doesn't mean any harm . . . Oh, but I *love* music. I like *all* sound, but music in especial. You can hear it so well. Well, except when it stops, of course. Its breadful when it stops. I missed it terribly in the jungle. Listen to those bells again. I wish I had my tape-recorder here.

Hilda Oh, you've got one of those things, have you?

Gland Oh, yes, wonderful they are. Beauty becomes fadeless thereby.

Hilda Sure.

Gland I make Reeve come round and help me with it sometimes.

Hilda That's where he gets to, is it?

Gland Yes. Reeve and I spent one whole evening a few weeks ago recording a very loud and beautiful chromium-plated bicycle-bell. I bought it specially. Breadfully tiring to the thumb, of course, but oh, it was worth it. It was worth it. We got two complete tapes of it – about four hours it plays for altogether. The bell was completely worn out, of course, by the time we'd finished, but we've got it for good, in a sense. Preserved. A thing of beauty is a joy for ever.

Hilda Its loveliness increases.

Gland Yes, there's a special knob for that. Very loud you can get it. We had the police up one night.

Hilda Oh-ah?

Gland They thought there was a fire. Wasn't, of course. (*wistfully*) I miss it, being away from it. But of course I'm very very grateful to be coming on this cruise, Miss Tablet.

Hilda And *I'm* very grateful to think you're going to act as our guide, General. It's most kind of you.

Gland That, Miss Tablet, is my privilege. I've suggested to the others we all go ashore, to the harbour, for dinner.

Hilda Good idea; see you later, then, eh? (*she goes*)

Gland Yours ever to command, Miss Tablet . . . All right, Reeve, you can come back now. What are you staring at, man?

Reeve I . . . I was just watching the sunset.

Gland Where? . . . Oh, yes.

Reeve Wonderful sight, isn't it?

Gland (*sceptically*) S'pose so, yes. It may be some lack in myself, of
course, but it always seems to me there's something breadfully
inaudible about a sunset. Still, enjoy it. While it lasts.
(*fade*)

Reeve There was indeed something about that first Mediterranean sunset
over Algeciras most potently evocative. It recalled, inevitably,
some of Richard Shewin's memorable descriptions. Would the
great man himself had been with us to see it. (*expansively*) The
splendid luminary . . . (*more modestly*) . . . the . . . the sun . . . was
descending in immen . . . considerab . . . in all its splendour
behind the . . . the hills, which were splendidly spil . . . silhouetted against the powerful . . . light of the . . . the descending
lumi . . . sun, as it went down . . . in . . . ah . . . behind the hills.
(One couldn't of course hope to express the sight as Shewin
himself would have done.)

Stephen And what are you contemplating with such absorption, Mr
Reeve?

Reeve Ah, good evening, Mr Shewin. I was watching the sunset.

Stephen And recalling no doubt the descriptions of it with which my late
brother was wont to bedizen his opening chapters?

Reeve Well, no . . . Well, yes, a little, perhaps.

Stephen Yes. (*a pause*)

Reeve What a . . . lot of enormous jellyfish there seem to be on the sea
at this point.

Stephen Yes.

Reeve Rather . . . horrible, aren't they?

Stephen They are as God made them, Mr Reeve.

Reeve They seem to be turned inside out.

Stephen That happens to many of us on the ebb-tide of life, Mr Reeve.

Reeve Y-yes, I suppose so.

Stephen Yes.

Reeve I wonder if they sting.

Stephen Oh, no, Mr Reeve. They are not human enough to sting.

Reeve I . . . I haven't seen Mrs Shewin yet. She's well, I hope?

Stephen My lady-wife is her usual flamboyant self. She has repaired to her
cabin, to attend to the wants of her feline retinue.

Reeve B-but, Mr Shewin, do you mean that Mrs Shewin has actually
brought the pussies . . . her cats, *with* her? On the boat?

Stephen I am afraid so, Mr Reeve. Indeed, I encouraged her to do so.

   I live, of course, only for her happiness. I am sorry if the thought of their presence incommodes you.

Reeve No, no, only I . . . I was thinking of when we get back to England.

Stephen Yes, Mr Reeve?

Reeve The poor creatures will surely have to stay in quarantine for six months?

Stephen Yes, Mr Reeve.

Reeve Does Mrs Shewin know that?

Stephen No, Mr Reeve, not yet.

Reeve But, Mr Shewin, how will she bear to be separated from them for six whole months?

Stephen Oh, I trust there will be no question of separation, Mr Reeve. I am sure she will insist on staying with them till the crack of doom, if need be. With such of them, that is to say, as do not slip overboard during the voyage . . . Ah, here come my lunátic sister-in-law and her unseemly brood.

   (*Owen, George and Brian approach. Nancy is a little behind them. There are effusive greetings*)

Brian Hello, Mr Reeve, isn't this spiffing?

George Jolly glad you've come too, Mr Reeve.

Reeve How d'you do? It *is* good to see you all again.

Owen Good evening, Mr Reeve.

Reeve Hello, Owen.

George Whacking great boat this, isn't it, Mr Reeve?

Reeve Yes, George: super. Still writing songs, Owen?

Owen Well, I hope to, while I'm here, of course.

Reeve I'm sure you'll find plenty of inspiration here.

Brian Yes, we're all going to look for some now. In the harbour.

Nancy Good evening, Mr Reeve. I was so hoping you'd be here too. It is kind of dear Miss Tablet to ask us, isn't it? We are all most grateful. I'm so sorry I can't come with you all to the town. I'm sure it will be lovely.

Reeve Oh, are we *all* going to the town?

Stephen Yes, we are all to be conducted thither to enjoy ourselves under the guidance of my brother-in-law, General Gland. Whether in single file or double he has not yet permitted himself to divulge.

Nancy I should so like to come too, but I have so much unpacking to do. And poor Janet has sprained her ankle. But perhaps I can go down there tomorrow – I adore seeing strange places.

Stephen Yes. I'm sure.

Hilda (*approaching*) Hello, folks. Are we all ready?

Owen I think so, Miss Tablet, yes. Except . . .

Hilda (*shouts, rather than calls*) Elsa!

Elsa (*very distant*) Com-ing!

Hilda Hello, Steve dear.

Stephen Hello, Hilda dear.

Hilda Coming ashore with us?

Stephen Of course, Hilda dear; you don't think I'm going to let you go without me, do you, my dear?

Hilda *Dear old Steve!*

Stephen *Dear old Hilda.*

Hilda (*calls*) ELSA!

Elsa I am already here.

Hilda Good. Are we all set?

Stephen Save for my dear brother-in-law, yes. We can't, of course, be expected to budge without him.

Connie (*distant*) Stephen!

Nancy Connie is calling you, Stephen.

Connie (*distant*) Stephen, dear!

Stephen (*meekly*) Ask her what I have done wrong *now*, will you, please?

Nancy (*calls*) What has he do . . . Oh . . . What is it, dear?

Connie (*unclear*) It's rather chilly. Doesn't Stephen want something to put round his neck?

Nancy She says don't you want something to put round your neck, dear?

Stephen No, thank you. Tell her I have my millstone.

Nancy (*calls*) He says he has his millstone, dear.

Connie (*distant, mollified*) Very well. Have a nice time, all of you!

Some of them (*call*) Thank you . . . good-bye . . .

Hilda (*suddenly*) Where's Evelyn?

Elsa I could not find him anywhere.

Hilda Well, where is he?

Elsa (*placidly*) Perhaps he is drownéd?

Hilda Don't be silly. He's sulking because I wouldn't let him bring that ghastly mum of his.

Gland (*approaching voraciously*) Now, then, are we all ready? Are we all ready? Are we all ready to go?

Stephen Only when you give the word, Arthur. How do you wish us to proceed?

Gland Oh, open order, I think, don't you? Open order. Nothing too formal. Just all keep close in behind me.

Hilda Bertie, do go and look for Evelyn and bring him along, will you? We'll go on, shall we, General? Bertie can follow us.

Gland Yes, all right. So long as he doesn't straggle. Don't *straggle*, will you, Reeve?

Reeve No, no, of course not.

Gland Good, then let's away.

(*the sound of the others departing in the background*)

Nancy (*calling*) Do be careful, George, do be careful! Owen, hold on to Brian! George, mind the gang-plank, do be careful, Owen . . . !

Reeve (*calling tentatively*) Evelyn . . . are you there, Evelyn? Evelyn . . . Are you anywhere about? (*pause*) Oh, is that you, Evelyn?

Janet (*a little way off*) No, it's me, I'm afraid.

Reeve (*uncertainly*) Who's that . . . ?

Janet (*approaching*) Hello, Mr Reeve. You won't remember me, I expect. I'm Janet Shewin. Owen's sister.

Reeve Oh, but of course I remember you, Miss Shewin. How nice to see you again.

Janet Nice to see you. I haven't seen you since the second time you came down to Mulset.

Reeve No. My visits always seem to have been when you were away at Cambridge.

Janet Yes. Pity.

Reeve I'm so sorry to hear about your ankle.

Janet M'm? Oh, that's nothing much.

Reeve How did it happen?

Janet Dunno, really. Just due to guilt, I expect.

Reeve To what?

Janet Guilt. Most sprained ankles are, after all.

Reeve (*benignly*) Well, I'm sure *you* have nothing to feel guilty about, Miss Shewin.

Janet (*casually*) Good God, who hasn't? Are you still writing that biography of Uncle Dick, Mr Reeve?

Reeve Well . . . I haven't actually begun to *write* it yet.

Janet How's that?

Reeve Well . . . (*weakly*) I still have rather a lot of data to sort. And . . . there have been other things.

Janet Oh, yes, they say you're writing a book about Miss Tablet.

Reeve Yes, I'm afr . . . Yes, I am.

Janet I didn't know you were an authority on music.

Reeve Oh, I'm not. Far from it. Though it's always been my second love, so to speak.

Janet Been what?

Reeve My . . . my *second* love. Hilda's . . . is *another* biography I'm supposed to be writing. (*ashamed*) Actually, I haven't really quite begun that either, so far.

Janet Oh. Interesting that you haven't begun either of them.

Reeve (*ruefully*) Well, I . . . I think it might be more interesting if I *had*.

Janet (*thoughtfully*) Yes. You'll have identified Richard Shewin with your father, of course.

Reeve (*surprised*) Oh, I really don't think . . .

Janet And Miss Tablet with your mother.

Reeve (*horrified*) No, no, God forb . . . (*suddenly abashed*) Well, I mean Hilda's always been very kind, of course, but . . .

Janet (*pondering*) I think I see why you can't *begin* the biographies. Not that I'm in any way an authority, but (*kindly and slowly*) I should think it's probable that the combined parent-image in the super-ego has been projected outwards on to Shewin and Miss Tablet; and the reason you can't begin to work on either of them separately may be simply due to unconscious fear of punishment at the thought of disturbing their embrace. You know?

Reeve B-b-but, Miss Shewin, such a thought never entered my head! I . . . know of course that Richard Shewin did want to marry Miss Tablet years ago, but Miss Tablet assured me that . . .

Janet (*lightly*) Oh, the phantasy would be purely unconscious, of course.

Reeve I . . . I think I ought to get on with looking for Evelyn.

Janet I saw him going ashore half an hour ago.

Reeve Oh, in that case I suppose I'd better go on after the others.

Janet Sorry, I can't come. It's this damned ankle.

Reeve I hope you'll still be up when we get back.

Janet Well, there's always tomorrow.

Reeve Yes. It's lovely to get away for a bit, isn't it? Do you know the Mediterranean?

Janet Not really, no.

Reeve Oh, you'll love it, Miss Shewin.

Janet Expect so, yes . . . Isn't it all a bit overrated?

Reeve (*earnestly*) Oh, *no*, Miss Shewin, I always think of it as the source of . . . of all that's finest and most enduring in our culture.

Janet So people say.

Reeve (*resolutely*) But of course it is, Miss Shewin. I always think the Mediterranean is the . . . the primal scene, as it were, of western civilisation.

(*pause*)

Janet The . . . the *what*, Mr Reeve?

(*we are plunged at once into the climax of a violent flamenco song. After the song, and wild cheers, only the throb of a guitar is heard behind the voices of Owen, Brian, etc. Café noises throughout*)

Brian (*reverently*) It's absolutely *it*, of course, isn't it?

George It's jolly well *it*.

Brian If that isn't *it*, I dunno what *is* it.

Owen It's the real McCoy.

Gland It's marvellous, absolutely marvellous. And so loud and clear. Isn't it, Miss Tablet?

Hilda (*gloomily*) You're telling me.

Elsa It is the pure flamenco. I should so like to sing such music.

Stephen I'm sure dear Hilda could write some for you, Miss Strauss.

Hilda No, dear Steve, dear Hilda couldn't.

Elsa It is so *vibrous and fluctuating*; and I so much like that. It is a music rich and well nourished. Perhaps one should try to *eat* a little more.

Brian Jolly fine music, isn't it, Miss Tablet?

Hilda S'pose so. Apart from being a stupefying bore, I suppose it is, yes.

Gland I *like* it. (*thoughtfully*) It's *novel*, of course, but . . .

Hilda It damn well isn't, old cock. It's as old as your aunt Amy.

Gland No, but what I mean is it's . . . *novel*. It makes a good sound, and it's what I call redolent.

Hilda It's what I call hell.

Gland And it's vital.

Hilda No, it isn't.

Gland (*judiciously*) I would say it's somehow redolent, and full of vitality.

Hilda Well, *I* would say it's got about as much life in it as a potted shrimp.

Gland Well, I think we're probably both trying to say the same thing in different words.

Hilda Oh-ah? What do *you* think, Steve?

Stephen Oh, *I* agree with *you*, Hilda dear.

Gland Oh, so do *I*.

Hilda *Dear* Steve . . .

Stephen *Dear* Hilda . . .

Evelyn (*suddenly*) Hel-*lowe*.

> (*murmurs of 'Hello, Evelyn'*)

Evelyn '*lowe* . . .

Hilda Where on earth have *you* been?

Evelyn Been for a little walk.

Hilda What, all by yourself?

Evelyn No, dear.

Hilda Who with?

Evelyn My friend Pedro.

Hilda Who's he?

Evelyn The one over there, in the white jersey.

Hilda Oh. You seem to have made friends pretty quickly. We've only been in the place a couple of hours.

Evelyn Yes, dear.

> (*the flamenco song is suddenly resumed. Hold and then down behind Reeve*)

Reeve What a wonderful experience it was for us to be there in the Spanish *bodega* that evening, with Richard Shewin's own kith and kin! How well he had known such places himself! We could picture him on just such an evening as this, watching the life of the old *puerto*, and sipping a glass of the sweet, warm, local, rather heady . . . ah . . . *drink*. How well he himself could evoke such scenes! We could never, alas, hope to emulate him, but none the less we felt a touch of a not unsimilar inspiration as we contemplated the smiling, dusky, sun-bronzed faces of the young men and women bending over their immemorial stringed instruments, and strumming ancient . . . music, from the str-strings of them, smiling from their sun . . . dus . . . dusky, sun-bronzed faces as . . . as they str . . . as they did so. Yes. Richard Shewin will have heard this subtle music on more than one occasion.

> (*a violent musical yelp from the singers*)

Janet (*earnestly*) Mr Reeve . . .

Reeve (*surprised*) Oh, Miss Shewin . . . I thought you'd hurt your ankle?

Janet Oh, it's not really very bad. And I felt I had to come . . . Look, Mr Reeve, I'm so sorry. You must have thought me a frightful idiot just now.

Reeve Oh, but why, Miss Shewin?

Janet I really must apologise for what I said about Uncle Dick being a father-figure and Miss Tablet a mother-figure.

Reeve Oh, no, Miss Shewin, please. I confess I was a little mystified, but . . .

Janet What I *ought* to have said, of course, was that it's actually Miss Tablet who's your father-figure, and Uncle Dick who's your mother. His novels probably reproduce archaic feeding-memories for you. They represent milk. You suck them in with your eyes, so to speak.

Reeve B-b-b . . .

Janet And Miss Tablet, of course, is a father-figure. (*remorsefully*) I ought to have seen that at once, when you said music was your *second* love. The father always appears as a love-object later than the mother, naturally.

Reeve (*cautiously*) Indeed?

Janet And of course Miss Tablet as a father-image will probably have been reinforced in the current situation by her habits of dress.

Reeve (*loyally*) I . . . *have* seen her wearing a . . . sort of blouse. Once.

Janet Did your mother ever dress as a man?

Reeve No. God bless my soul, no!

Janet Nor your father as a woman?

Reeve No, no, no . . .

Janet You're quite sure?

Reeve Well, yes, I think so.

Janet Well, of course, I can't claim to be an authority, but . . .
(*a further squawk of music from the singers*)

Reeve We English have the sea in our blood. That has been often said of us, by friend and foe alike. And what splendid appetites it gives us! There can be no meal on earth so satisfying as a good breakfast taken on shipboard . . .
(*breakfast noises up*)

Elsa And what I so much like about the continental breakfast and the English breakfast, is that when there is a choice, one is able to have *both*. First the one, and then the other.

Hilda Well, hurry up over it, Elsa. Some of us are on this cruise to work, not to idle. I'll see you in the music room in fifteen minutes.

Stephen And how is the new opera proceeding, Hilda dear?

Hilda It isn't proceeding at all, as yet, Steve dear. I can't think of a ruddy subject. Plenty of ideas for the score of course. But nothing to *drape* 'em over.

Evelyn Have you tried one of those new plastic clothes-horses, dear?

Hilda (*coldly*) Evelyn. Have you finished your breakfast?

Evelyn Yes, dear.

Hilda Then kindly go.

Evelyn I'm on my wa-ay! (*he departs*)

Hilda Don't forget what I said, Elsa. (*off*) Fifteen minutes.

Elsa (*mouth full*) Fifteen minutes.

Nancy Has anyone seen Janet this morning? Have *you*, Mr Reeve?

Reeve No, not yet, Mrs Shewin.

Nancy It was so kind of you to talk to her last night, Mr Reeve. I . . . I hope she didn't say anything to you?

Reeve Say anything, Mrs Shewin?

Nancy Well, I'm so worried about her.

Stephen I don't wonder.

Muffy Miaow.

Connie Hush a bright Muffy, mummy's here.

Muffy Miaow.

Reeve I hope there's nothing wrong with Miss Shewin?

Nancy (*evasively*) No. Not exactly wrong. Not exactly.

Gland The girl seemed all right to me. Seemed as sound as a bell. Well, almost, I mean . . .

Stephen What is the nature of her affliction?

Nancy Well, it isn't exactly an affliction – except for the rest of us, a little, perhaps.

Stephen What further degradation is about to fall on our hapless family? Is she with child?

Connie ⎱ Stephen!

Muffy ⎰ Miaow!

Nancy Oh, no, no Stephen, *dear*! No, it's . . . (*she pauses*)

Gland Shall us chaps go away?

Nancy No, no, *please* . . . you're bound to know sooner or later . . . Janet is psychoanalysing herself.

Gland Good gracious. What's wrong with the poor girl?

Nancy Oh, nothing, nothing at all.

Stephen No?

Elsa (*mouth partly full*) I think it is a so good idea. I have been psycho-analysed myself. In Vienna.

Gland What for?

Elsa Anorexia nervosa.

Gland What's that?

Elsa Loss of appetite. I was a martyrdom to it.

Gland Did yer get it back?

Elsa Not entirely. But it enabled me to hold on to my top C for longer than anybody else in Mittel Europe.

Nancy Yes, I'm sure it's very nice. But I didn't know anyone *could* psychoanalyse themselves.

Stephen Professor Freud psychoanalysed himself. In 1897.

Connie (*quietly*) And a little Muffy pussy-analysed herself. In 1955.

Stephen And I myself have psychoanalysed myself for the last twenty-seven years.

Nancy Yes, I know, Stephen dear, that's what's worrying me . . . oh, I didn't mean . . .

Stephen (*angrily*) Oh, you may calumniate me as much as you wish, Nancy Shewin. My deep self-knowledge enables me to take *any* affront with equanimity. I would like to know how else I could have acquired the fortitude that has enabled me to put up with what I have had to put up with in all these years. Anyone else in my position would have been riddled with internal persecutors, *riddled* with them; but my internal persecutors are all external ones, as you have only to look around you to see. And I continually turn the other cheek. Continually.

Gland (*interested*) Do they ever slap that one?

Stephen Invariably.

Gland Oh, I say, that's rotten.

Stephen (*savagely*) I am used to it.

(*brief pause*)

Nancy (*plaintively*) Well, Janet's doing the same. Perhaps it runs in the family.

Stephen Never.

Nancy I dare say it's very modern, but some of the things she says are so very broadminded. About me too. Of course I know I'm only her mother, but . . .

Connie And a Muffy says broadminded things about a mummy some-times, doesn't a Muffy?

Nancy (*with sudden passion*) It's all very well for you to make light of it,

Connie. You wouldn't joke if you heard what Janet said about you
and the pussies.

Connie What! How dare she? *What* does she say about pussies?

Nancy She says they're . . .

Muffy Miaow!

Connie Hush, Muffy. *Well?*

Nancy She says they're children. She thinks.

Connie (*delighted*) But of course they're children, a dear little pussies are.
They're little *kiddy*-cats. Aren't you, darlings? Of course you are.

Stephen (*sombrely*) A hedge, backwards. A veritable dartboard.

    (*fade on last line*)

Reeve How deep, mysterious, and secretive are the workings of the
human mind. We had had no idea, so reserved had Jan . . . Miss
Shewin been on the previous night, that her interests embraced so
wide a field. But was it not to be expected? It was the impulse to
spiritual exploration so often encountered in the novels of her
uncle. And how his fearless and questioning spirit would have
approved! Yes, even on this a bright and carefree day with
the sea sparkling joyously around us, he would have approved.
And he would have approved of the sea also. How he would have
distilled such a mid-ocean day as this, with the small light waves
dancing . . . and . . . and hopping . . . from the horizon to the . . .
(*a pause*) from here to the horizon, with the morning sun poised
questioningly over it . . . them . . . as though to ask these . . .
small light waves what they were doing, . . . hop . . . d-dan . . .
flowing so brightly from the . . . from here to the horizon. Yes, by
heaven, Shewin would have had the words for it.

Gland Well, I'm all for them.

Reeve For whom, General Gland?

Gland The psychoanalysists. I once went to one myself. A splendid body
of men. The one I went to was a woman. I went to her for about a
couple of months. But somehow after a bit she seemed to break
up. They had to put her away, poor woman.

Reeve Oh, really, why?

Gland Well, she somehow got it into her head that she was the Bell Song
from *Lakmé*. Strange, the deep underworkings of the mind. She
wasn't, of course.

Reeve No . . . I suppose not.

Gland I think I might let Janet have a go at me. Of course, I'll have to make her promise not to stop My Dream. I wouldn't like that. No, by golly . . . Do *you* dream, Reeve?

Reeve Not very often, no.

Gland Really? (*modestly*) I . . . I dream quite a bit, myself. Only when I'm asleep, of course. Curious thing is it's always the same dream. Would yer believe that now? Always the same. Not that I mind, of course. I'm not one to hanker after change the whole time.

Reeve No.

Gland No. Good dream, it is. (*invitingly*) I'm . . . quite pleased with it really. (*there is a long pause*) Well, if you really insist on knowing, it's about fireworks, actually.

Reeve I see.

Gland Yes, it's always bonfire night in My Dream. There's a lot of things going off round about, of course. Roman candles – that sort of thing. Sparklers. Small stuff, all right of its kind, but breadfully *small*.

Reeve (*sympathetically*) Yes.

Gland There's always a lot of nice people there. Plenty of fun, the old king and queen bobbing about, of course, and so on. I've always got me tails jacket on, nothing else, just the jacket; and as things wear on (it's a nice long dream, very leisurely, the sort most people don't have these days), but as things wear on, I become aware of feeling rather hot round the coat-tails, and before I know where I am, I've turned into one of those spanking great rockets they have. Oh, terrific.

Reeve How very alarming.

Gland Say?

Reeve I . . . Yes.

Gland Yes. I'm a rocket. And suddenly, up I shoot. Right up in the air, till eventually . . . I *explode*, don't-yer-know?

Reeve Oh dear.

Gland Well, I say explode. I don't want to be dogmatic, it may just be the sound-barrier I break through at that point, I can't tell. I'll ask Janet. But whatever it is, there's a whopping great *bang*. Supremely impressive.

    (*pause*)

Reeve And . . . and then what happens?

Gland Say?

Reeve What happens next?

Gland When?

Reeve After the explosion.

Gland (*after a pause*) Reeve: I like you very much, personally. But what I *can't* stand is this eternal note of carping criticism the whole time. I've told you. There's a whopping great bang. Isn't that enough? *I* find it enough. Why shouldn't anybody else? Say?

Reeve No, no, General, please don't think . . .

Gland It's the attitude of mind I don't like, Reeve, forgive me for saying so. There seems to be no end to it; what you must have put poor Stephen and Hilda through, I can't . . . Why, there she is! Hi! Janet!

Janet (*distant*) Hello, uncle!

Gland Can you come here for a minute, my dear?

Janet OK, uncle, coming . . .

Gland And please don't start taking the rise out of poor Janet, Reeve. You'll have not a friend left in the world the way you're going on, by Golly . . . Ah, Janet, my dear.

Janet Hello, uncle Arthur. Good morning, Mr Reeve.

Reeve Good morning, Miss Shewin.

Gland (*kindly*) Janet. Your mother tells us you've taken to the psychoanalysis.

Janet Well, that's a bit of an exaggeration, uncle, I . . .

Gland I'm very glad. Every girl needs a quiet indoor hobby, and as a little encouragement, Janet, I'm going to let you psychoanalysise *me*. There!

Janet (*laughs*) Don't be silly, uncle.

Gland We'll start tomorrow . . .

Janet Don't talk nonsense, uncle. I couldn't psychoanalyse anyone for toffee. And even if I could, uncle dear, it'd be totally improper to try to analyse a member of one's own family.

Gland I disagree with that most emphatically, my dear. These things are like charity – they should begin at home. Think of your dear uncle Stephen, for example. We'll start tomorrow morning.

Janet (*firmly*) No, uncle. It's out of the question.

Gland Who says so?

Janet Everyone: Freud, Ferenczi, Abraham, Ernest Jones, Melanie Kl . . .

Gland (*shocked*) Janet! You're not taking any notice of what a crowd of foreigners say, I hope and trust?

Janet (*laughs*)

Gland (*persuasively*) Go on, Janet, don't be a spoil-sport. And I'll buy you a whacking great box of chocolates for your birthday.

Janet No, uncle.

Gland Very well, Janet. I shall speak to your mother about this.

Janet Can't help that, dear.

Gland I shall speak to her at once. I've been very patient, Janet, but I won't stand insubordination. Good morning to you. (*he departs, muttering*) A breadful prospect we all face, if this is allowed to go on.

Janet (*laughs affectionately*) Dear old uncle.

Reeve (*also laughs, though decorously*) Yes. Haha. Yes.

Janet Terrible old narcissist, of course.

Reeve Did I hear him say you had a birthday, Miss Shewin?

Janet Yes – end of next week. Twenty-two.

Reeve Ah, a beautiful age.

Janet So people say. It gives me hell, sometimes.

Reeve (*concerned*) Oh, I do hope not, Janet . . . Miss Shewin.

Janet Oh, do please call me Janet. I can't bear Miss Shewin. Reluctance to grow up, I suppose.

Reeve Thank you . . . Janet. I do hope you'll reciprocate by . . .

Janet Oh, thank you. I'll call you Bertie, shall I?

Reeve (*suddenly*) Oh, no, Janet, please, for God's sake. Herbert. Please call me Herbert.

Janet But Miss Tablet always calls you Bertie.

Reeve Yes . . . I'm afraid she does.

Janet You resent it, obviously.

Reeve Well . . . not resent, actually, but . . .

Janet I expect you feel she's split off part of you, and incorp . . .

Reeve Janet, I . . .

Janet Yes, Hurtie . . . Berb . . . Herbert?
　　　(*they both laugh slightly*)

Reeve It was just that there's a . . . ping-pong table in the billiard-room and I thought we might . . . play a game of . . . ping-pong on it.

Janet (*pleased*) I'd love to. Let's. It'll help to work off our aggression. Come on.

Reeve (*happily, as they recede*) Well, I don't play a very aggressive game, I'm afraid . . .

Janet That's OK. Come on.

Reeve The still-admirable Third Programme has suffered rude mutilation in recent times, a point we shall return to later. At the moment we must content ourself with observing that that is the reason we cannot give any very full account of all the delightful places we visited on our voyage . . . Nice, Portofino, Lerici, Naples (dear, dear Naples . . .). We could say how much, how very much, of them, but we feel we must concentrate on certain important moments in the lives of our own friendly adventurers. That life was by no means all play. We ourself had our two biographies to . . . to ponder on. Hilda had her opera, whose gestation she would frequently enlighten us about.

    (*a few explosive bangs on the piano*)

Hilda I've never been in such a hell of a sweat over anything. I can't get the ruddy thing to *move*.

Reeve (*sympathetically*) No . . . I . . . no.

Gland Well, it sounds beautifully loud.

Hilda Oh, it is, I grant you. And what there is of it's good. Well, listen.
    (*four chords*)
But it's the ruddy subject of the thing that I still can't get. I do think you great hulking chaps might give a girl a bit of help.

Reeve Yes, I . . .

Gland I am always yours to command, Miss Tablet.

Hilda Well, I've already commanded you. Think me up a good heroic classical subject. Damn it, you're a classical scholar, General.

Gland (*musingly*) Yes. Have you ever thought of Robin Hood?

Hilda Never, General. And the subject has to be classical: Hellenic.

Gland Yes, of course. How about Julius Caesar?

Hilda No, General dear: Greek.

Gland Greek. Ah, yes, Greek. (*energetically*) Well, Miss Tablet, I am ever yours to command, and the minute I think of anything, I shall lay it at your feet.
    (*fade on 'minute'*)

Reeve Nor were others less creative. Our young friend Owen Shewin, Janet's brother, was to find – as who has not? – fresh inspiration in the waters, the skies, and the shores of fair Italy, that admirable land . . .

Owen (*fade in*) Well, of course, you'll understand that this is still in rather an experimental state at the moment, Mr Reeve.

171

Brian So is the lyric, of course.

Reeve Yes, yes, of course.

Owen I mean this is all a big new experience to us. You feel you have to absorb new sensations . . .

Reeve Yes, indeed . . .

Owen . . . and new techniques. So if this piece does sound rather . . . sort of *avant-garde* . . . you'll be a bit patient with us, I'm sure . . .

George You will, won't you, Mr Reeve?

Reeve Oh, by all means, my dear fellows.

Owen It's a little number called *Speriamo*.

Brian It means 'Here's hoping'.

Reeve Yes, of course.

Owen You come and slap the piano, Brian.

George I'll take the tambo.

> (*Owen plays a few introductory chords on the guitar, and breaks off to remark:*)

Owen I'm afraid it's also a bit experimental in . . . in language as well, Mr Reeve. But anyway you'll see , . . .

Owen (*sings*)

> *Under the moon*
> *And the sweet-scented palms,*
> *It was summer, and soon*
> *You lay in my arms*
> *And murmured so gently those sweet foreign words.*
> *They sounded to me like the song of the birds . . .*

> *Hasta la vista, you said, je vous aime.*
> *I knew not the meaning, but I loved you the same.*
> *Tre mila lire, you said, s'il vous plaît:*
> *And I knew there was something stood in our way.*

> *Yes, something was wrong then,*
> *Between you and I,*
> *And oh, I could see*
> *From the look in your eye,*
> *That arrivederci*
> *Meant 'good-bye'.*

. . . But, as you see, Mr Reeve, it's all rather *fragmentary* at the moment.

Brian We haven't even worked the *title* in yet, Mr Reeve . . .
(*fade*)

Reeve It will scarcely be denied that the still-admirable Third Programme has been rudely abbreviated of late, a point to which we must later revert. We mention the fact here merely that we may be forgiven for saying almost nothing of the ship's company. Nevertheless a ship, be she the veriest sloop, scow, yawl, smack or lugger, is as naught without her captain. The master of the *Jokasta* was Captain Smithers, always approachable, and often approached. We all of us respected, nay, revered the man. General Gland in particular had that almost shy adoration for him, so often found among army men in their contacts with the navy.

Gland Evening, Cap'n Smithers.
Smithers Evening, General Gland. Nice night.
Gland Yes, very. Very clear.
Smithers Calm. Yes. Very calm.

(*fade up and hold in distance young people singing 'Greensleeves'*)

Gland Yes, 'tis. (*after a pause*) I expect you . . . like it calm, Cap'n?
Smithers Yes. Nice calm night. Peaceful.
Gland Yes. A storm *might* blow up though.
Smithers Oh, no, no. No. Impossible this time of year.
Gland M'm. Ever . . . ever *been* in a storm, Cap'n Smithers?
Smithers God, yes. Hundreds.
Gland Where?
Smithers Everywhere.
Gland M'm. Ever been off Kamchatka in winter?
Smithers No. Can't say I have. You?
Gland No. Not exactly. No.
Smithers No. Bad spot. Best avoided. Worst spot in the world probably.
Gland (*sceptically*) Well . . . have you ever been in a *jungle*, for example, Cap'n Smithers?
Smithers No, never.
Gland Thought not . . . Have you ever *seen* a jungle?
Smithers Only from a distance, of course.

    Gland Where?

Smithers Off Sumatra, in '37.

    Gland M'm . . . yes, well, you might call that a jungle, I suppose. Breadfully small one, of course. Still, I expect you were wise to steer clear of it.

Smithers Yes.

    Gland Yes.

       (*music up a little louder*)

Smithers (*pleased*) Ah, listen. The young people. Singing.

    Gland Yes. (*gloomily*) Progressive jazz. Breadful.

Smithers Oh, come, come. I expect they enjoy it.

    Gland Ah, they may think they do. But it's a sign of the times, Smithers. I don't like it.

Smithers No?

    Gland No. I don't like what it portends. Well, just listen to 'em. (*they do so for a few seconds. The music is clear and joyful*) Yes, by Golly, it's an angry generation, Smithers, an angry generation.

Smithers Angry? What about?

    Gland They don't know, Smithers. That's the trouble. They don't know.

Smithers No?

    Gland No. But they're not pleased, Smithers.

Smithers Oh, no?

    Gland No. Not pleased with us, and not pleased with themselves, and not pleased with the world. Dissatisfied.

Smithers S'pose so. Yes.

    Gland Angry. And not afraid to say so.

Smithers No.

    Gland Not afraid to speak out. Crisp modern dialogue.

Smithers Yes.

    Gland Yes. (All the same, I'll make young Janet psychoanalysise me, if I have to swing for it.)

Smithers What's that?

    Gland Crisp.

Smithers Yes.

    Gland (*with sudden curiosity*) Have you ever shot an albatross, Cap'n Smithers?

Smithers Good God, no.

    Gland Why not?

Smithers Cruelty to animals. Can't stomach it. Beastly.

Gland An albatross isn't an animal, Cap'n Smithers, it's what's known as a bird.

Smithers Same thing. Same sort of cruelty. Abominate it. Same as rhino-hunting.

Gland (*amiably*) Ah well, I've never met anyone before who thought an animal was the same as a bird.

(*at this moment the young people break into 'Nymphs and Shepherds'*)

(*sombrely*) God bless my soul, listen to that now. (*after a pause*) Ah, Smithers, they're tired of the old shibboleths.

Smithers Yes, yes, I suppose so.

Gland Tired of 'em.

Smithers Yes.

Gland Think they're exploded.

Smithers Yes.

Gland Outdated. Ex-moded. Sick of the old shibboleths. (*after a pause, curiously*) Do you . . . do you *remember* any of the old shibboleths, Cap'n Shivers?

Smithers No. Can't say I do. Not off-hand.

Gland No. Nor me. Pity . . . (*thoughtfully*) There must have *been* some, sometime, I suppose.

Smithers Well, General, I must turn in.

Gland Yes, yes, you do. You turn in. It's . . . quite calm. And thanks for the chat.

Smithers Thank *you*, sir . . . Good night, General.

Gland Oh . . . just one thing, Cap'n Smithers . . .

Smithers (*off*) Yes, General?

Gland Have you . . . (*delicately*) Have you ever seen a *white whale*, Cap'n Smithers?

Smithers (*jovially*) Never, my dear fellow, never. There's no such thing.

Gland What?

Smithers (*farther away*) Somebody's obviously been trying to scare you, General. There's nothing to be scared of in the Med. Just don't let yourself get jumpy, that's all. Good night to you.

Gland (*overcome*) God bless my . . . (*faintly*) Good night, Cap'n Shibboleth. (*he listens to the music, happy and distinct, and after a moment or so is heard to murmur gloomily*) God help us. Listen to them! Where's it all leading to?

(*music up, then out*)

Reeve It is, perhaps, a strange feeling to be a guest aboard a ship, and yet never to see one's host. But Mr Aphanisis himself, our kindly benefactor, and Hilda's new patron, had still not appeared. Indeed, Hilda had assured us that we might not see him at all before we arrived in Greek waters, if then. Nevertheless, one evening as some of us were sitting chatting in our deck-chairs under the jib-boom, with the brilliant moon almost overhead in the soft, almost palpable sky . . .

(*fade in desultory chatter behind last sentence. Grown-ups only and Muffy*)

Nancy (*faded in*) But I've tried my best with her, Arthur, I'm terribly sorry . . . but I do see her point.
Gland She's a bad wicked girl, Nancy; and bad will become of her.
Muffy (*loudly*) Miaow!
Connie No, Muffy dear, Uncle Arthur wasn't talking about you, he was talking about Janet.
Muffy (*dubiously*) Miaow.
Nancy I do see your point, Arthur dear, but then I see Janet's point too. Don't you, Mr Reeve?
Reeve Yes. And . . . yes.
Stephen What *is* the unfortunate girl's point?
Gland Fancy refusing her poor old uncle a simple little thing like that. It galls me. And stop fidgeting, Reeve, I've told you before.
Stephen Psychoanalysis is never simple, Arthur. Though I am sure you would derive great benefit from it.
Hilda As *you* have, Stephen dear.
Stephen As *I* have, Hilda dear.
Connie And as a Muffy has, hasn't a Muffy?
Muffy Miaow.
Gland I promised her a great box of chocolates.
Stephen Our family has frequently been offered bribes. It hasn't always refused them. My late brother Richard, on several occasions . . .
Hilda (*suddenly*) Good Lord, look there!
Gland Where?
Hilda Up on the bridge. With Captain Smithers. Can you see?
Nancy Who is it, dear?

Hilda It's the great man himself. Our host. Aeschylus Aphanisis.

Connie Keep quite quiet, Muffy.

    (reverent pause)

Gland A striking figure.

Stephen Yes.

Gland Very striking and impressive.

Stephen Yes.

Gland Very remote. Shrouded in a golden enigma . . .

Stephen Yes.

Gland . . . you might almost say.

Stephen (Thank you.)

Gland Inscrutable. Like Captain Ahab in *Moby Dick* . . . Well, apart from still having the extra leg, of course.

Hilda Bother, he's going below.

Connie ⎱ *(in disappointment)* Aah!
Nancy ⎰

Stephen Well, that was your new patron, Hilda dear.

Hilda That was my new patron, Stephen dear.

Gland Gone below. Pity. Only old Smithers there now.

Nancy What a charming man Captain Smithers is – so courteous and refined.

Gland Yes. Interesting mind, too. Thinks a rhinoceros can fly.

Hilda Thinks it can *what*?

Gland Fly. A deep-rooted obsession with the man, in a very real sense. I wanted to ask Janet about it, but the girl seems to hide half the time . . .

    (fade on last remark)

Reeve To approach the magical city of Venice from the sea is the experience of a lifetime. Even on a Third Programme so rudely stunted (a point to which we must shortly return) we feel compelled to linger awhile over the magic of that sea-girt city. How many pens have evoked and preserved her for us! And none more certainly than that of Richard Shewin. How deeply the Queen of the Adriatic had entered his lofty spirit! And whose indeed would she not? Even now as we contemplated the blue waters of the incomparable lagoon flowing from the church of Santa Maria della Salute along the esplan . . . the front . . . the . . . that part of the sea-girt city that . . . faces the sea – the water of the blue lagoon lapping and . . . flowing as far as Santa . . . San . . . the church at the other end. There was something about her that would have inspired even the most sluggish pen.

Janet It's heavenly, isn't it? Especially from the sea.

Reeve Incomparable. What a lovely colour on the Doge's Palace, especially at this time of day. You know, I never see it without thinking of . . .

Janet I know: part two, chapter seven of *The Bang and the Whimper*, by my late respected uncle.

Reeve (*reproachfully*) Oh, Janet.

Janet Well, if you can take that, you can take anything.

Reeve I know there have been one or two rather malicious parodies of it, but, oh no, Janet, it's incomparable.

Janet That I do grant.

Reeve Oh, Janet. (*pause*)

Janet Herbert. You do know about *idealisation*, I suppose?

Reeve Idealisation?

Janet Idealisation is the result of excessive splitting in the superego. It goes very deep. It's one of the root causes of schizophrenia.

Reeve (*cheerfully*) Well, haha, let's hope I don't develop *that*, Janet.

Janet Let's hope not. Oh, Lord, Uncle Arthur's coming this way. Do tell him I've gone to change, will you? See you later . . .

Gland (*approaching*) Was that Janet you were talking to, Reeve?

Reeve Yes, General.

Gland Ah, she's a bad wicked girl, Reeve. I shan't give her a birthday present tomorrow.

Reeve Oh, yes, of course, it's tomorrow.

Gland I would have given her a large box of chocolates if she'd only consented to psychoanalysise her poor old uncle. Now, I shan't even wish her many happy returns.

Reeve Oh, I'm sorry to hear that, General.

Gland (*mildly*) Have you ever been to Bangkok, Reeve?

Reeve N-no, General, never.

Gland They call it the Venice of the East; did you know that?

Reeve No, I don't think I did.

Gland I expect they call this the Bangkok of the West. Well, must do, of course, must do. Stands to sense. Beautiful place, remarkable.

Reeve Oh, incomparable.

Gland Some very fine jungles in the hinterland. I used to take Sister Martin and the two nurses out there in a rickshaw on Sundays. We

178

used to get lost sometimes. Still, there's always plenty to do in a jungle . . . Oh, just listen to those lovely bells!

(*town noises in background*)

Reeve As we wandered about the enchanted sea-girt city, observing the ever-moving, motley crowd in the vast piazza, or admiring the glitter and flash of the antique shops in the narrow, crowded *calli*, it crossed our thoughts how often, with his superb, unfailing eye for detail, his immediate and immense capacity for entering into the foreign scene, how often, how very, very, very often . . . bloody old Richard Shewin must have gone mousing aroun . . .

(*long pause*)

(*in quiet horror*) Wh-what had we just heard ourself say to ourself? 'How often bloo . . .' No. No. It must have been some other voice. Such things do happen. Voices *are* heard. Some . . . some trick of the heat, working on the overtired brain, can at times, it has been well said, produce extraordinary feelings of the most shameful and degrading disloyalty towards people and objects we normally venerate. Perhaps *our* brain was a little overtired? Who could say? Perhaps we ought to . . . to sit down? We . . . we sat down.

(*sounds of outdoor café and orchestra*)

We sat down and began to collect our thoughts.

Waiter Prego, siòr?

Reeve Oh . . . una . . . una tazza di tè, s'il vous plaît . . . per favore.

Waiter (*in excellent English*) China or Indian tea, sir?

Reeve (*absently*) Oh, both . . . I . . . Indian, please. Prego.

Waiter Subito, siòr.

(*a brief pause*)

Evelyn (*suddenly*) Hel-*lowe*.

Reeve Oh, hullo, Evelyn.

Evelyn 'lowe.

Reeve I . . . I didn't see you.

Evelyn Saw *you*, though.

Reeve Yes. (*with an effort*) Have you been exploring?

Evelyn Been for a little walk with my friend Nino. Can I come and sit down?

Reeve Yes, please do. I didn't know you had friends in Venice, Evelyn.

Evelyn It's the one in the white T-shirt over there. Like to meet him?

Reeve Well, I'm just about to do a little hurried shopping, Evelyn.

Evelyn OK. So'm I. I'll go and send him away. Back in a moment.

Waiter Ecco il tè, siòr.

Reeve Oh, grazie.

Waiter Prego, siòr . . .

    (*pause*)

Evelyn Here I am. Isn't it hot? What are you going to buy, Mr Reeve?

Reeve Well, I have to try and buy . . . a sort of bangle. A bracelet.

Evelyn Jolly pretty. (*brief pause*) Which wrist are you going to wear it on, Mr Reeve?

Reeve What? Oh . . . haha . . . it's not for myself, Evelyn.

Evelyn Ooooh! Who's it for, then?

Reeve Oh . . . no one in particular.

Evelyn (*sedately*) I bet.

Reeve I . . . y . . .

Evelyn Jolly nice place, Venice, isn't it?

Reeve Oh, incomparable.

Evelyn What's that tower in the corner, Mr Reeve? I've seen it before, at the movies.

Reeve Yes, I expect so. It's the tower of St Mark's.

Evelyn Why does it look so new, Mr Reeve?

Reeve Well, actually it *is* fairly new. It was built about fifty years ago to replace the old one.

Evelyn (*intelligently*) Why, did the old one get worn out?

Reeve No, Evelyn, it . . . suddenly collapsed one day into the square.

Evelyn Gosh! Were lots of people killed?

Reeve No, the marvellous thing was, it killed nobody at all. Everyone was in church at the time.

Evelyn Jolly *lucky*. Everybody?

Reeve Well, it's rather odd you should ask, because as a matter of fact, there *was* one person who saw it collapse, and . . . and that was Mr Richard Shewin, the subject of my biography.

Evelyn Oh yes, I know who *he* was . . . And he actually saw the tower fall down?

Reeve Yes, Evelyn. He saw it fall.

    (*pause*)

    (*reproachfully*) You mustn't say that, Evelyn.

Evelyn (*much surprised*) Say what, Mr Reeve?

Reeve What you just said.

Evelyn But I didn't say anything, Mr Reeve!

Reeve (*worried*) Are . . . are you *sure*, Evelyn?

Evelyn (*hurt*) Of course.

Reeve Well, I'm terribly sorry, Evelyn. Please don't be hurt.

Evelyn (*severely*) What did you think I said, Mr Reeve?

Reeve Well, it's very silly, but I . . . I made sure I heard you say:
'A pity it didn't hit him.' (*distressed*) It's . . . it's very *close* today,
don't you think, Evelyn? (*fade*)

(*suddenly, loud and clear, the family are heard singing*)
Happy birthday to you,
Happy birthday to you,
Happy birthday, dear Janet,
Happy birthday to you.
(*this is followed by affectionate cheering: 'Good old Janet', etc.*)

The Boys Speech, Janet! Come on, Janet, speech!

Owen Speech, Janet.

Janet (*embarrassed and happy*) I'm jolly well not going to make a speech,
and you jolly well know it. But thank you, *thank you, everyone,*
for all the lovely presents you've given me. I . . . I adore getting
birthday presents, well, we all do of course. If . . . if one doesn't
get birthday presents, it can remobilise very painfully the persecu-
tory anxiety which usually follows birth . . .

The Boys (*groan histrionically*)

Nancy (*anxiously*) Janet, dear . . . not on your *birthday*.

Janet (*cheerfully*) So thank you again everybody very much. I feel very
very happy, and full of good objects.
(*general cheers. Hold conversation behind*)

Janet I've never spent a birthday at sea before, have you?

Reeve N-no, I don't think I have.

Janet Very interesting it is, actually, bec . . .

Gland (*sombrely*) Janet.

Janet Oh, Uncle Arthur . . .

Gland (*gravely*) I'm sorry I was not here for the official ceremony, Janet.

Janet Oh, it wasn't exactly a –

Gland (*sadly*) And I know that you are not very fond of your old Uncle
Arthur these days, my dear; but I trust you will not be offended if,
in wishing you many happy returns of the day, I offer you this
small token of my devotion.

The Boys Ooooooooh! Look!

    Janet Uncle, darling! Thank you! It's . . . it's enormous!

    Gland (*with melancholy pride*) It's the largest box of chocolates in Venice.

    Janet It's wonderful, Uncle Arthur. I *must* give you a big kiss for it.

    Gland (*tearfully*) I'm very sorry if it offends you, Janet . . .

    Janet (*affectionately*) Don't be a great silly, uncle dear. Offend me, indeed! Can I open it now?

    Gland (*sadly*) Only if you don't think it offensive of me, Janet dear.
(*the box of chocolates is opened behind the next lines. Exclamations of admiration*)

    Gland (*gloomily*) Good morning, Reeve.

    Reeve Good morning, sir.

    Gland Have *you* any uncles, Reeve?

    Reeve Oh, yes, indeed. Several.

    Gland Old ones?

    Reeve F-fairly old, yes.

    Gland (*wistfully*) Have you ever refused to psychoanalysise any of the poor old things, Reeve?

    Reeve Well, none of them has ever actually approached me with . . .

    Gland Ah, Reeve, my dear fellow, it's a very sad day for an uncle when that happens.

    Janet (*pleading*) Uncle . . . No, Brian, don't touch!

    Gland Well, I've no wish to disturb this happy gathering. No doubt I shall see you later, Reeve . . . (*he withdraws*)

    Janet Oh, dear . . . what am I to do? I feel so awful. I can't make him understand.

    Reeve (*sympathetically*) Yes, it's a very difficult . . .

    Janet I know! Let's go after him.

    Reeve What do you propose to do?

    Janet Come on. Excuse me, everybody (*the noise of the others fades*) . . . I'll give him an association-test.

    Reeve (*anxiously*) Whatever's that?

    Janet I needn't listen to the answers. And it can't do any harm. Or good, for that matter. (*darkly*) It was invented by Jung.

    Reeve But wh-wha . . .

    Janet (*suddenly stopping*) Oh . . . and Herbert . . .

    Reeve Yes, Janet?

    Janet Thank you *again* for my lovely bracelet.

    Reeve Oh, it was . . . j-just a small tok . . .

Janet It's beautiful! Look at it! Thank you very much, my . . . (*suddenly calls*) Uncle! Uncle Ar-thur!

Gland (*distant*) Yes? Did you call me?

Janet (*as they approach*) Uncle Arthur . . . I . . . I . . .

Gland Yes, Janet?

Janet I . . . I . . . well, uncle, of course I don't really know anything about the subject, but I . . . I could give you an association-test.

Gland (*guardedly*) Will *that* psychoanalysise me?

Janet Well, it's still used, I think, sometimes, as a sort of . . . beginning.

Gland (*much pleased*) That's quite good enough for your poor old uncle, my dear. Good. (*once more a man of action*) Now, then. How do we start? Just give me an idea of the rules.

Janet (*nervously*) Well . . . I simply say a word . . . and *you* j-just say the first thing it suggests to you.

Gland Good. Splendid. I can do that. All right. I'll stand over here. You stand there. And you can stand there, Reeve, and act as referee.

Janet Well, uncle, there's no . . .

Gland No, not there, Reeve. Two short paces to the left. That's right. (*amiably*) Don't slouch, man. Shoulders back. That's right. Stomach well in. That's better. Now then, Janet. Are you set?

Janet Y-yes, uncle.

Gland Right. Ready. Steady. Off!

Janet (*after a pause*) I . . . I . . .

Gland Come on, Janet. I'm all set.

> (*in the following, Gland's replies, except where otherwise indicated, are very prompt. It is Janet who is occasionally disconcerted and hesitant*)

Janet Mother.

Gland Father.

Janet Brother.

Gland Sister.

Janet Blue.

Gland Blood.

Janet Cat.

Gland Mint.

Janet Plate.

Gland Teeth.

Janet . . . Glass.

Gland Teeth again. I like this. Go on.

Janet Watch.

Gland Out.

Janet Bottom.

Gland Note. (Haha, that got you!) Go on.

Janet Dog.

Gland M'm . . . Oh, teeth again, obviously.

Janet Foot.

Gland Flat.

Janet White.

Gland Teeth.

Janet Girl.

Gland . . . Another girl.

Janet Back.

Gland Teeth.

Janet Red.

Gland Nasturtiums. (*pause*) Go on.

Janet Yellow.

Gland Teeth.

Janet Front.

Gland Teeth.

Janet . . . Horse.

Gland Voice.

Janet What?

Gland Not.

Janet No, no, uncle.

Gland Yes, yes, aunt. Go on.

Janet . . . Tea.

Gland The tee on a golf-course, or the sort you drink?

Janet It . . . doesn't matter.

Gland 'Course it matters, girl. Supreme difference.

Janet (*nervously*) Well, then, the tea you drink.

Gland (*after a brief pause*) Caddy. Go on.

Janet Bell.

Gland . . . Half a mo. Less think. Bell . . . No, sorry. Can't do that one. One to you. Go on.

Janet I can wait. Bell.

Gland No, no, no. Skip that one. Go on.

Janet Bell. (*pause*) Bell.

Gland Janet: I don't want to have to speak to your mother about this.

Janet (*hastily*) Very well, we'll pass on.

Gland I should think so.

Janet Mouth.

Gland Teeth.

Janet Eye.

Gland Teeth.

Janet Cow.

Gland Hilda. (*hastily*) No, no, no, no, don't put that down. Accident. Slipped out. Very naughty.

Janet . . . Gold.

Gland (*after a pause, judiciously*) Tooth.

Janet Boy.

Gland (*indifferently*) Girl.

Janet Teeth.

Gland (*solemnly*) Out.

Janet Well . . . I think that'll do, to go on with, uncle.

Gland Jolly splendid. How many did I get?

Janet Get?

Gland Yes. How many marks?

Janet But, uncle, this isn't a *game!*

Gland I know it isn't, my dear. But you must have marks. Otherwise you can't tell who's won. I shall give *you* marks.

Janet *Me!*

Gland Yes, of course I shall. It's your turn now. You come over here. I'll go over there.

Janet But, uncle . . .

Gland Come on, Janet, be a good girl. I've got some good ones for you. I'll stand over here.

Janet But . . .

Gland Ready? Steady? Go! Buttercups. (*pause*) Come on, **girl**, you know buttercups. Easy.

Janet (*faintly*) Daisies.

Gland Of course. But you're too slow. We won't count that one. Start again. Ready? Monkey.

Janet P-puzzle.

Gland That's better. Robinson.

Janet Crusoe.

Gland Good. Rhododendron. Come on, girl c'mon, c'mon . . .
(*fade*)

Reeve And now at last, we were steaming towards Greek waters. In less hurried times, how glad we would have been to record a full account of every island we touched at, every monument, albeit ruined, that we saw. Alas, the still-admirable Third Programme, so rudely pollarded of late, is no longer a place for such deliberation: a point we must discuss anon. Yet, cursory as our survey must of necessity be, let it not be thought that our experience was a less than momentous one. Or that we were not all brimming with excitement in our anticipation of it.

(*fade in conversation*)

Hilda Oh, it'll be wonderful to be there again. I can hardly wait. I haven't been to Greece since before the war.

Stephen (*roguishly*) Before which war, Hilda dear?

Hilda Now, dear Stephen wouldn't be trying to pull poor Hilda's leg, by any chance, would he?

Stephen Of course he wouldn't, Hilda dear.

Hilda Well then: before the war. It'll be wonderful seeing the Acropolis again . . . and the islands . . . and prowling about the village markets in the Peloponnese, and the monasteries on Mount Athos.

Stephen Mount Athos, Hilda?

Hilda Sure.

Stephen But Hilda, ladies are not allowed on Mount Athos.

Hilda (*nonchalantly*) Oh? Aren't they? Well, *I've* been.

Stephen But *how*, Hilda dear?

Hilda (*modestly*) Oh . . . I managed. And what a girl can do once, she can do twice.

Stephen *Yes*, Hilda.

Hilda Greece is really my spiritual home. Well, I don't have to say . . .

Stephen No, Hilda, you don't have to say.

Hilda (*with jocular menace*) Steee-phen!

Stephen (*coyly*) Hil-da!

Gland I think that Greece is the spiritual home of *all* of us, in a very real sense.

Nancy Yes, indeed, my husband was British Consul in Athens for some years, you know. He spent a *very* happy time there.

Stephen Nancy dear, let us not wash the family's dirty linen in public, even in such beautiful drying weather as this.

Connie (*nervously*) Stephen, dear . . . Hush, Muffy.

Nancy (*indignantly*) Whatever do you mean, Stephen? I'm sure Edward never did anything to be ashamed of.

Stephen I was merely asking you not to allude to the case of your late husband and the Greek ballet-dancer, my dear. (Have you heard of that, Mr Reeve?)

Reeve (*nervously*) N-no, Mr Shewin.

Stephen Oh no, of course. It is my other brother's sombre record that principally concerns you. I had momentarily forgotten that.

Nancy Edward and a ballet-dancer! *What* ballet-dancer?

Stephen The one who changed her sex so frequently. And her *name* even oftener, according to some accounts.

Nancy But Ste . . . !

Hilda General Gland: perhaps you will go on with what you were telling us about Mycenae?

Gland Yes, certainly. Yes, I will. Where had I got to?

Hilda The fall of the House of Atreus.

Gland Yes, well, the ins and outs of that have baffled scholarship for many years. (*learnedly*) It's known that it did come a breadful cropper, though probably not as badly as poor Edward. The exact details are still in dispute; the only point relevant to our immediate purpose is the problem of Electra's feet.

Hilda Electra's feet?

Gland Yes, it says in Sophocles that she took exactly the same size shoes as her grown-up brother Orestes, a breadful situation for a young woman. In the upshot, she murdered her mother and married her father (a fact I am afraid we *can't* gloss over, much as we might wish to). At that point, the ancient legend diverges somewhat from the story of the ballet-dancer and poor old Edward, who as we all know married poor old Nancy here.

Nancy Yes. In 1923.

Plankton (*young and impeccable*) Excuse me, ladies and gentlemen . . .
(*murmurs of 'Not at all', etc.*)

Plankton I am Mr Aphanisis's secretary.

Hilda Oh, yes, I expect it's me you want.

Plankton No, madam. Which is Mr Reeve, please?

Reeve Oh, ah . . . that's . . . I. I am Herbert Reeve.

Gland (*sternly*) I can confirm that, if necessary.

Plankton Mr Aphanisis asks if you would kindly call and see him in his stateroom in seven minutes' time, sir.

Reeve M-me? I?

Plankton Yes sir. The steward will show you the way. Good morning, sir.
(*he departs*)

Reeve Well, haha, this is an unexpected honour.

Hilda What's he want with *you*, I wonder.

Reeve I can't think.

Stephen It depends entirely on what you have been up to of late, Mr Reeve.

Gland Well, I've nothing against you personally, Reeve, and I hope I shan't have cause to have.

Reeve I . . . I think I'd better go straightaway. Excuse me.

Stephen (*on a long fade*) Tell me, Hilda dear, have you ever read the passages about social climbing in the work of Marcel Proust . . . ?

Reeve It was with considerable trepidation that we approached the forbidden territory in which Mr Aphanisis held his domain. We rather wished we had been a little more formally dressed, but the instruction, 'in seven minutes' time', had not seemed to permit of interpretative latitude . . .

> (*Mr Aphanisis is never far from tears, and is very often in the midst of them. He gives the impression of knowing more about different ways of weeping than anyone else in the world. He has just received rather perturbing news*)

Aphanisis (*faded in*) All right Plankton. What is it?

Plankton Mr Reeve is here, sir.

Aphanisis (*after a brief pause sniffs, and says*) Sit.

Reeve (*petrified*) Thank you, sir.

Aphanisis (*sadly*) Sit. (*after a pause*) Mister, you ever been to a place called British Museum?

Reeve Oh, yes, sir, many times.

Aphanisis (*tears welling up*) So have I.

Reeve You . . . enjoyed it, I hope, sir?

Aphanisis Enjoyed it? (*in tears*) Mister . . . mister. For God's sake. (*he yields temporarily to a small bout of weeping*) Bear with me, mister. Please. Bear with me a minute.

Reeve I'm terribly sorry sir. Is there anything I can do?

Aphanisis I hope and pray so, mister. I need them . . . I want them . . . I've asked for them . . . Listen, mister: I love the English. I've always loved them. I love you too. I'm Greek. I've got the Greek spirit, I've imbibed the Greek experience. Nobody could be Greeker than I am. Sometimes when we're cruising through them islands, I could cry like a baby at the very sight of them, I'm that Greek. And I cry the English. Who owns it?

Reeve (*lost*) Owns . . . what, Mr Aphanisis?

Aphanisis That British Museum.

Reeve Well, I don't think . . .

Aphanisis Who manages it? I got his name some place here . . .
    (*rustle of papers*)

Reeve I . . . don't think I quite rem . . .

Aphanisis (*quietly and sadly*) I'll break him.

Reeve Break . . . ?

Aphanisis I shall have to. It's only right. I'll ruin him. (*fighting down a sob*) I'll fix that . . . *bad man*, so he'll be glad to beg a nickel for a hamburger on Park Lanes. I want them. I *told* him I wanted them. Sent him cables. I must have them. I ought to have them. (*parenthetically*) The Elgin marbles. I offered him two million for them, cold. I know what things are worth. I wasn't asking for nothing on the cheap, was I? I know they're valuable, but everything's got its price. And I've got the price. On me. The Elgin marbles.

Reeve (*astounded*) You mean you've tried to buy the . . .

Aphanisis 'Course I have. The Greek Government would be delighted, mister, delighted . . .

Reeve (*eagerly*) Oh, I see, sir! Yes, it's a splendid ideal, one which many people cherish, to . . . to see the Elgin marbles back in Ath . . .

Aphanisis (*has not heard him*) The Greek Government wouldn't stand out a couple of days against me. I know they wouldn't. If I can tell 'em I've got the London lot, they *can't* refuse to sell me the others. I'd like to see them goddam try.

Reeve Oh, I . . .

Aphanisis (*indignantly*) I got the *place* for them, mister. *Ready.* At Florida Keys. I've bought Florida Keys. (*heart-brokenly*) Look, mister, I love the English. I love you. But *I'll fix that bad man.* He's trying to break my heart. I'm getting old, mister. We all get old. A man wants his little collection around him when he gets old. Wants 'em so he can see 'em, all in the same place. I've *got* the place. At Florida Keys, with me Picassos and me Matisses and me Gainsboroughs and me little Coronation mug. It's just the place. Sun all the year round. What they want. People'd come from far and near to see them. I wouldn't let 'em in, but they'd come. I could . . . (*plaintively*) I could *guarantee* it. (*suddenly he bellows*) I feel terrible, mister!

Reeve Sir, I'm . . .

Aphanisis (*in great distress*) It's the penalty of riches, mister. People cheat you right and left. I've bought sculptures all over the world. Commissioned 'em. Picasso. Matisse. Gainsborough. Commissioned. (*with simple pathos*) And whadder they do? They try to cheat me. Why,

    mister, I love the English, but do you know a sculpture-guy the
    name of Henry Moore?

Reeve Well, yes, I have a very great admiration for . . .

Aphanisis (*loudly*) So had I! I commissioned the damn greatest carving in the
    world from him. Henry Moore. In granite. I paid for it to be sent
    all the ways out to Florida Keys. (*he falls to weeping again*) I sent it
    back. I sent it back, mister!

Reeve Wh-why, sir?

Aphanisis (*almost strangled by the memory*) There was a damn great hole in it.
    He thought I wouldn't notice! Thought I'd be too busy. I'll break
    him too. Oh, mister, bear with me. (*as though seeing the object
    before him*) You could have drove a couple of horses through that
    goddam hole. (*suddenly a thought strikes him*) Horses. (*he calls*)
    Plankton!

Plankton Sir?

Aphanisis Those horses. You never let me know!

Plankton The signals have only just been decoded, sir.

Aphanisis What do they say?

Plankton May I say in front of the gentleman, sir?

Aphanisis Yeah, sure. I love him.

Plankton They can provide eighty Arabian horses for you, without delay,
    and by private contract.

Aphanisis White ones?

Plankton Some twenty of them will be brown, sir.

Aphanisis Why? Are they trying to pull a fast one on me? Who's the
    info from?

Plankton Parmenides, sir. He managed to contact a former eunuch from
    the court of the ex-Khedive of Egypt.

Aphanisis (*tearfully*) What do you mean 'a former eunuch'? Once a eunuch,
    always a eunuch. I'll only buy the whites. The others can get the
    hell. Send a signal tonight. Buy them. And buy the eunuch as
    well. I won't be left out in the cold like this the whole time. (*to
    Reeve*) I want *everything*, mister. People try to stop me right and
    left.

Reeve I'm very sorry, sir.

Aphanisis (*drying his eyes*) Never mind. You're the one. I knew the minute
    I saw you.

Reeve The one?

Aphanisis I love the English. I love them all. I like the way they look at you.

Reeve (*presumably looking away*) I . . . yes.

Aphanisis And I love you. And you'll do it. I know you will.

Reeve Well, sir, if I can be of any help . . .

Aphanisis Thank you, mister. The Elgin marbles. There's only one thing I don't want. I don't want you should use the knife.

Reeve The . . . the knife, sir?

Aphanisis No. It's dirty. You'll use the powders.

Reeve P-powders, sir?

Aphanisis I shan't give 'em you till the end of the trip. (*virtuously*) It wouldn't be right. Three of them. I'll give you three. They never fail.

Reeve Fail . . . ?

Aphanisis The minute we get back to Gibraltar you'll fly to London in one of my planes. You'll invite Mr Henry Moore and the British Museum guy, either together or separate, to afternoon tea. The powders are tasteless in tea. There's one for each of them. The third's for yourself.

Reeve M-*myself*?

Aphanisis A present. You never know when it might come in handy. We all have our enemies. It's terrible, but we do.

Reeve B-b-but, Mr Aphanisis . . .

Aphanisis Decency, mister. That's what I like about you. I love you. And I know you love me too.

    (*fade*)

Reeve The consequences of our interesting interview with Mr Aphanisis were indeed strange and far-reaching. Alas that the rude shearing of the Third Programme in recent times should entirely preclude further reference to them. Greece must be our theme. How happily we lingered in the blue Aegean waters! What pen could convey the charm of those island nocturnes? The Greek *taverna*, with its dancers, moving slowly and gracefully on their shapely . . . legs, to the ancient evocative music which seemed to impel the . . . dancers to move their . . . lim . . . legs in time to . . . it, their shapefully-swinging sk . . . garments revealing to . . . to . . . the full, the . . . in the *taverna* . . . the beautiful movements of their . . . l-legs, as they weaved in and out of the dance on their (*long pause*) . . . in the *taverna*. (*a faint blush has slowly spread over his voice*)

    (*dance music and murmurs behind*)

Hilda Magnificent, isn't it? Disturbing in some strange way. A sort of primitive, archaic quality about it.

Gland About what, Miss Tablet?

Hilda This dancing.

Gland (*politely*) If you can call it dancing, Miss Tablet.

Hilda Well, damn it, it *is* dancing.

Gland No, no, not really.

Hilda General Gland. This dance is absolutely authentic.

Gland No, no. It's just a debased copy of the things Sister Martin and the two nurses used to do in the jungle on their afternoon off. A Thursday, usually.

Hilda Well, really, General, you seem to have been very lucky in that jungle of yours.

Gland Oh, I was, Miss Tablet, very.

Elsa I should so like the dance-routine in my next opera to have some such motion as this, Hilda.

Hilda Well, dear, if any of these bright boys ever so much as suggests a ruddy subject for a girl . . .

Gland I am ever yours to command, Miss Tablet.

    (*music up and out*)

Reeve And Athens herself, the goal of every traveller with western culture in his heart! How fortunate we were to have a soldier-scholar for our guide, one who could disentangle the romance from the grim reality in the classic past.

Gland (*impressively*) This, my friends, is . . . the Parthenaeum. Breadful state of disrepair it's in, of course, but let us all hope (and fervently) that Time, the great healer, will one day see it restored to its former glory. Don't *finger* it, Reeve, I've told you before. That's the way it's got the way it is.

Reeve No, General, I was only . . .

Gland And let us not brawl in public, Reeve.

Reeve Sorry.

Gland Not at all. If you'll all look up there, you'll see the remains of what is called a frieze, very casual of course the way it's been left there, just a few chaps' legs, and some horses' heads, but let us all hope (and fervently) that, if ever the world enjoys settled peace once more, they will all be returned to their original place in the British Museum.

Hilda Oh, I say, General, damn that for a game.

Gland Exactly, Miss Tablet. And now, turning southwards, the harbour of the Piraeum, together with a magnificent spectacle of sea and sky, can be seen out yonder, just behind my sister-in-law.

Nancy *(hastily)* Oh, I'm so sorry. I always get in the way. So stupid of me. *(with a sudden little yelp)* Ooooh!

Connie Darling!

Nancy I'm so sorry, could someone help me up, please? I seem to have slipped. Thank you so much.

Elsa What a beautiful sight! It makes me wish to sing it. *(she begins to)* 'Cielo e mar! L'etereo velo . . .'

Hilda Elsa!

Elsa *(louder)* 'Splende come un santo altar!'

Hilda Elsa, do you mind?

Elsa *(mutters)* I shall go back to . . .

Hilda You were saying, General?

Gland It was here, on that fateful day, centuries ago, that the Trojan fleet, a thousand strong, landed their forces for the great war of Troy.

Stephen No, they didn't, Arthur.

Gland *(mildly)* Yes they did, Stephen. Here the great war of Troy commenced. Even to us today, with the experience of global war behind us . . .

Stephen And before us, Arthur.

Gland And behind us, Stephen. We can have no conception of what the Trojan war meant to the ancient world. It lasted exactly a hundred years, and very few of the people who were in on the beginning managed to get out at the end. It has been so in many wars.

Stephen No, it hasn't, Arthur.

Gland Yes, it has, Stephen. It was during the Trojan war that one of the most noble efforts at restoring peace that have ever been made was made. I refer of course to the bold action taken by the Greek heroine Lysistrata and the women of Athens, as recounted in the celebrated comedy by Aristophanes: a work of double significance to us today, inasmuch as we enacted it on VJ day in the officers' mess in Rangoon. I took off the part of Lysistrata myself. It was an all-male cast, naturally in an officers' mess. The few men's parts were lightly sketched in by Sister Martin and the two nurses. To the best of my recollection, it is the only occasion on which I have ever shaved my chest. The moustache, of course, I was allowed to keep because of the victory parade the next day, but I don't think anybody in the audience noticed it . . .

Hilda (*suddenly and loudly*) Heaven and Earth!

Gland You spoke, Miss Tablet?

Hilda (*vibrantly*) My Subject!

Gland Yes, Miss Tablet?

Hilda Why in the Lord's name did I never think of it before? The Lysistrata. Of course. (*a long chortle*) Why it's the perfect subject for me, perfect. It'll be better than *Butter*, even. God bless you, General, an angel alighted on your tongue this afternoon, Posterity will remember you for it.

Gland Yours ever to command, Miss Tablet.

Hilda Bertie!

Reeve Yes, Hilda?

Hilda The minute you get back to the yacht, be sure and make the exactest possible notes of this occasion for the biography. Give full credit to General Gland, and make a complete list of all the people who were present.

Reeve Y-yes, Hilda.

Hilda Together with their reactions.

Reeve Yes, Hilda.

Hilda (*resolutely*) Come on, Elsa. Back to work! What a magnificent occasion!

Evelyn (*suddenly*) Hel-*lowe*.

Hilda Hello, where've you been?

Evelyn Been for a little walk.

Hilda Who with?

Evelyn My friend Spiro.

Hilda Who's he?

Evelyn The one over there. In the white jersey.

Hilda Well, my lad, you missed the experience of a lifetime this afternoon.

Evelyn Oh, no, I didn't, dear.

Hilda (*receding*) Come on, Elsa! And God bless you, General Gland!

Elsa I am already so exhaust. And I am feeling so *much* the need of some tea and tost.

Gland (*to the others, a little worried*) Well, of course, I may find it a trifle difficult to actually *sing* the rôle. Still, one can but try one's best . . .

> (*fade*)

Janet (*teasingly*) Well, *Bertie* . . . ?

Reeve No, Janet, please . . .

Janet You will remember that you have to record everyone's reactions to the great annunciation, won't you?

Reeve Y-yes, Janet.

Janet You'll be able to say that the moment Hilda vanished towards the city, Janet Shewin, the famous novelist's niece, asked, with marked curiosity, 'Mr Reeve, do you . . . ?'

Reeve J-Janet, do be careful.

Janet . . . 'Do you ever have phantasies about Miss Tablet in which you imagine you are cutting or tearing her to pieces, gouging her, scooping her out, roasting her, or stuffing bad excrements into her?

Reeve Well . . . not *scooping her out*, Janet, certainly not that. We're . . . very good friends of course.

Janet Does the thought of *eating* her repel you?

Reeve Well . . . it's not a thing I've so far given much thought to, Janet.

Janet Or do you ever feel she has eaten *you*?

Reeve (*after a moment's thought*) Well, it's interesting you should mention that, because last Wednesday afternoon I did have rather a strange . . . (*fade*)

(*a brief piano passage from Hilda's new opera is heard, with Elsa vocalising and Hilda murmuring:* Gooooood! Lovely!)

Hilda Well, that's all so far, Mr Aphanisis. Just the opening bars, you understand.

Aphanisis (*moved*) You've written all that in just these five or six weeks?

Hilda (*modestly*) That's so, Mr Aphanisis. It's been coming along.

Aphanisis (*quietly, in wonder*) It's a miracle. You're not rushing ahead too fast with it, are you? Just to please *me*? I don't want it to be scamped.

Hilda I think I can promise that.

Aphanisis I want it to be all mine.

Hilda It shall be, Mr Aphanisis.

Aphanisis (*plaintively*) I wish it could be *solid*, so I could hold it in me arms like me Picassos and me Matisses.

Hilda I'll be . . . pretty solid.

Aphanisis I want it all written on my yacht and all mine. I want you to be surrounded by everything you need, your friends, all the time, whenever you want 'em.

Hilda Every man jack of them is helping me tremendously.

Aphanisis In that case tell 'em we'll extend the cruise. Tell 'em all to make arrangements to stay on the yacht for the next two years. Circulate that in the form of a memo, Plankton, to everyone on board.

Plankton Yes, sir.

Aphanisis And send a cable to Nilsson, telling her to come to Athens for an audition for the chief part.

Elsa (*outraged*) I shall go back to Vienna! (*bursts into sobs*)

Aphanisis (*kindly*) What's the matter at you, Miss Strauss? You hungry again, or something?

(*seagulls*)

Janet Hello, Herbert.

Reeve Hello, Janet.

Janet What's the matter? You look rather in the depressive position, this morning.

Reeve Perhaps I am a little, Janet.

Janet It's quite healthy of course.

Reeve Is it? Yes. You see, Janet, I've . . . I've just made a great decision. I . . . I think.

Janet What is it?

Reeve It's about Hilda.

Janet Are you going to tell her to go to hell?

Reeve Good heavens, no, Janet. I'm very fond of her. I merely intend to ask her if she could possibly see her way to . . .

Janet You *tell* her, Herbert, not *ask*. Just tell her. Not that it's my business, of course . . .

Reeve It's going to be very painf . . . Oh, good morning, General.

Gland Morning, Reeve.

Janet Hello, unk.

Gland Morning. Sorry I am not at liberty to stay and converse. Very busy, much preoccupied.

Janet With what, uncle?

Gland No, no, Janet, I'm sorry, but I have no time for the psychoanalysising this morning. Very busy, much preoccupied.

Janet Oh, sorry, uncle.

Gland No matter, you shall have your chocolates just the same. Excuse me. (*he goes*)

Janet You were saying, Herbert, it would be very . . . ?

Reeve Painful, Janet, painful. Still it must be faced. I . . . I must face it.

Janet When?

Reeve Oh, I hadn't exactly thought when. Tomorrow, perhaps. Or Sunday.

Janet Compulsive postponement.

Evelyn Hel-*lowe* . . .

The Others Hello, Evelyn.

Evelyn '*lowe*. Got a message for you, Mr Reeve, from old Hilda. Wants to see you straightaway. On the poop-deck.

Reeve Oh . . . well, thank you, Evelyn.

Evelyn (*after a pause*) Shall I go away now?

Reeve Well . . . just as you like, Evelyn.

Evelyn I'm on my wa-ay! (*he departs*)

Reeve Well, I ought to be on mine too, I suppose, and see what she wants.

Janet Yes, Herbert.

Reeve Janet . . . there is one thing I wanted to tell you. I . . . it was about the first time I came down to Mulset. I expect you've forgotten, but . . .

Hilda (*off*) Bertie! Where are you?

Reeve Oh, please excuse me a moment. (*calls*) I . . . I'm here, Hilda. (*on fade*) Just coming . . . (*after a pause*) Hilda?

Hilda Ah, Bertie. I . . . I wanted to talk to you. Rather seriously, Bertie.

Reeve Yes, Hilda?

Hilda As you know, Bertie, I've had very little to crow about in my life. No . . . no advantages to speak of, little happiness, no great experiences, except of my own creation. (*clears her throat*) It's been different with you, Bertie. You've always been lucky.

Reeve I sometimes wonder how anyone can imagine that, Hilda.

Hilda (*shocked*) Bertie! Damn it, Bertie, that's a bit ungrateful, isn't it?

Reeve How, Hilda?

Hilda Well, damn it. Bertie. You've . . . known *me* for several years, and been the recipient of my most intimate confidences. Don't . . . don't estimate that so ruddy lightly, old cock.

Reeve No, Hilda . . . I won't.

Hilda It's been different with me. I've had nothing like that at all. (*wistfully*) No one has ever said to me the sort of things I've said to you, Bertie.

Reeve N-no.

Hilda No one. And that's what I wanted to talk about. Because you see, others are unlucky too, besides me. And somehow I'm beginning to believe the luck in this world ought to be a bit better shared out than it is.

Reeve Yes, Hilda.

Hilda And for several years past, as I say, you have been able to – (don't think I've grudged it you, Bertie, please don't think that) – to sit wallowing luxuriously in this biography of my humble self you've been working on. Oh, I know you've not begun it yet. In a way, that makes what I have to say a little easier.

Reeve Wh-what is it, Hilda?

Hilda You saw what happened at the Acropolis the other afternoon. How old Arthur Gland suddenly gave me my Subject. I was deeply moved, Bertie. You see, he, like me, is another chap who's not had much luck in his life, poor old thing.

Reeve No.

Hilda And I'm grateful to him. And I want to do what I can for him in return. So . . . though I know this is going to hurt, Bertie . . . I . . . I'm going to take my *Life* . . . out of your hands and put it in those of Arthur Gland.

Reeve He . . . *he's* going to write it, you mean?

Hilda (*solemnly*) He is, Bertie.

Reeve (*after a very long pause*) Oh.

Hilda Take it like a man, Bertie, with your chin up. And for God's sake don't cry, will you? I hate to see a man cry.

Reeve I . . . I'll try not to, Hilda.

Hilda Good. It's not been an easy thing to say to you. I know you're a scholar, Bertie, and a very fine one. But General Gland is a *soldier*-scholar; and I somehow feel that's tremendously important in my case.

Reeve Yes. May I say, Hilda, that I wish him . . . well?

Hilda I like you for saying that, Bertie. And, oh damn it, Bertie, we've had the hell of a lot of good times together, haven't we?

Reeve (*warmly*) Oh, very, Hilda.

Hilda And shall again. OK, Bertie. That's all. And thank you.

Reeve Thank you, Hilda.

Hilda (*slightly receding*) And we shall see each other at dinner, eh? (*after a brief pause, she is heard very loudly calling*) ARTHUR! ARTHUR! ARTHUR!

(*fade. Brief pause*)

Reeve (*almost chattily*) And what I wanted to say, Janet, was about the occasion of my first visit to Mulset. To me it was a . . .

Janet But what about Hilda?

Reeve . . . wonderful exper . . . what?

Janet What did Hilda say?

Reeve (Oh, that's perfectly all right. I needn't bother about it any more.) It was a wonderful experience to be on your uncle's native heath for the first time, to breathe his air, to see the sights he knew so well.

Janet But what about Hilda's biography?

Reeve (We came to an agreement about that. I'm to give it up.) And everything about that first visit is wonderfully distinct to me still, Janet.

Janet But wasn't Hilda terribly angry?

Reeve I know you and I had many interesting conversations about . . . (No, I honestly don't think she minded . . .) about literature. But for me there was one thing that transcended even literature. It was the first time I saw you . . .

Janet But does this mean you don't have to write the biography at all?

Reeve (No. There was no difficulty, none whatever.) It was the first time I saw you. You didn't see me, I'm afraid. But you were with the others in the meadow at the back of the house. It was . . . something you called out.

Janet What was it?

Reeve It wasn't so much what it was – though it was very appropriate to the moment, of course – it was the way you said it. There was something about it – you won't laugh at me, will you, Janet?

Janet Of course not.

Reeve There was something about it . . . oh, so young and heroic and ardent, Janet. You threw back your head, I remember, and cried out, simply cried out, '*Come on, Humphrey, bowl!*' Oh Janet . . .

Janet But Humphrey was too small to bowl.

Reeve (*sincerely*) It somehow didn't stop you saying it, Janet. It . . . was magnificent. When I think back on that moment, Janet, I realise that I have always loved you as I shall never love anyone else. I have always hoped that one day you might be my wife. For on that day, Janet my darling, you were magnificence itself.

Janet (*after a long pause*) No, Herbert . . . I wasn't.

Reeve Oh, yes, Janet.

Janet You're so honest, Herbert . . . you make me feel such an awful fake.

Reeve Fake, Janet?

Janet (*almost in tears*) You're so sweet and noble, Herbert; and of course I'll be delighted and honoured to marry you . . .

Reeve (*irradiated*) Janet!

Janet I love you more than I've ever loved anyone. But . . . you say I didn't see you, when I shouted 'Come on, Humphrey, bowl', but I . . . I did. I saw you standing by the stile there and watching us . . . I knew you were there.

Reeve (*enfolding her*) Janet, my darling.

Janet (*weeping bitterly*) It's . . . my beastly exhibitionism the whole time. You . . . you . . .

Reeve Yes, my sweet?

Janet (*gulping*) You . . . urethral sadism, the whole bloody time.

Reeve My only one . . .

Janet And now you know . . . I'm awfully sorry . . . (*fade*)
   (*some sort of music up and hold intermittently in background*)

Reeve Love . . . art . . . scholarship . . . the classical heritage: even a Third Programme that has recently been (as our dear, dear Janet would say) so rudely castrated, must find a place, a brief moment, to honour them. What more can we ourself do but recall the warm friendly moments that attended the announcement on shipboard of our engagement?

Gland Yes, well I've no objection at all, highly delighted in a very real sense. Congratulations, Reeve. I've never had much against you personally, and I'm very glad to think that after being friends so long, we shall also be relations.

Reeve Yes, indeed. Thank you, sir.

Gland (*anxiously*) It . . . won't be *blood* relations, will it?

Reeve N-no, sir. No,

Gland No. Oh, well, there's that about it, then.

Stephen (*kindly*) And in any case, blood relation or not, you have the advantage of knowing, Mr Reeve, that Janet will eventually inherit the house in Mulset and a very large part . . .

Connie Stephen!

Stephen And a very large part of her late uncle's so-called literary estate.

Reeve I . . . I didn't know that, Mr Shewin, no!

Stephen Oh, I am sure you will have the spirit not to let the thought embitter you, Mr Reeve.

Gland No. Never become embittered, Reeve, whatever happens.

Connie And the dear little pussies are delighted, Mr Reeve.

Reeve Oh . . . thank you, I'm so glad.

Gland The important thing is to see that there are *bells* at the wedding. I often attribute much of my own marital misfortunes to the absence of those.

Connie But you were never married, Arthur dear!

Gland Well, you could never be sure with Sister Martin and the two nurses about the place. I remember one Saturday night, they . . .

Hilda Dear, dear Bertie! This is splendid! Give us a kiss.

Reeve Oh, thank you, Hilda.

Hilda (*privately*) Mind you, I've always had my doubts about these marriages on the rebound. But (*louder*) you're lucky, Herbert, you've always been lucky. And perhaps you'll be lucky in this. Let's hope so, eh?

Reeve I'm sure I shall be, Hilda.

Hilda That's what I like to see in a chap. Pluck. And I shall certainly write the anthem for the wedding. I can promise that.

Reeve Thank you, Hilda.

Elsa And I shall sing it, Mr Reeve. Who are you getting to do the wedding-breakfast? I ollways think that is of prime importance.

Gland Well, I think bells are the most important thing.

Elsa Toh! No one can eat a bell. And Mr Reeve: I should so like to call you Herbert.

Reeve Oh, please, Elsa, I always thought you did.

Evelyn Hel-*lowe* . . .

Reeve Oh, hello, Evelyn.

Evelyn '*lowe* . . . Congratulations.

Reeve Well, thank you, Evelyn.

Evelyn What are you going to wear at the wedding, Mr Reeve?

Reeve Oh . . . I . . . a morning-suit, I expect.

Evelyn Jolly pretty, Mr Reeve.

Reeve I . . . I think you too ought to call me Herbert, too, after all these years, Evelyn.

Evelyn (*firmly*) No, Mr Reeve. It's too late now.

Reeve Well, I . . .

Gland Yes, it's a habit *I* can never use meself to, either.

(*for a few moments past there has been friendly argument among the Shewin boys*)

Brian Go on, Owen, *you* ask him.

George You're the eldest.

Brian Go *on*.

(*semi-silence falls*)

Owen (*embarrassed*) Mr Reeve. My brothers and I do wish to congratulate you very much. We've always been very fond of Sister Janet, and we're very glad to think of you marrying her, we've always sort of hoped you would. And my brothers and I would consider it a great honour if you would accept a new little number which my brothers and I have specially written for this occasion.

Reeve (*much moved*) My dear fellows, thank you enormously . . .

Owen And also, Mr Reeve, now that you're marrying Sister Janet my brothers and I have asked me to ask if you think we might begin to use your Christian name?

Reeve My dear dear fellows, please. I don't know why you didn't ages ago.

The boys (*sincerely and gratefully*) Thank you . . . Bert.

Owen The song is called 'English Lane' . . . and it . . . sort of goes like this:

> There's many a place for a honeymoon tour
> From Venice and Rome to Rocamadour,
> There's the Costa Brava and Cap Ferrat,
> Marrakesh and the Old Bazaar.
> > But there's only one place for you and for I
> > To watch the pageant of life go by;
> > The only thing that will always remain
> > Is the dear old sight of an English lane . . .

(refrain)

> The gentle sigh of an English breeze
> And rivers and hills and fields and trees
> And sea and summer and air and sky
> And clouds and cows as the days roll by.
> > If I've said it before, let me say it again:
> > The only place is an English lane.

Elsa (*loudly*) But it is beautiful! I must learn it myself!

(fade congratulatory murmurs behind dialogue)

Nancy And I . . . I shall be Granny Shewin, shan't I?

Janet Really, mother, you're shameless.

Nancy I shall be, shan't I, Herbert? I've always wanted to be Granny Shewin.

Reeve *(traditionally)* Well, I assure you I shall do *my* best, Mrs Shewin.

Nancy Do, my dear.

Janet What a very lowering conversation.

Nancy Oh, I think Connie is waving to me. Excuse me, my dears . . . *(goes)*

Janet Well, you heard what she said . . .

Reeve Yes, my sweet, I agree with her most emphatically, don't you?

Janet Of course I do.

Reeve My love.

Janet It's just . . .

Reeve What, my dear?

Janet There's only one thing I . . .

Reeve Yes, dear?

Janet I know you always like to have your own way, Herbert, and it's quite right you should, but . . .

Reeve What is it, darling?

Janet I know what I'm going to say is a bit sentimental . . . but I want you to promise me that you won't insist on having the children psychoanalysed before they can actually *speak*.

Reeve *(loyally)* No, no, my darling, certainly.

Janet Any time after the age of two and a half, of course, but . . . oh, I know you'll think I'm mawkish, but . . . let's wait till then, shall we?

Reeve Yes, my darling, we shall. We . . . we will.

Janet Dear, sweet Herbert. *(she kisses him)*

Elsa *(loudly)* I shall sing it at the wedding! And I shall ollso sing it now! Play!

> I've loitered . . . in the streets of gay Vienna,
> I've lingered . . . in palaces of old Siena.
> I've waited . . . in a café in Montparnasse.
> But what is there left when these things pass?
> > The only thing that will always remain
> > Is the dear old sight of an English lane.

(refrain)

Where English sun and clouds roll over
English sheep and English clover
And the scent of an English tree in leaf
And the honest taste of English beef.
I have said it before and I say it again:
The best place on earth is an English lane.

All

The gentle sigh of an English breeze
And rivers and hills and fields and trees
And sea and summer and air and sky
And clouds and cows as the days roll by.
If I've said it before, let me say it again:
The only place is an English lane.